ROUTLEDGE LIBRARY]
SCOTLAND

Volume 32

THE CHANGING SCOTTISH LANDSCAPE

THE CHANGING SCOTTISH LANDSCAPE

1500–1800

IAN WHYTE AND KATHLEEN WHYTE

Routledge
Taylor & Francis Group

LONDON AND NEW YORK

First published in 1991 by Routledge

This edition first published in 2022
by Routledge
2 Park Square, Milton Park, Abingdon, Oxon OX14 4RN

and by Routledge
605 Third Avenue, New York, NY 10158

Routledge is an imprint of the Taylor & Francis Group, an informa business

© 1991 Ian and Kathleen Whyte

All rights reserved. No part of this book may be reprinted or reproduced or utilised
in any form or by any electronic, mechanical, or other means, now known or
hereafter invented, including photocopying and recording, or in any information
storage or retrieval system, without permission in writing from the publishers.

Trademark notice: Product or corporate names may be trademarks or registered
trademarks, and are used only for identification and explanation without intent to
infringe.

British Library Cataloguing in Publication Data
A catalogue record for this book is available from the British Library

ISBN: 978-1-03-206184-9 (Set)
ISBN: 978-1-00-321338-3 (Set) (ebk)
ISBN: 978-1-03-200210-1 (Volume 32) (hbk)
ISBN: 978-1-03-200223-1 (Volume 32) (pbk)
ISBN: 978-1-00-317319-9 (Volume 32) (ebk)

DOI: 10.4324/9781003173199

Publisher's Note
The publisher has gone to great lengths to ensure the quality of this reprint but
points out that some imperfections in the original copies may be apparent.

Disclaimer
The publisher has made every effort to trace copyright holders and would welcome
correspondence from those they have been unable to trace.

THE
CHANGING
SCOTTISH
LANDSCAPE

1500–1800

Ian and Kathleen Whyte

London and New York

First published in 1991
by Routledge
11 New Fetter Lane, London EC4P 4EE

Simultaneously published in the USA and Canada by Routledge
a division of Routledge, Chapman and Hall Inc.
29 West 35th Street, New York, NY 10001

© 1991 Ian and Kathleen Whyte

Set in 10/12pt Times by Intype, London

Printed in Great Britain by TJ Press (Padstow) Ltd, Padstow, Cornwall

All rights reserved. No part of this book may be reprinted or reproduced or utilized in
any form or by any electronic, mechanical, or other means, now known or hereafter
invented, including photocopying and recording, or in any information storage or retrieval
system, without permission in writing from the publishers.

British Library Cataloguing in Publication Data
Whyte, I. D. (Ian D.)
The changing Scottish landscape 1500–1800 – (The History of the British landscape).
1. Scotland. Human geographical features, history
I. Title   II. Whyte, Kathleen A.   III. Series
304.209411

Library of Congress Cataloging in Publication Data
Whyte, Ian (Ian D.)
The changing Scottish landscape, 1500–1800 / by Ian and Kathleen Whyte.
p.   cm.
Includes bibliographical references and index.
1. Scotland – Historical geography.
2. Landscape – Scotland – History.
3. Land use – Scotland – History.
I. Whyte, Kathleen A.   II. Title.
DA850.W48 1991
911′.411–dc20
90–24524

ISBN 0–415–02992–9

For
Rebecca and Ruth

Contents

Plates

Maps

Acknowledgements

The authors would like to express their thanks to the National Trust for Scotland and to Dr Douglas Lockhart for supplying some of the illustrations. We would also like to thank Mr Owen Tucker for drawing the maps, and members of the Photographic Unit at Lancaster University for preparing many of the illustrations.

Introduction

In 1500 Scotland was a poor country with a small population and a backward, underdeveloped economy, impoverished by two centuries of war with England. Further debilitating conflict was to follow during the first half of the sixteenth century, starting with the devastating defeat at Flodden in 1513. In some respects Scotland had only recently emerged as a clearly defined nation state. Orkney and Shetland had been acquired from Norway during the fifteenth century. In the Western Highlands and Islands the Lordship of the Isles was virtually a separate kingdom until its forfeiture to the Scottish crown in 1493. Even the Border with England was not completely fixed. An area in the lower part of Eskdale and Liddesdale, known as the Debateable Land, was claimed by both countries. A definitive boundary was only settled in 1552 when an embankment and ditch were constructed between the Rivers Sark and Esk. The Scots Dike is the first landscape feature relating to our period that visitors from south of the Border will encounter if they enter Scotland along the A7.

The period from the sixteenth century to the end of the eighteenth saw increasing contact and progressive integration between Scotland and her wealthier, more powerful southern neighbour. Milestones along the way were the Reformation of 1560 which gave Scotland a Protestant church, the Union of the Crowns under James VI and I in 1603, and finally the Union of the Parliaments in 1707 under whose terms Scotland was integrated politically and economically with England though preserving some of her established institutions, including church, law and education system. By 1800 Scotland was industrialising rapidly alongside England: population was concentrating in the towns and already Scotland was one of the most highly urbanised societies in Europe. The countryside was being altered out of all recognition by changes in agriculture. The rate of transformation was certainly rapid enough to justify that often misused term 'Agricultural Revolution'.

This book examines how the Scottish landscape changed in these crucial three centuries during which medieval gave way to modern. The themes which have been chosen reflect those aspects of change which were most significant and had the greatest expression in the landscape. Another volume in this series will cover the development of Scottish towns so the focus here is on the Scottish countryside.

In England there is an established tradition of interdisciplinary research into the landscape which has been undertaken by a variety of specialists and many highly skilled amateur fieldworkers. In Scotland far less is known about the development of the landscape and much less detailed local research has been carried out. Although historians, archaeologists, geographers and others have made important contributions to our understanding of particular aspects of the Scottish countryside there have been few general overviews of the evolution of the landscape. In part this reflects a different history of landscape development. In England landscape change was a more gradual, evolutionary process from late medieval times onwards. In Scotland the changes which occurred in the later eighteenth and nineteenth centuries were more revolutionary in character and more traces of the pre-existing landscape were swept away. Investigation has also been hampered by the poorer quality of surviving Scottish archive sources. The pre-sixteenth-century record is often sparse, making it difficult to examine continuity and change in the landscape from medieval times. However, these excuses have been used far too frequently. There is still a wealth of untapped information in Scottish archives awaiting the attention of the enthusiastic researcher. To an even greater degree the landscape itself still holds innumerable fascinating puzzles which more detailed research work may help to solve. It is our hope that this book may stimulate interested people, Scots and visitors alike, to look more closely at the Scottish landscape and to undertake investigations of their own.

To cover landscape change over three centuries in a country as diverse as Scotland within a single book is a daunting task and inevitably we have had to omit much interesting material. We have tried to achieve a balance between generalisation and the description of specific sites. Many of the places mentioned will be easily found with the aid of a good road atlas. National Grid references are given to features which are more difficult to locate. The description in this book of any site is no guarantee of a right of access to it. Permission should be obtained before entering private land and cross-country walking in upland areas should be avoided during the grouse-shooting and deer-stalking seasons. Ordnance Survey maps at scales of 1:50,000 and 1:25,000 will greatly enhance the exploration of the landscape of any part of Scotland.

1

Rural settlement before the improvers

The rural settlement pattern is a fundamental aspect of the pre-improvement Scottish landscape. The problem is that we still know very little about it in either the Highlands or the Lowlands before the mid-eighteenth century when detailed estate plans first become available in quantity. The lack of cartographic evidence for the sixteenth and seventeenth centuries, and the limitations of documentary sources, make it difficult to establish the character of settlement in 1500, and how this had evolved from medieval times.

Another difficulty is that few medieval and post-medieval settlement sites have been excavated in Scotland. In England excavations at a number of deserted villages, notably the long-continued dig at Wharram Percy, have added greatly to our understanding of the construction of late-medieval peasant houses and how the settlements they made up evolved. In Scotland excavation has focused on prehistoric and Roman sites rather than those from later times. A further problem is that excavated medieval and post-medieval sites have often provided few artefacts making accurate dating impossible in some cases. In addition there has been a lack of field surveys of the surface remains of deserted sites although the position has improved in recent years with detailed work in areas as far apart as Caithness and the Borders.

The settlement pattern immediately preceding the period of rapid improvement and change in the later eighteenth century is recoverable in the Lowlands from estate plans and in many parts of the Highlands from abundant remains on the ground. There has been a natural, but dangerous, tendency to look at settlement in this late period and project its features back into the more poorly documented medieval period. This has been particularly true of the Highlands whose wealth of deserted settlements from the late eighteenth and early nineteenth centuries deserves more detailed study than it has received. The remains are as widespread, and far better preserved, than those of deserted medieval villages in England. However, as we will show, such settlements belong to a short-lived phase which was demonstrably uncharacteristic of earlier centuries.

Because most of the pre-improvement settlement pattern has been wiped out in the Lowlands due to subsequent intensive exploitation of the land, deserted settlement sites generally occur on the fringes of improved land, often in marginal semi-upland locations. Such sites may not have been representative of those in the Lowlands which have been obliterated.

Dispersed settlement: ferm toun and clachan

The rural settlement pattern of Scotland between the sixteenth and later eighteenth centuries was mainly a dispersed one of small hamlets and isolated dwellings. It had many similarities with other outlying areas of north-west Europe such as Ireland, Wales, south-west England and Brittany. It was well adapted to conditions where extensive areas of freely drained fertile soil, capable of supporting large communities, were infrequent and to an economy oriented towards livestock rearing. Nevertheless, the fact that the same basic settlement pattern occurs in districts like Strathmore, which have large areas of high-quality land, and are known to have concentrated on arable farming in the pre-improvement period, should make us wary of being too deterministic about the development of this dispersed settlement pattern. There must also have been powerful influences within Scottish rural society which prevented the development of larger villages in such areas.

The origins of this settlement pattern are hard to determine. In other areas of hamlets and farmsteads, like south-west England, prehistoric roots for it have been suggested. It is likely that the basic frameworks of the settlement pattern that existed in Scotland in 1500 go back to pre-medieval times. The standard settlement unit was the hamlet cluster or 'ferm toun' as it was known in the Lowlands. The equivalent term in Gaelic was 'baile'. In a Highland context the name 'clachan' has also been applied to this type of settlement. Although clachans were, strictly speaking, places possessing a church or chapel the label has been used more generally by archaeologists and geographers to describe all Highland hamlets, similar to its usage in Ireland.

The ferm toun has usually been portrayed as a cluster of between six and a dozen households, mainly tenants working a joint farm. Contemporary estate plans and surviving deserted settlements show that the buildings comprising most ferm touns were loosely scattered or strung out in an irregular line without any sign of planning. This was partly due to the fact that before the later eighteenth century most dwellings in such settlements were flimsily constructed. Rebuilding on adjacent sites was frequent. The positions of houses and outbuildings tended to move over time as a result. An English traveller in the Highlands in the early eighteenth century described the buildings in the settlements he visited as 'all irregularly placed, some one way some another', a description that would fit most hamlet clusters, Highland or Lowland. As well as being fluid in layout the actual locations of ferm touns and clachans could change too, as we shall see presently.

Some ferm touns had a semblance of regularity where their dwellings were built along a slope with the same general alignment. Certain deserted hamlets in the south-west Highlands, and the excavated example from Lix in Perthshire which will be described below, had a more planned linear layout. There is a close association between such sites and estates of landowners like the dukes of Argyll where agricultural improvement began relatively early in the mid-eighteenth century. These more regimented clusters probably represent a preliminary phase of rationalisation before the clachans were cleared and abandoned.

The social composition of the ferm toun could vary. In its ideal form it comprised a joint farm worked by several tenants holding equal shares. However, hamlets might also contain cottars. These were smallholders who sublet portions of the arable land from the principal tenants in return for providing labour. In deserted Highland clachans the cottars' dwellings can sometimes be distinguished from those of the tenants. They were smaller, lacking attached byres and barns, and were often more poorly built. Some touns consisted of a large consolidated farm worked by a single prosperous tenant with the aid of several cottars. Others were exclusively inhabited by cottars. 'Cottoun of X' is a common type of place name and as most cottars also had a part-time trade such as weaving or shoemaking, these touns acted as minor service centres for the local population.

Pre-improvement ferm touns and clachans have not survived in the modern settlement pattern in any numbers. The amalgamation of holdings and farms from the seventeenth century has replaced them by the consolidated single farms which are prominent in the modern landscape throughout the Lowlands as well as in the southern and eastern Highlands. However, some impression of their character can be gained from two examples which have survived with relatively little change. Swanston stands on the outskirts of Edinburgh at the edge of the Pentland Hills. Its old cottages, thatched, whitewashed, and possibly dating back to the seventeenth century, are laid out around a small green with a later school and farmstead. Auchindrain, in mid-Argyll on the road from Inveraray to Lochgilphead, is a Highland clachan which, almost uniquely, has survived into modern times. Appropriately it now forms a museum of rural life. In 1800 it was a classic hamlet cluster with twelve tenants paying rent to the Duke of

Figure 1 The hamlet of Swanston near Edinburgh, whose thatched cottages may date back to the seventeenth century, preserves the character and layout of a pre-improvement ferm toun.

Argyll for shares in the farm. Unlike other joint farms in the area it escaped obliteration with the onset of improved agriculture and one house was inhabited until 1954. The site has twenty buildings including long houses with house and byre combined, barns and cottages. In between them are kailyards for vegetables, stackyards for the corn, enclosures and access ways. The interiors of some of the houses have been furnished to show what they were like in earlier times. Making allowances for the neatness of the site, it gives a good impression of how many Highland and the Lowland settlements must have appeared in earlier times.

Many hamlets were merely ferm touns, purely agricultural in function, but larger settlement clusters also developed under the influence of various nucleating forces. In the Lowlands the parish church generally provided the focus for a larger hamlet, the kirk toun. In the Highlands such nucleations were rarer and it was more common for churches and chapels to stand in isolation. However, some kirk touns did exist and have retained their original character, like Kilmory in Kintyre (NR 702751). In the modern landscape many kirk touns have lost their original form. Some developed into small burghs in the sixteenth and seventeenth centuries, others into planned villages in the eighteenth and nineteenth. Elsewhere kirk touns have been split up as a result of agricultural improvements or have declined because of the development of planned villages within their parish.

Nevertheless, kirk touns surviving as small, scattered hamlets can still be found in some areas. They have proved more durable than ordinary ferm touns and are probably the principal surviving element of the pre-improvement settlement pattern in the modern landscape. Their buildings, with the exception of the parish church, rarely predate the later eighteenth century but their size and layout have probably not changed very much. Some parish centres are still named 'Kirkton of X' and a glance at the Ordnance Survey map of areas like Aberdeenshire, Angus or Ayrshire will show that a substantial proportion of parish centres are still small hamlets loosely grouped around the church. There is a whole line of them along the well-drained slopes above the Carse of Gowrie on the northern side of the Firth of Tay. Today, as well as the kirk, you may find a post office and a hotel but rarely much more in the way of service facilities. Insufficient research has been carried out to see to what extent the layout of such kirk touns has changed from the eighteenth century, when many of them are recorded on estate plans, to the present day.

Other nucleating elements are emphasised by place names which recur again and again on the modern map; 'bridgeton' 'castleton', 'chapelton' and 'milton' are self-explanatory. Along the coast fisher touns reflected a distinctive way of life quite separate from that of neighbouring agricultural communities. They are particularly numerous in the north east from the coast of Angus to the Moray Firth. Most of them were developed between the sixteenth century and the mid-eighteenth by landowners who wanted to increase their revenue and ensure local supplies of fish. They should not be confused with the planned fishing villages of the later eighteenth and nineteenth centuries which served the same purpose on a grander scale. These earlier fisher touns are usually laid out in one or more rows close to the shore, the houses built with their gables to the sea for protection from wind and weather. Pennan in Aberdeenshire (NJ 8465), or Crovie (NJ 8065) and Whitehills (NJ 6565) in Banffshire, are good examples.

'Mains' is another common place-name element in Lowland Scotland. The mains was the home farm of an estate, the descendant of the medieval demesne lands which were worked under the direct management of a feudal lord. In the sixteenth and seventeenth centuries the mains was usually a large farm close to the landowner's residence. It was sometimes leased to tenants but even in the early eighteenth century many proprietors still supervised the cultivation of the mains in person and retained traditional labour services to help work it. Tenants might be required, as a condition of their leases, to undertake a certain number of days' work each year on the mains, ploughing, harrowing, sowing, harvesting and spreading manure. The castle or mansion with the mains and often an attached cottar toun frequently formed a substantial settlement in its own right.

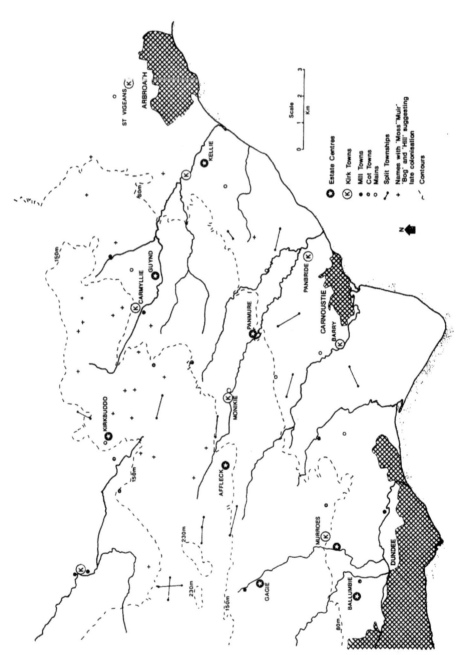

ST VIGEANS

ARBROATH

KELLIE

Scale

0   1   2   3
         Km

● Estate Centres

Ⓚ Kirk Towns

●○ Mill Towns

○○ Cot Towns

⌐ Mains

+ Split Townships

Names with 'Moss' 'Muir'
'Bog' and 'Hill' suggesting
late colonisation

Contours

N

150m

150m

GUYND

CARMYLLIE

PANMURE

PANBRIDE

CARNOUSTIE

BARRY

KIRKBUDDO

MONIKIE

150m

AFFLECK

230m

230m

150m

MURROES

GAGIE

BALLUMBIE

DUNDEE

80m

Map 1 Elements of the pre-improvement settlement pattern in southern Angus.

Nucleated settlement: village and burgh

Most villages in the modern Scottish landscape did not exist in 1500. They are either small burghs of barony dating from the sixteenth and seventeenth centuries or planned estate villages from the eighteenth and early nineteenth. However, one part of Scotland, the Lothians and the Merse, has many nucleated villages whose origins appear to go back to medieval times. In West Lothian industrial development has obscured much of this pattern of village settlement. Around Edinburgh former villages like Corstorphine and Duddingston have been absorbed by suburban expansion though they still preserve some of their original identity. The pattern of ancient villages is best seen in East Lothian and the Merse. There you can find villages laid out in rows or focusing on greens with the parish church, the market cross and sometimes the gates of the local 'big house' nearby in a style strongly reminiscent of north-east England.

The origins of this settlement pattern and the reasons for its distinctiveness are unclear. The names of many of the villages have Anglo-Saxon origins and this has prompted some historians to look to the Anglian occupation of the area between the seventh and ninth centuries as a period in which they might have been established. However, the idea of large numbers of Anglian migrants establishing villages and field systems on a classic 'English' pattern does not fit the available historical evidence or recent ideas about the development of villages in England.

There is a gap of some 600 years between the Anglian settlement of the Lothians and the Merse and the first documents relating to villages in this region, a gap during which many changes in the settlement pattern could have occurred. It can be shown that some of these places were already villages in the thirteenth century. It is likely that many of them grew with the build-up of population in medieval times which ended in the early fourteenth century. Many may have been established by incoming Anglo-Norman landowners in the twelfth and thirteenth centuries. The plan of some green villages like Dirleton, Denholm and Midlem suggests links with north-eastern England where layouts around greens are known to have originated in medieval times. A similar process may have operated in south-east Scotland but the poorer documentary record makes this difficult to prove. For Dirleton, estate papers show that the village's present plan existed in the late sixteenth century and was not the result of a comparatively recent replanning exercise. But, with many other green villages like Ancrum, Bowden and Maxton, there is a suspicion that their regular layout may have been due to replanning when they were granted market charters during the sixteenth and seventeenth centuries.

In some areas villages developed on monastic estates. During medieval times Cistercian abbeys like Melrose worked their lands using groups of

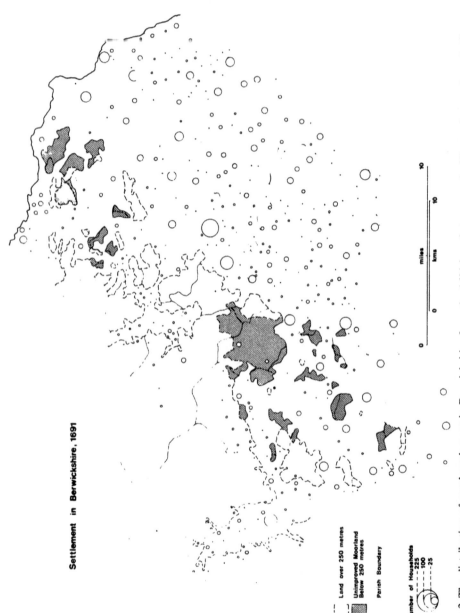

Map 2 The distribution of rural settlement in Berwickshire from the 1691 hearth tax records. The ancient nucleated villages stand out clearly in the pre-improvement landscape.

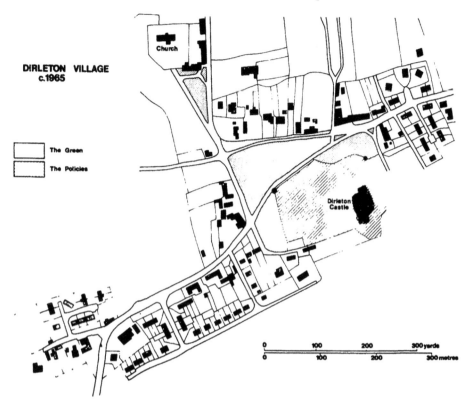

Map 3 The modern village of Dirleton in East Lothian clustered around its central green and baronial castle.

lay brothers living in communal farms or granges. In the fifteenth century this system was abandoned in favour of leasing the land out to lay tenants, a system which had been used from earlier times by other monastic orders. On the best lands some large settlements were created. During the early sixteenth century, when the Scottish crown was pressing the church hard for money, the lands in many of these townships were granted to the sitting tenants in perpetuity in return for substantial cash payments. This fossilised the old landholding pattern and its associated settlements. A number of these villages on former monastic lands can still be seen. A group surrounds Melrose Abbey: Darnick, Eildon, Gattonside and Newstead are examples. Others are scattered through the Merse, including Auchencraw, Coldingham, Eyemouth and Reston which belonged to Coldingham Priory. Some of these communities had as many as forty small proprietors and although their holdings were gradually bought up and amalgamated into larger units, a clustered settlement pattern has remained.

Another type of nucleated settlement in Lowland Scotland was medieval

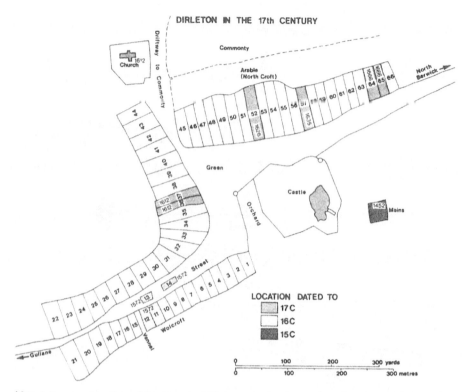

Map 4 A reconstruction of the layout of Dirleton in the sixteenth and seventeenth centuries.

Figure 2 The mercat cross still stands on the green of the village of Ancrum, testifying to its former status as a burgh of barony.

royal burghs which had never grown beyond the level of villages. In the early sixteenth century even the larger royal burghs held only a few thousand inhabitants but many centres had remained much smaller. Good examples are the old royal burghs of Inverurie and Kintore, which at the end of the seventeenth century had only about 300 inhabitants each. A new group of burghs was created in the Lowlands during the sixteenth and seventeenth centuries with the foundation of large numbers of burghs of barony. Scotland was one of the few parts of Europe in which the vigorous foundation of new towns was still continuing in the seventeenth century. Between 1500 and 1707 some 260 burghs of barony were authorised with the aim of improving internal trade.

The new baronial burghs were not allowed to engage in overseas trade until 1672 and were overshadowed by existing royal burghs. Relatively few of the new foundations developed into towns of any size and many never developed at all. Only about 25 per cent of the new centres had populations of over 500 by the end of the eighteenth century. The failure rate was high. Some centres were founded simply because it was fashionable or as a result of rivalry between neighbouring landowners. One-upmanship between the families of Wemyss of Wemyss and Scott of Balwearie explains the cluster of four baronial burghs; Balnakilly, Balnald, Dalnagairn and Kirkmichael, situated within a few kilometres of each other in Strathardle, Perthshire, which were granted charters in 1510–11. Others were founded in good faith and failed to develop. The laird of Penkill in South Ayrshire received a charter authorising the establishment of a market centre and, according to a contemporary source, he laid out the lines of its streets and erected a pole to mark the site of the intended mercat cross on a new site near the Water of Girvan. However, he was unable to attract settlers to the new market centre and not a single house was built there.

The charter authorising the establishment of a burgh of barony or regality gave landowners the opportunity to lay out a planned town, establish burgesses, a burgh council and a court. Sometimes, as at Langholm, founded in 1621, and Thurso, established in 1633, this helped to create successful communities which grew into real towns. In other cases prosperity and growth were more elusive. Crawford, in upper Clydesdale, was created a burgh of barony in 1510–11 and twenty plots of land were granted to the first burgesses. Yet Crawford never developed into anything grander than a hamlet; by no stretch of the imagination could it be considered a town, although its inhabitants chose to call it one. At the end of the eighteenth century the original burgess plots were still being worked as smallholdings and although their proprietors maintained a weekly burgh court this was largely an excuse to adjourn to a nearby alehouse!

The plans of the burghs of barony that did achieve a modest amount of growth were often conventional medieval ones; a single straight street widening into a market place in the centre, with long, narrow building plots running back at right angles to form a herringbone pattern. Some landowners financed the construction of a tollbooth, a public building which acted as a burgh courthouse, prison and place where market tolls were collected. More usually a mercat cross is the only affirmation in stone of a settlement's elevation to burghal status. Few developed on such a grand scale, though. Most landowners were probably only seeking to attach market rights to an existing kirk toun, with as little expenditure as possible. In many cases they may merely have been legalising existing customary markets with the aim of gaining an extra income from market tolls. Such places remained mere parish centres with nothing about them to denote their newly elevated status.

In the later seventeenth century another class of market centre was established in large numbers. These were not accorded burghal status but were nevertheless given the right to hold markets and fairs. In south-east Scotland many villages which had not already been created baronial burghs obtained market charters. In many cases this was probably only legitimising existing customary assemblies. Often the only indication of their former status, as with many small burghs of barony, is a mercat cross. One of the finest of such crosses stands in the village of Preston in East Lothian. The settlement has been overshadowed by the growth of the adjoining industrial centre of Prestonpans but still retains a village atmosphere. The cross stands on a stone drum nearly 4 metres high with a series of niches with stone seats around the base. A small doorway and flight of steps gives access to the platform at the base of the cross from which proclamations were read. The shaft which rises from this base is topped by a unicorn holding an armorial tablet. Like many of these 'crosses', the shaft is topped not by a cross but by a heraldic design though some, as at Ormiston, do have proper crosses, in this case almost certainly reused from a former pre-Reformation churchyard cross.

Settlement continuity

As in any settlement pattern, elements of continuity and change can be identified in the Scottish landscape. Elements of change tend to be more obvious, leaving evidence in the form of deserted sites and attracting more attention than continuity, which is an unobtrusive process. Nevertheless, the importance of settlement continuity should not be underestimated. For Lowland Scotland a comparison of almost any sixteenth- or seventeenth-century estate rental with a modern large-scale map shows that a high proportion of the old settlement names still survive, despite the changes caused by the agricultural improvements of the eighteenth and nineteenth centuries. Many of the settlements may have changed their form from

Figure 3 This weathered cross is the only visible sign of the former baronial burgh of Preston, south of Dumfries.

ferm toun to farmstead but continuity of name and, in most cases, of location, is evident.

On a longer timescale the excavation of some key settlements has demonstrated continuity of occupation extending back for centuries or even thousands of years. One of the most fascinating settlement sites in Scotland is Jarlshof at the southern tip of the mainland of Shetland. In the middle of the site stands a seventeenth-century laird's house christened 'Jarlshof' by Sir Walter Scott in his novel *The Pirate* (1821). Around it, only discovered from under blown sand in 1933, is a long and complex sequence of settlement; a fourteenth-century farmstead, a Viking-period settlement of rectangular long houses, a Pictish broch and wheelhouses, and circular huts going back to Bronze Age and late Neolithic times. Jarlshof may not have been occupied continuously but its settlement history clearly extends over several millennia. Another classic site illustrating this kind of continuity is The Udal in North Uist, where nineteenth-century and medieval settlement levels are underlain by a sequence going back to Pictish and prehistoric times.

Although the continued use of particular sites over thousands of years can only be established by excavation, surface features often hint at prolonged occupation. At the deserted settlement of Rooal in Strathnaver, Sutherland, which was abandoned in the early nineteenth century, remains of prehistoric hut circles, a burial cairn and a souterrain were found within the improved area of the township indicating occupation at several periods in the past. In an environment like Strathnaver sites suitable for settlement and cultivation are comparatively few and it is hardly surprising that they should have been used and reused in this way.

On deserted sites, including those which have been excavated, there often appears to be a major gap in the chronology of occupation. Throughout Caithness and Sutherland, for instance, and more widely throughout the Highlands, one can find settlements where the latest buildings date from the early nineteenth century and the earliest probably do not predate the eighteenth century. Prehistoric remains often occur close by but there is a hiatus in the settlement record between them and the later structures. Field archaeologists have suggested that in Caithness and Sutherland the sites of the immediately pre-clearance townships were first settled by the Norse in pre-medieval times and have been occupied ever since. Repeated rebuilding of houses and the reuse of foundation stones have removed all traces of buildings predating the eighteenth century although careful excavation might provide some evidence of them. More careful survey of the visible remains on some of these deserted sites may indicate that not all surviving foundations relate to the late eighteenth or early nineteenth centuries and show that there is more of a palimpsest in the landscape than has sometimes been believed. In the Lochtayside area of Perthshire, for instance, a comparison of a detailed plan of 1769 with features on the ground has provided evidence that houses at several sites predate the survey. They are of more primitive construction than those which were standing in 1769; but without excavation their date remains uncertain.

In the Lowlands continuity of use of sites from the sixteenth century to the present helps to explain why there is so little trace of the medieval settlement pattern. Much of it must underlie modern farmsteads. A detailed study of crop mark sites on the gravels of the Lunan valley south of Montrose identified plenty of prehistoric sites. Medieval, or at least pre-improvement, features like ridge and furrow plough marks, field boundaries and trackways were found, but not a single medieval building. It may be that medieval dwellings were less substantially built than the ring-ditch houses of Iron Age times which showed up so clearly on aerial photographs, but even so the implication was that there were few medieval settlements awaiting discovery.

At the same time, there is likely to have been considerable continuity from prehistoric times into the medieval period. If the considerable changes of the Agricultural Revolution have failed to alter settlement patterns in areas like the Lunan Valley the more gradual changes of the first millennium AD are likely to have had even less impact. Continuity from earlier times can also be seen in the Highlands in the use of seemingly prehistoric settlement forms into the post-medieval period. These include crannogs, lake dwellings of timber constructed on artificial stone islands in freshwater lochs, which have a pedigree extending back to the Iron Age or earlier. However, one in Loch Tay was garrisoned with forty men by Campbell of Glenorchy in 1646. This was probably an unusually late and exceptional use of a crannog but there is evidence that they were in more general use in the sixteenth century and that new ones were being built as late as the 1580s. The excavation of some duns, small, thick-walled stone forts which are characteristic of the Iron Age and Dark Ages, has also provided evidence of occupation from medieval and later times. Such structures may have been used at a late date by petty chieftains who could not afford a tower house (Chapter 4).

Settlement change: expansion

The importance of settlement change can easily be overemphasised because it is often easier to detect than continuity. Nevertheless, in a country like Scotland where settlements were small and dispersed, and where both field and documentary evidence is often poor, the scale and chronology of settlement change can be hard to determine. It is important to consider how rural settlement changed during the 250 years or so from the early sixteenth century to the onset of the most rapid phase of agricultural improvement in the later eighteenth century.

During the sixteenth and early seventeenth centuries the population of Scotland increased substantially. Estimates of the scale of this increase are only guesses but one sign of population growth is an expansion of settlement. It has been suggested that in early medieval times the rural settlement pattern of Scotland, even in the most fertile areas, had an undeveloped, patchwork character. During succeeding centuries the gaps were gradually filled in as population increased until, by the early sixteenth century, the landscape was fairly intensely worked and settled. Much of this expansion was purely local, small-scale infilling with the creation of new touns on the margins of the existing improved area. Often this involved the reclamation of poorer-quality land on higher, more exposed sites or in poorly drained valley bottoms. Place names often provide evidence of this process of reclamation and infilling. Old-established settlements often have names containing elements which can be traced back to pre-medieval times, like Pit- and Bal-, while later settlement names are often purely topographical in character. Names like Muirton and Bogtoun often show the kinds of environment from which new farms were created. An increase in the number of ferm touns over time can be seen in many areas by comparing successive estate rentals, with new touns being created originally as dependencies of existing ones and eventually becoming separate and independent.

An important process of settlement change that can be observed from documents and place names, as well as in the landscape, was township splitting, where an existing ferm toun was divided into two or more separate settlements on different sites. Sometimes this occurred as a result of patterns of land ownership. Where land within a settlement was held by more than one proprietor a division into discrete units with separate settlements might be advantageous. But most townships appear to have been split simply because of population growth. When a ferm toun reached a size where the complexity of the division of its field systems started to become too difficult to manage, the normal policy on Scottish estates was to split the toun into smaller settlements rather than to allow unrestricted growth.

The modern map is dotted with groups of farms possessing a common name but distinguished by different prefixes like Easter, Mid and Wester, Over and Nether, Old and New. It was once thought that these split settlements had originated in the eighteenth and nineteenth centuries by the division of pre-improvement ferm touns into consolidated farms. However, documents often confirm that they originated as single townships but were split in pre-improvement times. The split townships were amalgamated to single farms by the improvers, but the names remain. Sometimes one or more subsidiary settlement was hived off from a parent one which retained its original site. In other cases new townships were established on fresh sites and the original one was abandoned. This is sometimes evident in the landscape where two modern farmsteads with names like Easter and Wester X a mile or two apart have the remains of a ruined church in between them marking the site of the old settlement. The business of township splitting became even more complex when it happened more than once, the townships created by an original division being themselves split at a later date.

This process has rarely left any documentation but its timing can often be established approximately by comparing sequences of rentals. Thus in Ettrick Forest a document of 1456 records the farm of Mountbenger, but by 1500 it had been divided into Easter and Wester Mountbenger. In the same area the farms of Deloraine and Kershope were similarly divided at a later date, while the original settlement of Eldinhope developed into three farms: Over and Mid Eldinhope and Eldinhopeknowe.

As well as the creation of new touns in the interstices between existing settlements there were still some new frontiers where colonisation on a larger scale was possible. These included royal and baronial hunting preserves which were disafforested at a late date. One of the largest of such areas was Ettrick Forest in the Borders which only returned to crown hands with the forfeiture of the powerful Douglas family in 1455. At this time it was a sparsely settled area inhabited mainly by rangers and wardens occupying forest stedes with some attached grazing rights. In the late fifteenth century the forest stedes were gradually converted to large sheep farms, some held directly by the crown, others leased to tenants. In the early sixteenth century most of the holders of these farms had their tenures converted from leasehold into perpetual feus which gave them hereditary possession of the lands. The original forest stedes still exist as large sheep farms in the valleys of the Ettrick and Yarrow Waters. Beside several of them stand the ruined tower houses built by the newly established pro-prietors during the sixteenth century (Chapter 4). In Glen Strathfarrer, which runs eastwards towards the Beauly Firth, the process of disafforest-ation and colonisation occurred even later. The area was retained as a hunting preserve well into the seventeenth century. From the late sixteenth century permanent settlement gradually pushed up the valley and by the end of the seventeenth century the glen had a considerable population.

In Glen Strathfarrer and elsewhere the expansion of settlement was often achieved by the permanent colonisation of shielings. These were groups of temporary huts associated with summer grazings beyond the margins of the improved land. The operation of shieling systems and their remains on the ground are discussed in more detail in Chapter 3, but here we consider the processes by which such temporary sites became permanently settled. Documentary sources sometimes provide details of this transition. For instance a report prepared in 1712 by one of the Earl of Mar's estate factors stated that the earl's Deeside feuars, though bound by their charters not to move their shielings from their traditional sites, were encroaching on the earl's deer forests between the head of the Dee, Glen Tilt and Glen Shee. The old shielings were being leased to tenants who were converting them to permanent settlements and were cultivating the ground around them. New shielings were being pushed higher into the deer forests at the expense of the game.

A steady build-up of population throughout the Highlands during the second half of the eighteenth century led to another wave of shieling conversion which, because of its late date, can be studied in detail in the landscape. In areas like Caithness, Sutherland and Upper Deeside there is a transition zone between permanently occupied farmsteads and the true temporary shielings in which traditional shieling huts are overlain by larger, more substantial buildings associated with the cultivation of small plots of ground. In the glens around Braemar the ruins of substantial farmsteads with outbuildings, corn-drying kilns and fields extend up to about 500m (1,640ft). Higher up the valleys are the remains of groups of temporary shieling huts but in an intermediate zone small circular shieling huts are sometimes overlain by rectangular buildings near which are found small cultivation plots. These may represent the efforts of landless squatters during the peak of population pressure. Given time and a run of favourable summers such sites might have become proper farmsteads, but the onset of the clearances for commercial sheep farming in the early nineteenth century fossilised their development in an intermediate state between shieling and farm. In other places, where the remains of old shieling huts occur in close proximity to modern settlements, as in upper Glen Sannox in Arran, the same process is likely to have occurred on a more permanent basis. The same transition can be shown to have happened at an earlier date in areas like the Borders by the place names of permanent farmsteads which incorporate elements like 'shiels' or 'shield', indicating that they were once shielings.

In some upland areas of England, like west Yorkshire, and in lowland wood-pasture areas like the west Midlands there was a good deal of new settlement creation in the sixteenth century by unauthorised squatting on waste land in areas where pasture was plentiful and manorial controls weak. Such areas were characterised by a high density of smallholdings occupied by families who devoted part of their time to industrial activities, such as textile manufacture, to supplement their incomes from farming. In Scotland this type of squatter fringe was uncommon. In part this was due to strong controls imposed by proprietors and estate officers who restricted indiscriminate squatting and undue subdivision of existing holdings. In addition, the balance between land and population in Scotland was more favourable. Because of the universal presence of cottars and subtenants who had some stake in the land, even in areas that concentrated on arable farming, there was no truly landless class in Scottish society. Thus there was no flow of displaced people from the more intensively cultivated lowland arable areas seeking opportunities beyond the head dyke. Where fringes of smallholding settlement were created on the margins of the improved land this was generally associated with the period of agricultural improvement and will be considered in Chapter 6.

Settlement change: desertion

The danger of generalising about settlement patterns in the pre-improvement Scottish countryside on the basis of deserted sites which may not have been typical has already been mentioned. Nevertheless, exploring an abandoned settlement and walking amid the grass-grown traces of former farmsteads and outbuildings, trackways, field boundaries and cultivation ridges can be an evocative and poignant experience which, to a greater degree than old maps or documents, connects one directly with the pre-improvement farmers who lived there and worked the land.

In England, it has been said, you are rarely more than a few miles from the site of a deserted medieval village. Identifying, surveying and sometimes excavating such sites has been a major growth area in landscape studies. In Scotland the study of deserted settlements has not advanced as far, for many reasons. In the Lowlands the landscape has been so thoroughly transformed by the improvers that the visible remains of deserted settlements are uncommon. An area like the Berwickshire Merse and lower Tweed valley contrasts with nearby Northumberland, where the earthwork sites of many deserted villages are still readily visible. The contrast probably relates to the greater intensity of cultivation in south-east Scotland compared with north-east England during the last 250 years. Away from south-east Scotland and its ancient villages the smaller size of settlement units in the Lowlands and the fact that the buildings in them were flimsily constructed means that they have often left little trace in the landscape compared with the more substantial peasant houses of late medieval England. This applies even in marginal areas which have not been cultivated since they were deserted.

In the Highlands, paradoxically, deserted settlement sites are ubiquitous. From the Western Isles to the Grampians and from Caithness to Argyll the glens are littered with their remains. They relate to the very end of our period, dating from the late eighteenth and early nineteenth centuries. Because of this their buildings are often relatively well preserved among the remains of the enclosures, access ways, corn-drying kilns and fields that surrounded them. Only one or two of these sites have been excavated. The work of Dr Horace Fairhurst on Highland rural settlement has been of major importance, especially his two excavations of sample sites, one at Rosal in Sutherland and the other at Lix near Killin in Perthshire. A number of other sites have been surveyed in detail and the relict settlement pattern in some limited areas has been mapped, but no general study of settlement desertion in the Highlands at this period has yet been attempted. Perhaps because they are so recent and the context of their abandonment seems so well known they have not attracted the interest and detailed study that they deserve.

In Lowland Scotland a number of nucleated settlements with ancient origins are known to have been deserted although the reasons are not always easy to pinpoint. Removal of a village to allow the extension of the parklands or policies (see p.147) around a country house was one cause of abandonment. When the Marquis of Tweeddale was laying out the policies around Yester House in East Lothian at the end of the seventeenth century he had the old village of Bothans demolished. It was replaced by the planned settlement of Gifford a short distance away at the entrance to the new park. The ruined parish church of Bothans close to Yester House marks the site of the original settlement. A similar process of relocation happened at Tyninghame, near Dunbar, in the eighteenth century. However, when Winton House, also in East Lothian, was constructed in the early seventeenth century the village of that name was removed but never rebuilt.

As in England, the remains of a ruined and isolated church may point to a deserted settlement site. Some places declined and vanished when parishes were amalgamated and churches went out of use. This could sometimes be a chicken-and-egg situation: parishes were often amalgamated because one centre had already declined. The East Lothian parish of Bara was merged with that of Garvald in 1702 and all that remains of the site of the village and church of Bara are traces of the old burial ground (NT 564697). Pitcox, near Dunbar, is an example of a shrunken settlement. It was originally a parish centre and a sizeable village but after the Reformation the church was moved to another village, Spott. All that is left at Pitcox is a farmstead and two or three cottages set around a small triangular green.

Other villages declined for no identifiable reason. Morham in East Lothian is one example. If you visit the site today you will still find the parish church hidden in a sheltered hollow at the end of a narrow lane. The building dates from 1724 but there has evidently been a church here from early times, as a fragment of an Anglian cross shaft was found embedded in one of its walls. The Ordnance Survey also marks the site of Morham Castle, of which there is no more trace than the adjacent village. There were still a few cottages at Morham in the 1790s but by the nineteenth century only the church was left. Its modest proportions suggest that the community was already tiny when it was rebuilt.

Many small burghs have also changed their site over time. Airth, in Stirlingshire, is an example. It was founded as a royal burgh in medieval times but it cannot have prospered as it was re-established as a burgh of barony in 1597. The original site, with the parish church, stood above the present settlement. By the early eighteenth century, however, the original burgh was in decline and the focus of activity was moving downhill towards the port. The earliest surviving structure in the modern centre of Airth is the mercat cross, dating from 1697. By 1723 the transfer of the settlement was well under way and the change of location was completed in 1820 when the old parish church on the hill was abandoned and the site of the medieval burgh was enclosed within the grounds of Airth Castle. At Greenlaw in Berwickshire the original settlement was on a relatively high, exposed site at Old Greenlaw, 1.5km (1 mile) away from the present town which lies in a sheltered valley. The original grant of burghal rights was to the old settlement but by the end of the seventeenth century it was already losing population. Markets and fairs were eventually transferred to the new location.

Other burghs were moved by landowners who wanted to extend their parks and at the same time smarten up the burghs which stood near their gates. One of the best known examples is at Fochabers in Moray. Old

Fochabers was too close to Gordon Castle so in 1774 the Duchess of Gordon persuaded her husband, who was extending the castle, to have the settlement moved. Despite opposition from some of the inhabitants who were reluctant to leave their homes, construction of a new town further from the policy walls was begun in 1776. The old, straggling burgh with its central market square was demolished and replaced with a carefully planned settlement. A similar process occurred at Inveraray in Argyll. The third duke of Argyll had conceived the idea of a new settlement to replace the existing cramped and partly ruinous burgh during the mid-1740s when he began to build a new castle at Inveraray. The old royal burgh, though small, was an important administrative, legal and trading centre, the focus of the large and widely scattered Argyll estates. Construction of the new town from the 1750s allowed the original settlement to be obliterated and the policies of the new castle were extended.

As already mentioned, many charters authorising both burghs of barony and non-burghal market centres were granted to existing kirk touns in the sixteenth and seventeenth centuries. Some of these centres developed into towns, others remained small. Some failed entirely including those which had been laid out on new sites. For example, Preston in Kirkcudbright received its charter in 1663 and was enthusiastically promoted by its proprietor, but it failed to prosper. At the end of the eighteenth century a mere three families lived here and today only the mercat cross remains within a small enclosure at the rear of a farmstead. Other market centres were eclipsed by the development of nearby planned villages during the eighteenth and nineteenth centuries. At Castleton in Liddesdale all that survives of the old nucleus of the parish is the churchyard, the remains of a series of old turf dykes, and a stone cross in the middle of a boggy field. The cross may have been erected in 1672 when the Duke of Buccleuch obtained permission from the Scottish Parliament to hold a weekly market and three annual fairs here. However, a century later the settlement was replaced by the large planned village of Newcastleton lower down the valley.

Deserted ferm touns also exist in the Lowlands and may be more common than has sometimes been believed. Some were abandoned as a result of farm amalgamation between the seventeenth and nineteenth centuries, others possibly at an earlier date. Most of the visible ones survive on the fringes of improved land in marginal areas. Few have been excavated and securely dated. One example is at Lour in the Tweed Valley above Peebles (NT 179356). Here you can see the foundations of a small tower house surrounded by a cluster of farm buildings set within an earthwork enclosure which is the reused rampart of an Iron Age fort. Around the settlement are traces of at least three types of ridge and furrow ploughing. The broader, more curving ridges may have been contemporary with the settlement. The excavators were fortunate to find

Figure 4 The rectangular foundations of a post-medieval farmstead stand within the circular boundary of a Romano-British homestead near Raeburnfoot in Eskdale.

artefacts such as clay pipes which showed that Lour had been inhabited into the seventeenth and eighteenth centuries.

Polmaddy in Kirkcudbright (NX 589878) is another deserted township, abandoned probably in the early nineteenth century, with remains of a mill and an inn as well as farmsteads, outbuildings, corn-drying kilns and field systems. A recent survey by the Royal Commission for Ancient Monuments in the Border valley of Eskdale has identified a number of abandoned farmsteads. Although their foundations are often barely traceable they stand out because, in such hilly terrain, the buildings were erected on artificial rectangular platforms. On some sites two phases of occupation can be detected; later steadings abandoned during the nineteenth century and earlier ones that probably date from the seventeenth or eighteenth centuries. Several of the sites are associated with extensive ridge and furrow ploughing and, superimposed on them, rectangular fields enclosed by turf banks which may reflect an early phase of agricultural improvement.

The problems of trying to interpret and date other deserted sites on the basis of their surface features alone are considerable. A site beside Douglas Burn, a tributary of the Yarrow Water, demonstrates the difficulties. The lower part of the valley of the Douglas Burn is dominated by a steep crag and scree slope. A series of buildings and enclosures are scattered along a river terrace at the foot of the slope, along a shelf on the hillside above, and at the top of the crag. Some of the buildings are long rectangular structures that may once have been farmsteads with attached byres. Some of the smaller buildings may have been cottages. The three groups of structures were probably occupied at different periods. It is possible that the highest ones were used by gold seekers, as a sixteenth-century source mentions this valley as a source of alluvial gold. The structures on the valley floor, which seem purely agricultural in character, may have been in use as late as the eighteenth century. Only excavation could prove this, and even then firm dating evidence might not be forthcoming.

In upland areas settlements may have been abandoned as a result of climatic deterioration. In a pioneering study linking climatic trends to changes in cultivation and settlement limits, Martin Parry has shown that in the Lammermuir Hills, between the Lothians and the Merse, high-lying settlements and fields were progressively abandoned from the fourteenth century to the eighteenth as the climate became cooler and wetter during the adverse phase known as the Little Ice Age. The remains of the settlements show up clearly on the ground and from aerial photographs. So far this approach has not been extended to other hill areas but there is plenty of scope for fieldwork. In upland areas of Aberdeenshire, such as the Cabrach and Montquhitter, many farms are known to have been abandoned at the end of the seventeenth century following a series of unusually severe harvest failures and it is possible that traces of these settlements still survive.

As well as climatic deterioration other natural disasters could lead to the abandonment of settlements. Coastal changes might cut a once-thriving port off from the sea. Old Rattray on the coast between Fraser-burgh and Peterhead is an example of a small port (albeit dignified with the status of a royal burgh) which eventually failed some time during the eighteenth century when the mouth of the Loch of Strathbeg, the inlet of the sea beside which it stood, was blocked by a belt of sand dunes. The remains of a medieval motte and a ruined chapel are all that mark the site today. One of the most spectacular disasters occurred at Culbin in Moray. The long-settled and prosperous barony of Culbin was completely overwhelmed by blown sand during a series of storms between 1693 and 1695 and the settlements within it, including the landowner's house, were abandoned. At various times the chimneys of the mansion have been visible as the sand shifted but much of the area is now planted with conifers.

In the Highlands it is likely that settlements were deserted at various periods as a result of damage inflicted by clan feuds down to the eighteenth century. However, most of the visible remains date from the later eighteenth and early nineteenth centuries. In the southern and eastern

Highlands the processes of settlement change were similar to those operating in the Lowlands. Holdings were gradually amalgamated into larger units and clachans were replaced by large consolidated farms. Unlike the Lowlands the ruined settlements have survived here because of the less intensive exploitation of the land. In the northern and Western Highlands change came later and was more traumatic. Whole groups of communities were cleared from the interior glens to make way for commercial sheep farms. In some areas the clearances began in the 1770s and 1780s though in the far north and west they were delayed until the early nineteenth century. Deserted clachans tend to be smaller in the southern Highlands, where improvement came earlier and was a more gradual process. In the north-west Highlands they are larger because clearance came later after a rapid build-up of population.

The settlements which survive from this period provide us with a last glimpse of the old peasant economy in its landscape setting. You can wander through abandoned settlements where the walls of the houses still stand almost shoulder high, surrounded by the fields, enclosures, corn-drying kilns and access ways of the former community. The Royal Commission of Ancient Monuments has surveyed some examples in Argyllshire and published their plans. One or two sites like Rosal (NO 689416) and Lix (NN 553299) have been excavated. At Rosal the township was cleared between 1814 and 1818 and its remains have been preserved within modern Forestry Commission plantations. Notice-boards help the visitor to interpret the settlement's features and indicate what is known of Rosal's history. The old improved area, which contained around 50 acres of arable land, was enclosed by a roughly circular ring dyke and formed an island of green among the moorland. The farmsteads, which at the time of the clearance housed seventeen families, were scattered in clusters around the perimeter of the improved area.

Some deserted settlements in Caithness and Sutherland actually post-date the clearances, being temporary townships which were created by tenants who had been evicted from their original homes. Badbea in Caithness (ND 087199), dating from the early nineteenth century, is an example, a scatter of several groups of houses stretching for 2 kilometres along the clifftops. In some of these clearance settlements on islands like Mull and Lismore, or on the West Highland mainland, you can see amidst the tumbled walls of the deserted clachans the shepherds' cottages which replaced them. They stand out because of their superior mortared stone construction and large windows, but they too are ruined. This emphasises how short-lived were the profits which Highland landowners made from commercial sheep rearing. When the bottom fell out of sheep farming in the mid-nineteenth century estate owners turned to an even less intensive form of exploitation, converting their sheep pastures to deer forest.

Dr Horace Fairhurst's research on the clachans at Lix illustrates many of the problems of interpreting such sites in the Highlands. A detailed estate plan of the area in 1755 shows that the layout of farms and cottages at that time bore no resemblance to that of the ruined structures which are visible today. The flimsy nature of the earlier structures had doubtless contributed to their obliteration. Even the locations of the settlement clusters have changed. The excavated remains seemed to date from no earlier than the 1780s when the three townships of Lix were each consolidated into two sheep farms. East Lix was later turned into a series of smallholdings for eight crofters. Remains of their houses are associated with a series of square fields laid out by a land surveyor but seemingly never completed. The combined house and byre dwellings of these crofters were poorly built even by the mediocre standards of their day and have a makeshift, temporary character. Subsequently a number of cottagers were allowed to settle at East Lix, swelling the township. The early sheep farms on Mid and West Lix were further consolidated into large single holdings and the township of East Lix was cleared some time in the mid-nineteenth century.

The evolution of the settlement at Lix, even within the brief period of the later eighteenth and early nineteenth centuries, was more complex than superficial examination of the surface remains suggested. Detailed search of the ground failed to reveal any trace of the buildings marked on the 1755 survey or indeed from any earlier periods. Only the head dyke, the shielings and some of the trackways through the settlement appeared to survive from the landscape portrayed on the mid-eighteenth-century plan. The lack of foundation trenches, the use of plain earth floors and flimsy walling materials like turf and unmortared stone combined to prevent the identification of earlier buildings. Houses of this type were designed to be recycled within the farming system; the thatch and the turf walls would have gone on the compost heap for spreading on the arable land, while the stones and timbers would be reused for new structures.

The paucity of the remains of the older settlements at Lix emphasises one of the major problems of reconstructing past settlement patterns in Scotland. Houses were so flimsily built that they have generally failed to survive in the landscape and do not always show up even in excavations. Nevertheless, when considering settlement patterns in abstract it is easy to forget that they comprised agglomerations of individial buildings. In order to understand pre-improvement Scottish settlement fully we need to know more about the character of rural housing and it is to this problem that we turn in the next chapter.

2

The pre-improvement landscape: house and home

A dearth of buildings

It is a paradox that we know more about rural housing in Scotland during the Iron Age than during the sixteenth century. In part this reflects the interests of archaeologists but it also emphasises the fact that many types of Iron Age hut have left a more permanent imprint on the landscape than their medieval successors. Very few houses of the ordinary rural population built before the middle of the eighteenth century have survived intact. One reason for this was the generally poor and flimsy nature of building construction, which gave most houses only a short lifespan. Another influence was the revolution in housing standards that occurred during the later eighteenth and early nineteenth centuries. The Agricultural Revolution brought increasing prosperity for farmers in the more progressive parts of Scotland and latterly housing conditions improved even for labourers and farm workers. As we shall see in Chapter 6, this was reflected in the building of farmhouses, cottages and outbuildings whose standards of construction and comfort were a vast improvement on what had been acceptable even a generation or two earlier.

The evidence for traditional housing in Scotland before the eighteenth century is much more limited than for England, where many houses have survived from Tudor times onwards and where a number of late-medieval 'peasant houses' on deserted village sites have been excavated. In Scotland, stone appears to have been relatively uncommon as a building material in many areas before the eighteenth century, being used only for the footings on which walls of clay or turf were constructed. Many houses must have had a lifespan of only a few years before they deteriorated enough to require major repairs or complete rebuilding. Excavation has shown that even nineteenth-century houses in the Highlands were built without proper foundations. The scanty remains of such flimsy structures were easily obliterated by the erection of later buildings on the same site, particularly recent ones with proper foundations. Thus there is little hope of tracing sequences of occupation in the way that has been possible for some deserted English villages like Wharram Percy.

Nevertheless, some traditional buildings survived into the nineteenth century as the homes of smaller farmers and farm workers, or as outbuildings. In a number of cases farmhouses built in the old style were downgraded to accommodation for cottagers, for animals or sometimes merely for storage, like the cruck-framed farmhouse and byre at Corrimony in Glen Urquhart which was converted into two cottages by upgrading the cowshed into a house! Many buildings which have survived from the later eighteenth century were improved in later times but their fabric often provides clues which allow reconstruction of their original state.

In the more remote areas of the Highlands like Skye, the Outer Hebrides or Caithness, some traditional styles of building, notably the Hebridean 'black house', survived into the present century. This is due in part to the prevalence of smallholdings and the peculiar regulations governing the tenure of crofts during the nineteenth century which made the tenant rather than the proprietor responsible for providing housing. In such districts some interesting examples, built mainly during the nineteenth century, are still intact. They provide indications of how houses may have been built in earlier times. Although many such buildings appear primitive by today's standards they were often transitional in character, embodying changes in layout and innovations in construction that were considerable improvements on what had been normal a century earlier. Despite this they provide a link with housing in earlier centuries which we can otherwise reconstruct only from historical references or excavation. Some traditional houses have been preserved as the centrepieces of museums of rural life. Although most of them were built after 1800, making some allowance for improvements in material conditions they nevertheless provide the visitor with the clearest impression of what the more primitive houses that they replaced must have been like.

Even in areas where housing standards improved rapidly in the later eighteenth and nineteenth centuries, rural craftsmen were slow to change their traditional building techniques and continued to use methods like cruck timbering, clay walling or stone and turf gables in buildings of improved design and construction, some of which are still standing. The study of such late survivals of traditional building techniques can provide further clues to the nature of pre-improvement housing as long as they are interpreted with caution.

The character of traditional housing can also be reconstructed by excavation and from documentary sources. Archaeology can provide valuable information about the size, layout and construction techniques of buildings which have been reduced to their foundations or which have left no visible traces on the surface. However, as mentioned in Chapter 1, there have been relatively few excavations of medieval and post-medieval settlements in Scotland, so that we have evidence from only a handful of sites.

Documentary sources supplement the scattered visible evidence in the modern landscape. The late eighteenth and early nineteenth centuries produced an unprecedented burst of descriptive writing about the Scottish countryside. Sources like the Old Statistical Account and the county reports on farming produced for the Board of Agriculture contain much information on contemporary housing. Although standards of living were changing rapidly by this time writers often described traditional buildings in some detail to emphasise the contrast between them and recent improved dwellings. The level of detail which such accounts contain is sufficient to establish some regional and local variations in building styles and materials. For the later seventeenth and early eighteenth centuries documents contained in collections of estate papers often provide information about house construction. However, as one goes back into the seventeenth century the number and detail of such descriptions tails off rapidly. For the sixteenth and seventeenth centuries the accounts of English and foreign visitors often contain interesting and pithy comments on the poor quality of Scottish housing.

In 1577 Martin Frobisher's expedition in search of the North-West Passage called at Orkney *en route* for the Davis Strait. The expedition's chronicler described the houses of the Orcadians with almost as much wonder as he would later write about those of the Eskimos of Baffin Island:

> Their houses are verie simply builded with pebble stone without any chimneys, the fire being in the middest thereof, the good man, wife, children and others of the familie eate and sleepe on one side of the house and their catell on the other verie beastlie and rudely in respect of civilitie.

Seventy years later a Cromwellian soldier described houses in the Lowlands as 'low thatcht cottages full of smoke and noysome smells. In many places their families and cattell be under one roof.'

Visitors only needed to venture a mile or two north of the Border to appreciate the difference in housing standards. Celia Fiennes did this in the later seventeenth century, having already described the houses that she had seen in the Lake District as primitive compared with those of southern England. Despite this, the ones that she found on the Scottish side of the Border seemed an order of magnitude worse. Perhaps it was because of this that she returned to England so promptly!

The poor quality of house construction was linked to the general poverty of Scottish society before the later eighteenth century but there were more specific reasons for low building standards. Until the later seventeenth century many tenants held their lands by purely verbal agreements which were renewed from year to year. At best they had written leases for only a few years. This did not encourage the investment of capital and labour in building solid and durable houses and outbuildings. In practice most tenants were fairly secure in the possession of their lands as long as they paid their rents but they were unlikely to receive any compensation for major improvements to farm buildings if they moved to another holding. Sub-tenants and cottars had an even less secure hold on their small plots of land. It was not usual, before the later eighteenth century, for land-owners to build houses for their tenants or even to allow them some remission of rent at the start of a lease in lieu of providing accommodation. Tenants and sub-tenants were expected to construct their own dwellings using whatever materials could be obtained locally; stones turned up by the plough for foundations, clay or turf for walling and a variety of materials for roofing. The only things which tenants in most areas could not easily obtain themselves were the main construction timbers. By the seventeenth century most of the Lowlands and substantial parts of the Highlands had been stripped of woodland, and good-quality construction timber, whether from remnants of natural woodland, landowners' plan-tations, or imported from abroad was scarce. Surviving timber reserves were strictly controlled by landowners, who were thus obliged to provide construction timber for their tenants.

Timber-frame construction and roofing

Apart from the Western and Northern Isles, where houses with thick stone walls were built with ordinary A-frame roof timbers, traditional houses almost everywhere in Scotland had roofs supported by frameworks of braced timber arches or crucks. The cruck frames transmitted the weight of the roof direct to the foundations rather than to the walls. This meant that the walls of such houses did not have to be load-bearing; they were generally constructed of flimsy materials which filled in the spaces between the crucks.

Where cruck-framed buildings have survived in Lowland Scotland their walls have generally been rebuilt with more permanent materials. These, rather than the timber framework, now support the roof and the crucks have simply been left in place out of inertia. In many parts of the High-lands you can find ruins of houses dating from the late eighteenth or the early nineteenth centuries with solid stone walls and gables which were perfectly capable of supporting the weight of the roof but which were still cruck framed. Although the houses are mostly derelict today and the crucks have been removed, their former existence is shown by the slots in the lower parts of the walls into which they fitted. There is no logical reason for such a 'belt and braces' solution to supporting a roof. It was probably an anachronistic survival from earlier in the eighteenth century when buildings in the Highlands were mostly cruck framed with flimsy turf walls. When the use of mortared stone became more usual it is likely that buildings continued to be constructed with crucks out of habit although they were no longer strictly necessary. On some deserted settlement sites in the south-west Highlands the stone foundations of two types of building can be seen, narrower houses sometimes being overlain by later, wider ones. It has been suggested that the narrower design was also an anachronism and that originally such dwellings had been built with cruck frames and walls of turf. The introduction of more solid stone walls allowed wider houses to be built but this was not appreciated at once.

The more versatile timber-frame technique of box framing, so familiar from lowland England, was not used in Scotland outside the larger towns, probably owing to the general poverty of the rural population and the high cost of suitable timber. The use of cruck frames imposed restrictions on the plan, height and width of buildings. Unless the crucks were made from very substantial pieces of timber or were mounted high up on very solid walls, only single-storey dwellings could be built with, at best, a cramped attic or loft. One of the few examples of a two-storey cruck-framed house to have survived is at Pitcastle, near Pitlochry (NO 973554). Here the crucks are bedded in solid walls of stone and clay mortar. However, this building was the home of a small laird and was distinctly superior in construction to the kind of house that an ordinary farmer would have possessed. Even lofts were rare before the eighteenth century; most buildings were simply open to the rafters. Because the crucks curved inwards it was impossible to extend buildings sideways, so houses were generally only one room deep, their width limited by the span of the timber arches. The most economical way to extend such a structure was lengthwise by adding extra sets of crucks. This led to a tendency to tack units on end to end, often producing very long ranges of buildings.

The cruck timbers were the most valuable part of a house. Oak or ash wood was preferred to pine or birch but at a pinch anything would do. In areas where peat mosses were extensive it was common to dig ancient tree trunks and branches out of the peat for house building. Crucks were often poorly constructed and makeshift. This is sometimes apparent in surviving examples where the cruck blades are fashioned from several pieces of timber fastened together rather than from a single piece of wood. In Caithness, an area that was very short of timber by the eighteenth century, surviving crucks tend to be barrel-shaped in section as a result of being made from odd bits of wood held together with wooden pegs. Because of the dearth of good timber thin pieces of birch wood were used along with bog timber and the ribs of abandoned fishing boats which at least had the advantage of being ready curved. In the Outer Hebrides, where only driftwood was available, roof timbers were very flimsy and cruck framing was not used at all. Elsewhere in the Highlands and in some parts of the Lowlands roof timbers normally belonged to the tenants who removed them when they left a farm at the end of a lease. Where timber was more plentiful the standard of cruck construction might be higher, as can be seen in a cruck-framed building at Priorslynn near Canonbie in Dumfriesshire (NX 394759).

More generally landowners provided the 'great timber' for house building including the cruck frames and sometimes the purlins and rafters. Inevitably, landlords were parsimonious, postponing the replacement of unsound crucks for as long as possible, which sometimes led to houses being in a poor state of repair. In 1682 the tenants of the baronies of Hailes and Traprain in East Lothian were forced to 'complean exceedingly with the badnes of there houses'. When they entered their holdings the proprietor had agreed to repair the buildings but had failed to do so. A late seventeenth-century inventory of tenants' houses in the barony of Thornton, also in East Lothian, records the provision of timber 'to John Murrays stable that fell and almost destroyed his horse' and to Adam Manderston 'for his dwelling house that fell to the ground'. Even in situations like these proprietors continued penny pinching by supplying short pieces of timber to shore up rotten crucks rather than replace them. A survey of repairs needed to houses on the Leven estate in Fife in 1682 contains entries like 'John Mitchell in Craigencatt is weak both in the couples timber and walls and some of his couples are broken and will be needfull to be taken down and repaired.' Small wonder that virtually no examples of this class of house have survived!

Various kinds of material were used for roofing. Straw thatch, with or without an underlay of turf, was widely used. Today the tradition of thatching has almost died out in Scotland and only a scattering of thatched houses survive, but this type of roofing was once widespread from Shetland to the Solway and from the Hebrides to Aberdeenshire. Modern thatching is far superior and more durable than the kind that was generally used in the seventeenth and eighteenth centuries. This was designed to be replaced almost annually. Wheat and rye straw were preferred for thatching when available though oats and barley straw were also used. In some areas, particularly the eastern Lowlands, straw thatch was daubed with a layer of clay to make it more weatherproof and longer lasting, while in the Kilmarnock area a covering of lime was used for the same purpose. In pastoral areas rushes or bent grass often took the place of straw. Heather formed a durable, if heavy, thatch which could last for a very long time. Buildings thatched with heather can still be seen at the museum of rural life at Auchindrain in Argyll and at the National Trust for Scotland visitor centre at Culloden Moor. Bracken, broom and gorse were also used and in many areas turf often formed the main roofing material, particularly for the houses of poorer families.

In parts of Caithness and in Orkney where thinly split flagstone was readily available, the houses of more prosperous tenants were roofed with it. Because of their weight, houses roofed with flagstones had low pitched roofs. Flagstone roofs were often covered with turf for better insulation and to protect the flagstones from frost, which might split them. Elsewhere slate was virtually unknown as a roofing material for ordinary houses. It was heavier than thatch, requiring more closely spaced roof timbers and, given the poor quality of cruck timbering, probably a liability. Its use was confined to the outbuildings surrounding mansions, castles and for home farms though even here straw and heather thatch were often used. The outbuildings at Castle Kennedy near Stranraer, the seat of the Earls of Cassillis, were roofed with heather in the late seventeenth century while straw thatch remained a common roofing material in small towns until well into the nineteenth century.

In east-coast areas pantiles, with their warm red tones, are widely used today for roofing both houses and outbuildings. Because they blend in so well with the landscape they give the impression of being an old-established roofing material. In fact pantiles only became fashionable in the later eighteenth century as a cheap and durable replacement for thatch. At first they were mostly used for outbuildings and the poorest cottages. It was only during the later nineteenth century that it became common to use them on more substantial houses. Traditionally pantiles were first brought over from Holland as ballast. There is no definite evidence for this but it is quite possible that original specimens were brought from the Low Countries and copied locally.

Walling

The use of solid stone walls, whether cemented with lime or clay mortar, appears to have been uncommon for ordinary houses in Scotland before the later eighteenth century. Stones turned up by the plough in the fields were usually too rounded to bond together well, unless they were set in a matrix of turf or clay. The labour and expense of quarrying building stone was rarely considered worthwhile for ordinary houses, except in areas like Orkney where the use of local flagstone for walling followed a tradition extending back to prehistoric times.

Turf was probably the most common walling material, either used on its own, on top of a stone footing, or laid in alternate courses with field stones. Some turf-walled buildings in north-east Scotland survived late enough to be photographed, but the lifespan of most simple turf dwellings must have been short. In the Highland parish of Kiltearn at the end of the eighteenth century such houses were demolished every five to seven years and added to the dunghill. Walls built from a combination of stone and turf were also common. Although less well insulated than solid turf walls, they were more durable and reduced the damage done to pasture by stripping off its turf. The turf needed for walls and roofs was pared from rough grazing land or even arable land in fallow. Admittedly much of the material was recycled back to the land via the dunghill when the houses were demolished but even so this practice must have done a lot of damage to the land. It was probably for this reason that the paring of turf was often strictly regulated by local baron courts. The use of turf or turf and stone continued into the nineteenth century in many areas; a turf gable can be seen on Old Leanach Cottage at Culloden. Documentary references suggest that wattle, sometimes plastered with clay, was also used for external walling though most surviving examples of wicker work of this kind come from internal partitions.

In many east-coast Lowland areas from Ross-shire to Berwick, as well as in Ayrshire and Galloway, clay mixed with straw or other binding agents was used as the main walling material. Provided that it was protected from the weather by an exterior cladding of harling or roughcast, clay formed a solid walling material capable of supporting the weight of a roof, one that could last for a long time. As a result there are still a number of clay houses surviving in various parts of Scotland though many examples have been demolished in recent decades. Errol in the Carse of Gowrie has some notable two- and three-storey clay houses. More 'clay biggins' and clay-walled outbuildings have survived than houses built with any other traditional walling materials. Clay was also used as a mortar into which dry stones could be bedded when lime mortar was not available. It allowed the construction of chimneys and gables. Clay was sufficiently durable for its use to be allowed in some nineteenth-century planned villages; some were still standing in the weaving village of Luthermuir in Angus in the 1970s.

House layouts

The standard house layout throughout Scotland before the Agricultural Revolution was one in which human beings and livestock were accommodated under a single roof, using a common entrance, with only a flimsy partition separating them. This arrangement is sometimes referred to as a byre-dwelling or, more generally, as a 'long house'. The latter name may be misleading. Where living quarters, byre and sometimes stable and barn were built end to end a very long structure could indeed result, as can be seen in some surviving Orkney farms. However, right at the bottom of the social scale, a house shared by a cottar family and their single cow was not necessarily very long. Nevertheless, the term has become so firmly established for this kind of dwelling that we will use it here.

Long houses were widespread in fairly recent times in Ireland, Wales and Brittany. They were also built in late medieval England but by Tudor times had been replaced in most regions by more comfortable houses with separate byres. As a result the survival of this primitive type of arrangement in Scotland was one feature which struck English visitors during our period. The origins of the long house go back to pre-medieval times. Clear examples have been discovered from the Norse settlements at Jarlshof and Underhoull in Shetland, and it has been suggested that the Norse may have introduced the design. At Jarlshof, however, long houses were a feature only of the later phase of Norse occupation and it is possible that the style was adopted from the native Pictish population. That long houses were common in medieval Scotland is suggested by recent excavations at Springburn Park near Kelso where three simple stone-walled, cruck-timbered houses were discovered. They had cobbled areas at one end which appear to have been occupied by livestock and were dated to the late twelfth or thirteenth century.

It was usual to build a long house on a slight slope with the byre downhill so that the liquid and solid manure did not flow back into the living area. The cattle were normally kept indoors for an extended period during the winter and this caused waste disposal problems. There was often a drain for liquid at the downhill end of the byre; the solid manure was removed either by breaking down part of the end wall or by using a muck hole which allowed the manure to be shovelled straight out on to the dunghill. The arrangement of the house uphill and the byre downslope was not an invariable one; the late eighteenth-century houses excavated at Lix in Perthshire actually had the byres uphill, a feature which can hardly have been conducive to the comfort of the human inhabitants. Written descriptions of houses and some early prints as well as structural remains of surviving long houses show that in the poorest dwellings the division between man and beast was only a low wooden partition. It was reckoned to be beneficial to 'let the coo see the fire'. The heat which the animals, and their dung, gave off must have helped to keep such houses cosy, if smelly.

In most houses before the eighteenth century the arrangement for heating and cooking was to have a hearth in the middle of the floor, with the smoke escaping through a hole in the thatch. A later development was a stone back-wall for the central hearth with a clay chimney or 'hanging lum' above to direct the smoke upwards. Gable ends with fireplaces and chimney stacks were late developments for most of the population. The houses of the poorest folk had a single multi-functional room in which everyone lived, ate and slept. During the seventeenth and eighteenth centuries it became more common for the houses of better-off tenant farmers to be divided into two main rooms: a kitchen and living area and a private apartment where the farmer and his family slept.

During the eighteenth century living standards improved and a greater degree of separation between the living area and the byre became common. At first this often merely involved building a more substantial partition wall between the two units, perhaps of stone instead of wood or wattle, but retaining the interconnecting door. The next stage was to re-design the house so that people and animals had separate entrances. A further step was to make a complete separation by building a new detached byre and converting the old one to extra living accommodation. A recent study of surviving traditional houses in Caithness has identified examples of each of these phases. At Laidhay, near Dunbeath, an example of one of these late eighteenth-century long houses, modified in the nineteenth century and inhabited until 1968, has been turned into a folk museum. Its structure shows some of the modifications which resulted from this process of upgrading.

By the end of the seventeenth century there are indications that housing standards, at least for the better-off tenants, were beginning to improve. Lime mortar was being used increasingly, although from references in contemporary documents it is sometimes difficult to decide whether lime was being used for making mortar or as an external coating on houses whose walls were built of other materials like clay. A survey of houses in the barony of Lasswade in 1694 indicates that by this time the homes of the larger tenants were of two storeys, built with lime mortar, with several rooms and glazed windows. A tenant's house at Bridgend of Lintrathen in Angus extended to eight sets of couples with a hall, back chamber, inner chamber and pantry. The windows were glazed and there was at least one chimney.

Closely comparable was the house of Thomas Innes, the Earl of Panmure's factor or steward at Belhelvie near Aberdeen, which was described in a detailed inventory dated 1705. It extended to fourteen couples, or sets of crucks, with walls of stone and clay mortar. There were four rooms with glazed windows on the ground floor. Part of the house at least was lofted with timber boards and the walls were built high enough for four glazed windows to light the first floor. One or more single-storey ranges of outbuildings including a kitchen, pantry, barns, byres and peat house adjoined the main block. It is difficult to know how widespread houses of this kind were at the opening of the eighteenth century. Innes' farm, which extended to a ploughgate of land, was not unusually large. However, although primarily a farmer he received a salary for his work as factor and also engaged in small-scale trading ventures, so he was probably wealthier than the average tenant.

George Robertson, writing in 1829 and looking back to the 1760s, described the farmhouses of the Lothians on the eve of the most rapid phase of improvement. They were low built with only a few small windows. Roofs were of straw thatch and turf. The farm dunghill was generally right outside the front door. Houses were divided into two main rooms, the 'but' and the 'ben'. The first was the kitchen and servants' apartment where the entire household met at mealtimes. The 'ben' was the farmer's private quarters where he and his family slept at night and friends were entertained. There was usually a low attic above, providing storage space and a place for the male farm servants to sleep. If this sounds primitive it was still a considerable improvement on earlier centuries. At least there was a proper fireplace and chimney stack in the gable instead of an open hearth in the centre of the floor and a hole in the thatch to let out the smoke, as was still normal for farmers in less prosperous areas and for cottars, even in the Lothians, in the 1760s. The houses of cottars at this date were still only mean hovels with walls no more than 5 feet high made of alternate courses of turf and field stones. The average cottar family lived in a single-room house only about 12 feet square.

Some early plans of farmsteads on the Penicuik estates near Edinburgh, dating from the opening years of the eighteenth century, show that farmhouse and outbuildings were arranged around three sides of a courtyard with a boundary wall enclosing the fourth side. This kind of layout was to become more common towards the end of the century. As the slow trend towards the amalgamation of holdings in many parts of the eastern Lowlands created larger farms requiring more extensive sets of outbuildings, the old pattern of building farmsteads in a single long line was no longer adequate.

Many of the houses which have survived from the eighteenth century have been preserved because of literary associations; Robert Burns' Cottage in Alloway is one of the last surviving examples of early eighteenth-century vernacular building in south-west Scotland. It was built around 1730, a typical thatched clay biggin with a but and ben layout and a byre at one end. Souter Johnnie's Cottage in Kirkoswald, a few miles away, is similar in some respects but, dating from c. 1785, is rather more sophisticated. Hugh Miller's cottage in Cromarty was built in 1711. Thatched but with solid stone walls and crow-stepped gables, it was built by a sea-captain. It extends to six rooms, showing that the people who occupied it were considerably more prosperous than the parents of Robert Burns. It gives a good impression of what many houses in Scotland's smaller burghs must have looked like during the eighteenth century. Some other surviving traditional buildings are linked with historical events like Old Leanach Cottage, which stood on the battlefield of Culloden in 1746. It has low stone walls and a heather thatch. Inside is a reconstructed hanging lum. The roof has been raised since the cottage was originally built but it retains its original central hearth and earth floor.

Although standards of housing improved rapidly towards the end of our period, so that all but fragmentary traces of earlier buildings were swept away, some echoes of the older housing tradition are still visible in the

Figure 5 Souter Johnnie's Cottage, Kirkoswald, is a good example of a late eighteenth-century thatched dwelling (National Trust for Scotland).

present landscape. The continued preference for single-storey homes with, at most, attic dormers, is evident throughout the countryside, in most planned villages, and in many small towns. This distinctively Scottish trait is one of the first to strike visitors from south of the Border. Scottish houses also still tend to be long and narrow. In many nineteenth-century cottages, built long and low, albeit with slate roofs and mortared stone walls, there is more than a hint of the old cruck-framed houses of the pre-improvement period.

Regional house types

For Lowland Scotland enough information is available from written sources and surviving structures to give a general impression of regional variations in the use of construction materials but not how they were combined to produce particular styles of housing. For the Highlands and Northern Isles we are more fortunate. Here improvements in housing standards came later and more gradually so that traditional types of house survived well into the nineteenth century and in some cases into the

Figure 6 Old Leanach Cottage at Culloden near Inverness is a good example of a mid-eighteenth-century house in this area. Note the heather thatch, turf gable and rough stone walls (National Trust for Scotland).

twentieth. An early study of Highland houses distinguished three main categories: the Hebridean 'black house' which was found in the Outer Hebrides and Tiree, the Skye House which occurred on that island and adjacent mainland areas like Ardnamurchan, Ardgour and Morvern, and the Dalriadian type which was characteristic of Argyll and Mull, the heartland of the ancient Scottish kingdom of Dalriada. Houses in Orkney and Shetland also had characteristic features which have been preserved in some surviving examples.

Perhaps the most distinctive type of traditional Scottish house to survive into recent times is the 'black house' of the Outer Hebrides. The name 'black house', or *tigh dubh* in Gaelic, seems to have originated during the early nineteenth century to distinguish these older dwellings from the more modern houses built with mortared stone and lime-washed (*tigh geal* or 'white houses') which replaced them. It has also been suggested that

Figure 7 This barn at Canonbie, dating from the end of the eighteenth century, has solid clay walls patched with stone, and preserves its original cruck timbers inside.

the name might have been descriptive of their dark, smoky interiors. The most characteristic feature of these houses was their massive walls, often over 2m (6ft) thick, formed from a double skin of dry stone with a core of peat or earth. This feature has parallels with some Viking-period houses which is not to say that there has necessarily been direct continuity between them.

The roof timbers of black houses were relatively flimsy, often fashioned from odd pieces of driftwood, and resting on the inner edge of the walls. The covering of straw thatch came down to the centre of the wall rather than overhanging its outer face, leaving a wide ledge all round which gave ready access to the roof when the thatch was being renewed. Rain draining off the thatch thus percolated through the earth core in the centre of the wall, helping to bind it together and make it more draught resistant. The stones forming the inner faces of the walls were laid so as to prevent moisture from trickling into the building. Nevertheless, in the later nineteenth century these houses had a bad reputation among health authorities as breeding grounds for tuberculosis on account of their dampness and lack of ventilation. The walls had rounded angles with a distinct inward slope or batter and the structures were hip-ended without gables so that they were thatched all round.

In appearance Hebridean black houses look weatherproof and streamlined offering minimum resistance to the gales which sweep the Long Island in winter. They also appear extremely primitive and ancient.

Despite efforts by Lord Seaforth, the proprietor of Lewis, the thatch of such houses was still being renewed annually until the end of the 1880s and houses were still being built on the old pattern in the early part of the present century. Considerable numbers continued in use as homes into the 1950s. These later black houses were often modified with stone gables, chimney stacks and larger windows. A number were still inhabited in the 1960s and early 1970s but virtually none are in use today. However, some former black houses still survive as outbuildings, and ruined examples are common throughout the Outer Hebrides. One has been preserved as a museum at Arnol on the west coast of Lewis. Built around 1875 and inhabited into the 1960s it is a classic long house with a byre at the lower end and a single entrance for people and animals. A barn was built parallel to the main block with a connecting passage between the two. The living end of the house was heated by an open central hearth but there was no hole to let the smoke escape, far less a proper chimney. The roof was of straw thatch, secured by straw ropes weighted down with stones. Windows were confined to small openings in the base of the thatch.

Superficially houses like these appear so primitive that one might think that their features had remained unchanged for centuries. Early writers did, in fact, believe that there was direct continuity from houses built by Norse settlers in the ninth and tenth centuries to these nineteenth-century examples. However, there are indications that a number of the features of the classic Hebridean black house were recent developments. Outer Hebridean houses at the end of the eighteenth century were even more spartan and simple but it is impossible to establish their character in earlier times. If there is a direct link between such houses and ones from Norse times, a gap in the archaeological record of 700 or 800 years still needs to be filled before this can be proven. Similarities in construction techniques between two widely spaced periods might merely be the result of independent adaptations to simpler environmental conditions using the same local building materials.

Descriptions of houses in the Outer Hebrides during the early nineteenth century indicate that the double-thickness stone wall was not usual then; walls were either of turf with an inner facing of stone or built with alternate layers of turf and stone. Earlier black houses may also have had proper smoke holes. The straw thatch on these houses was often renewed annually. The smoke from the peat fires that were kept burning constantly impregnated the thatch with soot, and the sooty straw formed a valuable manure. In early photographs of the black house at Arnol you can see how the thatch over the dwelling part of the building was much thicker than that over the byre. Each summer when some of the inhabitants and the cattle had been sent away to the shielings the thatch over the house was stripped off and the furniture stored in the empty byre whose thatch, further from the fire, was less sooty and was not renewed so often.

Figure 8 Inhabited into the 1960s this Hebridean black house at Arnol on the west coast of Lewis preserves many of the classic features of this distinctive house design.

Figure 9 The last village of inhabited black houses in western Lewis, at Garenin, photographed in 1974 shortly after their inhabitants had been rehoused.

It is thought that it was only with intensification of cultivation accompanying the rapid growth of population in the Outer Hebrides in the later eighteenth and early nineteenth centuries that the thatch became so prized as a fertiliser and was removed so frequently. The use of smoke holes declined so that as much soot as possible could be trapped among the thatch. The abandonment of smoke holes can be considered as an improvement in agricultural terms though not, surely, in terms of standards of comfort. It is little wonder that the faces of Hebridean crofters in early photographs often appear black! Thatch which was poorly laid and renewed so frequently was rarely completely watertight. As well as smoke, another hazard of living in such houses was the 'black drip' of soot-impregnated water that had percolated through the roof. This was particularly annoying when people were trying to sleep and was one reason why enclosed box beds were so popular.

Evidence from the surface remains of older black houses, and from archaeological research, suggests that houses in the eighteenth century were different in layout. The main house and byre unit was flanked on one side by the barn but also on the other by an additional block comprising a porch and store room. A good ruined example of this type can be seen immediately below the Broch of Carloway on the west coast of Lewis (NB 190413). Each of the three parallel units was roofed separately but the various rooms were inter-communicating via passages in the thick walls. There are even indications that in the eighteenth century or earlier large communal housing units accommodating two or three families may have been used, a layout recalling the Neolithic settlement at Skara Brae in Orkney.

The Skye house was similar to the Hebridean black house in being thatched and hip-ended but the walls were only single skinned, though often thick and inward-sloping. A good example, still with its heather thatch, can be seen in the village of Plockton in Wester Ross. Further south the Skye house gave way to the Dalriadian type which had sturdy stone gables and cruck frames. As explained earlier, houses of this type may have developed only in the second half of the eighteenth century.

In Orkney and Caithness a number of traditional farmsteads dating back to the eighteenth century have been preserved, partly as a result of the use of local flagstones for walling and roofing. These stones provided a building material which was durable and also versatile. The classic Orkney farmhouse was a really long 'long house'. There was a central two-roomed living unit, at one end of which was the byre and at the other the stable and barn. The barn had a clay threshing floor with twin doors which could be opened to provide a through draught for winnowing the corn. Right at the end of the barn was a massive circular corn-drying kiln. The harvest was often gathered late and wet and kilns for drying the grain were a necessity for every community. At many deserted settlements in the Highlands, like the one at Lix, communal kilns are found scattered throughout the townships but in Orkney, where arable farming was more important, they were an integral part of the larger farmsteads.

All the units were inter-communicating so that they could be reached from the dwelling area in bad weather without going outside. Kirkbister (HY 283253) is one of the few Orcadian farmsteads whose construction can be securely dated: in this case 1723. This was a higher-status building than most Orkney farmsteads, as is reflected in its more spacious and comfortable layout. Corrigall farm (HY 324193), dating from the later eighteenth century, has been preserved as a museum. It shows a more developed plan with three ranges of buildings: house, byre and barn, set parallel to each other and separated by paved areas.

Shetland has a different geology with a lack of good building stone compared with Orkney's ubiquitous flagstones. Yet in Dunrossness, the southern part of the Shetland mainland, the houses have many features reminiscent of Orkney. This relatively fertile area was settled by migrants from Orkney and mainland Scotland during the seventeenth century and they brought their own building styles and designs with them. South Voe croft museum, near Sumburgh, is a good example of one of these Orkney-derived farmsteads. It consists of a long house with a cross-passage between the byre and the living quarters, and a barn with a corn-drying kiln alongside. The house dates from the nineteenth century but probably reflects earlier styles in its thatched roof held down by ropes weighted with stones. It has gables, one with a stone chimney, but originally there was an open hearth and a smoke hole in the thatch has been reconstructed.

Doocots

One class of pre-improvement agricultural building is still a common feature in the Scottish landscape: dovecotes, or doocots. Doocots epitomise the old feudal order in the countryside. They were, by the seventeenth century at least, a perquisite of landowners and are often found close to their castles or mansions. This may help to explain why so many have survived, along with the old tradition that bad luck was liable to befall anyone who demolished a doocot. Pigeons were a valuable source of fresh meat during the winter, a change from the flesh of cattle which were slaughtered and salted at Martinmas. But pigeons made great inroads on surrounding crops. While a statute of 1503 had encouraged landowners to build doocots as a source of food, an act of Parliament in 1617 restricted their construction. It was stipulated that they could only be erected for proprietors who had a rental income of 10 chalders of grain drawn from lands lying within a radius of 2 miles of the proposed doocot. The aim of this was to ensure that the birds fed mainly at the expense of the land-owner's own tenants rather than those of other proprietors.

Figure 10 This pepperpot
doocot stands immediately
adjacent to the ruins of
Dunure Castle, Ayrshire,
reflecting its status as a
landowner's privilege.

Doocots were simply stone structures with hundreds of ledges inside for pigeons to nest on and holes for them to fly in and out. Nevertheless, variations in their design are interesting. The oldest surviving ones, to judge by datestones, were built in the later sixteenth century. These early doocots fall into two main types. The first is the beehive shape, circular in section and tapering towards the top like fat pepperpots. These generally have protruding string courses running round the outside to prevent rats from climbing in and destroying the eggs. Good examples of this type of doocot can be seen at Dirleton Castle and near Preston Mill, both in East Lothian, although examples occur as far north as Orkney. The other early style is a rectangular design known as a lectern because of its sloping top. Both single and double-width lectern doocots can be found.

Doocots generally faced south to give the birds a sunny surface to sit on, while sheltering them from cold northerly winds. Some areas, like Fife, have mainly beehive doocots. Others, like Angus, favour the lectern type. It has been suggested that the popularity of the round design in Fife was due to the lack of suitable slate or flagstone for roofing material; the lectern type required a larger roof. However, in other areas, like the Lothians, both types of doocots are found while beehive ones can be seen in Orkney which has plenty of good roofing stone. Other designs occur; one at Culloden House outside Inverness is octagonal and another at Boath, near Nairn, is circular with a conical roof. Some doocots, like one at Tealing near Dundee, which is dated 1595, are constructed like conventional buildings with pitched roofs and crow-stepped gables.

Although most doocots date from the sixteenth and seventeenth centuries they continued to be built in later times. Examples occur with classical columns and pediments. The smallest ones had boxes for about 500 pigeons but large ones could accommodate 2,000 birds. Inside, a revolving wooden ladder gave access to the boxes, though this has survived in only a few examples. It is possible to gain access to the interiors of some doocots, like the one near Preston Mill in East Lothian which is owned by the National Trust for Scotland, or the double lectern example at Tantallon Castle. While holding your nose against the smell it is worth reflecting that pigeon droppings, periodically cleared out from the bottoms of doocots, were the most highly prized manure available for spreading on arable land and vegetable gardens!

Mills

Grain mills were a ubiquitous feature of the pre-improvement countryside in Scotland. The most common type was the water-powered mill driven by a conventional vertical water-wheel, a design which was used in Scotland from at least the twelfth century. The evidence of charters suggests that there may have been at least 4,000 such grain mills in Scotland in the sixteenth and seventeenth centuries, possibly many more. Small water-powered mills were found in or adjacent to nearly every large nucleation. There was generally at least one mill on each estate because milling grain was, like possessing a doocot, a landowner's monopoly. Proprietors' feudal rights included thirlage, the right to compel their tenants within a defined area or 'sucken' to grind their grain at a particular mill. Landowners generally provided the capital for constructing the mill, which was then leased to a miller for a substantial rent. The miller recouped his rent and generally made a reasonable profit, by charging the tenants multures, a fixed proportion of the grain which they brought to be ground, usually somewhere between a thirteenth and a twenty-fourth, along with additional small payments to the mill staff. In addition, as part of their labour services, tenants were often required to help repair the mill, lade and dam, and bring home new millstones. Although it was widely resented by farmers, thirlage was so profitable to landowners that it was not

Figure 11 Preston Mill, East Lothian, dating from the eighteenth century, is a good example of the simple country grain mills which were once ubiquitous in the Lowlands.

abolished, in many areas, until the end of the eighteenth century. Complaints about thirlage in the Old Statistical Account of the 1790s show that it was still enforced in many parts of the Lowlands, only being generally abolished as a relic of feudalism in the early nineteenth century.

Because each mill had a monopoly over a limited area they were generally small, simple and not very efficient. Each mill served only a limited population and there was no competition. Most pre-improvement mills have disappeared from the landscape, leaving only a place name like Milton, or a few grass-grown foundations beside a stream, to mark their former location. A fine example has been preserved at Preston Mill in East Lothian. The National Trust for Scotland has restored this to working order and you can have a guided tour of the machinery and learn about the intricacies of milling. The fabric of the mill itself probably dates from the eighteenth century but the adjacent corn-drying kilns may be earlier. Originally the buildings were thatched but now they are roofed with pantiles. Their picturesque appearance emphasises how well such small-scale industry blended in with the countryside. Preston Mill was powered with water drawn from the nearby River Tyne but this stream was sometimes a fickle friend, subject to violent spates, as the various flood marks on the walls of the mill show.

Primitive mills like this remained normal until well into the eighteenth

Figure 12 This mill with its overshot wheel at New Abbey south of Dumfries, built in the late eighteenth century, represents a more sophisticated generation of mill construction.

century. Later in the century, however, a new generation of larger, better built and more mechanically sophisticated water-mills began to take their place. They were still built to serve local needs but often replaced two or three earlier, smaller ones. Sandy's Mill on the River Tyne upstream from Preston Mill, and East Saltoun Mill, also in East Lothian, are good examples but others can be found throughout the Lowlands. They generally have large, square corn-drying kilns built into the fabric of the mill. A working example has been preserved at New Abben near Dumfries, originally the site of a corn mill belonging to Sweetheart Abbey. The present mill dates from the later eighteenth century. Boardhouse mills at Birsay in Orkney is another interesting group with an eighteenth-century estate mill which was replaced by a larger nineteenth-century one. During the nineteenth century milling became further concentrated in the towns, and many country water-mills went out of business although some continued in operation until well into the present century.

In the Highlands and Islands thirlage was not imposed very strictly, or even at all. As a result, large water-mills with vertical wheels were rarer. More grain was ground at home using a hand-operated quern, a practice which was usually expressly forbidden in the Lowlands because it infringed proprietors' rights of thirlage. In the Northern and Western Islands many traces can still be found of a distinctive type of mill, the horizontal water-mill, or click mill. Often built to serve individual families or small groups of tenants rather than entire communities, such mills were tiny and the head of water needed was so small that almost any rivulet could be harnessed to power one. Water was taken from the stream by a stone-lined lade and drove not a vertical wheel but a set of horizontal paddles located in a lower chamber directly underneath the millstones. The millstones in the upper chamber were powered directly by the rotation of the paddles below without any need for gears, as with vertical wheels. The millstones themselves were little bigger than hand querns.

Horizontal mills were well adapted to an economy in which the amount of grain produced was modest and an environment where streams were numerous but too small to drive a vertical water-wheel. Their remains are common throughout the Outer Hebrides, particularly on the west coast of Lewis and in Shetland where there are estimated to have been around 500 in the early nineteenth century. There were fewer of them in Orkney due to a lack of suitable streams and because a system similar to thirlage restricted their use. Many of these mills continued in use throughout the nineteenth century and even later. Some have been restored to working order in recent years. One example is at Shawbost on the west coast of Lewis where the mill building is designed like a small black house. At Dounby, you can visit Orkney's last surviving horizontal mill. Another has been restored near the South Voe Croft Museum in Shetland. At Troswick, also in Shetland, one mill from a string of nine on the same stream has been restored.

The origin of this distinctive type of mill is uncertain. Horizontal mills are also known from Caithness, the West Highland mainland as far south as Kintyre, Ireland and the Isle of Man. This has caused some people to suggest that it was introduced by the Norsemen. However, there are indications that this distribution is a relict one; it may be that such mills were once more widespread in Britain but were replaced in many areas at an early date by mills with vertical wheels. There are scattered references to horizontal mills on Deeside in the eighteenth century and in the Angus glens in the sixteenth and seventeenth. Although the remains of many of these early mills may have been swept away by subsequent floods, careful fieldwork may yet reveal traces of them in the eastern Highlands. It is also possible that they may have occurred in the Lowlands during medieval times.

In some parts of Scotland, where streams were sluggish and there was insufficient water to drive a mill wheel, windmills were used. They were particularly popular in areas like Orkney where the wind seems ever present. East Lothian, with its low rainfall and gentle topography, also had a number of windmills, the remains of some of which can still be seen. One at Knockenhair on the outskirts of Dunbar has been converted into a house, as has an even larger one at Bielside a few kilometres away. Two main types of windmill were used in Scotland, the post mill and the tower mill. Post mills are recorded from as early as the thirteenth century but no surviving examples predate the eighteenth century. They were simple structures with a stone base and a wooden millhouse above. The whole superstructure was moved round to suit the wind by means of a long tail beam, sometimes fitted with a wheel for ease of movement. The remains of one of these can be seen at Peckhole on North Ronaldsay. One of the most imposing tower mills is at Dumbarney south of Perth. It has a tapered stone tower still nearly 6 metres high over a vaulted basement into which sacks could be lowered directly on to carts. Although modified at a later date the mill was probably built during the seventeenth century.

Individual buildings and the settlements that they made up formed the foci around which the remainder of the rural landscape was organised. Having considered settlement and housing in some detail we will now look beyond the farmstead and ferm toun to see what the rest of the pre-improvement countryside was like.

3

The pre-improvement countryside: field and farm

The face of the land

So far we have considered rural settlement and housing in pre-improvement times; but what did the landscape around the settlements look like and how did it change between 1500 and the Agricultural Revolution in the later eighteenth century? This is not an easy question to answer because, as we shall see in Chapter 6, the countryside has changed so much since then. Travellers' accounts and descriptions by Scottish topographers show us a landscape filtered through the perceptions of their authors. English visitors in the sixteenth and seventeenth centuries commented on the lack of woodland throughout the Lowlands: they rarely ventured into the Highlands. They also noted the absence of enclosed fields, the low standards of housing, and the general poverty of the inhabitants. English chauvinism sometimes led to spiteful, exaggerated comments about the Scottish countryside. Thomas Kirke, writing in 1679, described the landscape as 'being but one large waste surrounded by the sea'. Other, more fair-minded, visitors mentioned the fertility of arable areas like the Merse and the Lothians while criticising the backwardness of farming techniques, notably the lack of hay and the propensity of Scottish farmers to cultivate steep slopes in preference to draining the valley bottoms. The limited extent of enclosures and plantations around landowners' dwellings, and the grim, castellated appearance of their homes, also attracted comment.

Descriptions by Scottish topographers were as patriotic as English accounts were derogatory, emphasising to an improbable degree the fertility of the countryside and the abundance of its produce. Their descriptions of landscapes rich with corn and livestock refer to areas dismissed by visitors as bleak and barren. A good deal depended on what you were accustomed to! Many accounts by Scottish writers are mainly repetitive catalogues of the seats of the gentry and nobility within each district, and of the parklands or policies that surrounded them. This emphasises the extent to which landowners dominated Scottish society and how their castles and mansions dominated the landscape. The parks and plantations which surrounded landowners' seats must have stood out like islands of improved, enclosed and wooded land in an open, bare countryside which had few field boundaries and little woodland.

A similar image of the countryside is gained from the magnificent map known as the Military Survey which was produced by the army under the direction of William (later General) Roy between 1747 and 1755. The original sheets of the survey, drawn on a scale of one inch to 1,000 yards, are preserved in the British Library. The delicate watercolour tints of the original map depict streams in blue, settlements and roads in red, woodland in green, hill country in brown and arable land in yellowish tones. The Military Survey was carried out when the first effects of agricultural improvement were beginning to be felt in more advanced areas like the Lothians. Here the enclosure of policies and home farms was progressing steadily and the islands of improved land were starting to coalesce. Elsewhere, however, the estate policies with their enclosed fields, avenues and blocks of planting contrasted sharply with the unimproved countryside around them.

When information from individual sheets of Roy's survey is plotted at a small scale, broad patterns of land use throughout Scotland become clear. Some regional contrasts are abiding and are still evident today such as the concentration of arable land in the Lowlands and its relative sparseness in the Highlands. Even so the extent of cultivation in many Highland glens and Border dales in the 1750s is surprising as is the amount of unimproved land in many parts of the central Lowlands. Enclosed farmland was heavily concentrated in Galloway where it was linked with the cattle trade, around Glasgow, and in the Lothians with lesser concentrations in central Ayrshire, the Merse and Fife. Some remnants of natural woodland still survived in parts of the Southern Uplands, notably around Nithsdale, but forests were much more plentiful in the West Highlands.

Even by the second half of the eighteenth century the basic features of the pre-improvement Scottish landscape do not seem to have changed very much, to judge from Samuel Johnson's comments on his famous tour to the Hebrides with Boswell in 1773. His remarks on the open nature of the Lowland landscape, the lack of enclosures, and the small extent of plantations around gentlemen's houses all echo the comments of travellers in the sixteenth and seventeenth centuries. Johnson was particularly struck by the lack of trees. By this date even the West Highlands seemed devoid of timber. On Mull he lost his walking stick and wryly commented that he did not expect to have it returned: 'Consider, sir, the value of such a piece of timber here!'

Professor Jimmy Caird has described the modern Scottish countryside as the product of revolution rather than evolution. Compared to parts of England, where many features in the modern landscape can be traced back to pre-medieval and in some cases prehistoric times, this is true. So much of the pre-improvement landscape has been swept away by the pattern of regular enclosed fields laid out by the improvers that only fragments are recoverable on the ground. Many of its features can be reconstructed from surviving estate plans but only limited numbers of these predate the second half of the eighteenth century. Thus they portray the pre-improvement landscape in its final stage after centuries of evolution. It is much more difficult to study it during the sixteenth and seventeenth centuries and much harder to pinpoint changes than for the better-documented eighteenth century.

Nevertheless, it is evident that in the Scottish countryside continuity rather than drastic change was characteristic of the sixteenth, seventeenth and early eighteenth centuries. Although it will be argued in Chapter 6 that agricultural improvements began earlier than has often been believed, there was undoubtedly a rapid acceleration of progress from the 1760s and the subsequent rate of landscape change was much faster than anything that had gone before.

In many parts of Scotland the revolutionary character of the landscape can be appreciated from its rigid geometry, which is clearly a product of the 'Age of Reason'; sometimes enclosure boundaries cut right across traces of earlier cultivation. Yet the degree of continuity from pre-improvement times is probably greater in many areas than has been realised. This was emphasised in a study of landscape change in Ayrshire by J. Lebon published in 1946. Strangely, his interesting approach has not been repeated very often since then. Lebon compared pre-improvement estate plans with ones drawn after the landscape had been refashioned and with early Ordnance Survey maps. From this it was clear that in the more fertile arable lowlands of central Ayrshire the landscape had indeed been altered drastically but that in the surrounding pastoral districts there had been a greater degree of evolution and continuity from earlier times in the layout of fields, boundaries and roads. It is possible that in other parts of Scotland too the 'landscape of improvement' may have inherited more from earlier times than has usually been appreciated. In some areas, like the former estates of the earls of Panmure near Edzell on the fringe of the Grampians, it is possible to walk over the ground with a photocopy of a pre-improvement estate plan in your hand, noting the former location of the scattered parcels of arable land and matching them exactly with areas of present-day cultivation.

A further difficulty is that our view of pre-improvement farming has been heavily coloured by the writings of the improvers themselves who condemned it as archaic, inefficient and unchanging. They were, however, propagandists who had every incentive to present as unfavourable a contrast as possible between the old styles of farming and the improved methods which they advocated, so their comments arc often entertaining but are palpably biased. In fact, as we shall see, there was a good deal of change in the Scottish landscape between 1500 and the 1760s.

Field systems

Arable farming in pre-improvement Scotland was organised around a type of open-field system. In some of its basic features it was similar to the field systems which were found throughout Britain in medieval and later times. However, in the details of its operation Scottish cultivation practices had more in common with Ireland than with lowland England. The arable land belonging to each ferm toun had no permanent internal boundaries between the various strips and blocks; the cultivated area was divided from the rough pasture by dykes of turf or stone. The arable land fell into two main categories: infield and outfield. In most parts of Scotland the infield formed only a small proportion of the total cultivated area, often around a quarter. This was usually situated on the best land, close to the ferm toun, and was cultivated very intensively. It received most of the farmyard manure accumulated from the byres during the winter as well as the dung from animals that were pastured on the stubble after harvest.

Over most of Scotland the infield was kept in continuous cultivation with an endless succession of crops of oats and bere (a hardy form of barley). In Galloway a system in which only bere was sown on the infield was practised and in some other districts there was a simple division of the infield into two halves, one sown with oats and the other with bere. A more common system was to have a third of the infield under bere and two-thirds under oats in any year. In the most fertile parts of the Lowlands, particularly where additional fertilisers like seaweed or lime were available, wheat, a more demanding and less hardy crop than oats or bere, was also grown. In such areas crops of peas or beans were also taken between the cereals; farmers were aware that legumes improved soil fertility although they did not know why. Bare fallowing on the infield, to give it a rest between cereal crops, was used only in the most progressive areas. Infield rotations including wheat, peas, bere, oats and fallow were not uncommon in Berwickshire, Roxburghshire and the Lothians in the late seventeenth and early eighteenth centuries but they may have been a relatively recent development.

The outfield, much more extensive than the infield in most areas, was only cropped with oats, the hardiest cereal. The sole manure this land usually received was dung from livestock that were folded at night on the outfield during summer inside temporary dykes. Once the land was sufficiently dunged the dykes were thrown down and the plots were ploughed. After two or three crops a portion of outfield was generally worn out and yields had deteriorated so much that cultivation was abandoned and the land left to rest for a few years before being ploughed once again.

Although outfield husbandry has been described as a kind of shifting cultivation, with the implication that it was a primitive, almost haphazard system, in practice the outfields of most townships were cropped regularly. A system in which each plot was cropped for three or four years and then left for an equal period was common, particularly in the north-east. This intensity of outfield cropping was feasible mainly in areas where rough pasture was abundant and the use of the unploughed outfield for grazing was not crucial. In a sense it was a variant of the improved systems of convertible husbandry used in England, where areas of land were kept under arable for a few years and then permanent pasture for a comparable or longer period. The main element that was lacking in order to produce reasonable yields was the adequate application of fertilisers.

In summer the livestock of a township grazed areas of infield and outfield that were in fallow and the rough pastures beyond the head dyke. After harvest the animals pastured on the stubble of the infield and the cultivated plots of outfield. To help feed them in winter natural hay was cut from the rank grasses and sedges that grew beside streams or in marshy hollows. Even though livestock numbers were reduced in the autumn by selling off or killing surplus animals, lack of winter fodder was one of the principal shortcomings of the farming system. In spring the animals were often so weak that they had to be physically lifted out of the byres to the pastures.

Crop yields from this system were generally mediocre. A return of three times the quantity of seed sown was regarded as a break-even yield for a tenant farmer who had to set aside seed corn for the following year, feed his family and pay his rent. An old saying 'ane to saw (sow), ane to gnaw, and ane to pay the laird witha' expressed the notion that returns from cultivation were often around three to one, as did the practice of assessing the value of growing crops in the inventories of deceased tenants at three times the value of the grain sown.

Returns of oats on outfield land were often around three to one, sometimes lower, and the quality of the grain was sometimes so poor that the straw was considered the most valuable product. Yields on the best infields might rise to six or seven to one in a good year but were often around four or five to one. It must be stressed that our information on crop yields from Scottish pre-improvement farming is still very scanty. Much of the evidence takes the form of generalised comments rather than specific figures from particular plots of land. For one or two estates we have details of the quantities of grain sown and harvested on the mains under the proprietor's direct management but such details are sporadic. It is worth noting, however, that in one or two cases where long runs of data are available there was a significant increase in crop yields from the late seventeenth century into the middle of the eighteenth. The system was clearly capable of substantial improvement.

The simple model of infield–outfield farming outlined here is highly generalised. There were all kinds of regional and local variations. In the Highlands and the Border dales the cultivated land formed only a tiny proportion of the total area. Some large sheep farms in the eastern Borders during the late seventeenth century ran to as much as 500ha (1,235a) but only 25ha (62a) of this or even less might be under cultivation. In a survey of the district of Assynt in Sutherland in 1,779, many townships had over 1,000ha (2,500a) of land but less than 50ha (124a) of arable.

In the most intensively cultivated areas like the Lothians, the Merse and Strathmore a high proportion of the land was under the plough by the late seventeenth and eighteenth centuries, so permanent pasture was in short supply. Many lowland farms in such districts had all their lands under infield or outfield so that the only available pasture in summer was on the unploughed portions of the outfield. Outfield land on such farms was vital as a source of grazing.

In the past it has been suggested that infield–outfield farming was merely an adjunct to a basically pastoral economy which was not geared to large-scale cereal production. However, detailed study of sample estates in the Lothians suggests that the system could be adapted to quite intensive cereal production. On the Dundas estates outside South Queensferry, close to Edinburgh, Scotland's largest single market for grain, detailed documents allow a reconstruction of the farming system in the mid seventeenth century. The infield accounted for around 70 per cent of the arable area. With half the outfield in cultivation, 85 per cent of the arable area was under crop in any one year. Intensive rotations including wheat, peas, bere, oats and fallow were practised with lime as a fertiliser. Animal husbandry played only a minor part in the farming system and the estate was so short of pasture that the draught oxen had to be sent to summer grazing some 25 kilometres away from late May to early September. The farming system was becoming more intensive for the infield was continuing to expand at the expense of the outfield. Effectively, the farming system at Dundas involved the use of reasonably well-balanced four- and five-course rotations over most of the arable area.

However, infield–outfield cultivation was rarely this intensive. Surviving estate plans indicate that over most of Scotland the arable area was discontinuous, being broken into a number of small blocks on the better-drained land, separated by areas of rough pasture and boggy ground, a pattern which contrasted markedly with the huge, continuous open fields of lowland England. In the Hebrides cultivation by spade or a special foot plough called a caschrom rather than animal-drawn ploughs was common. These implements turned the soil over more thoroughly than conventional ploughs. Hand cultivation and the intensive application of seaweed as a fertiliser on small plots of land produced very high yields. Returns of ten, fifteen or even twenty to one are recorded. In less fertile upland areas the proportion of infield to outfield was very small and in some high-lying areas there might be no infield at all.

Infield–outfield cultivation has been described as a primitive system which combined two contrasting but simple types of agriculture: constant tillage and shifting cultivation. It has also been suggested that medieval English two- and three-field systems evolved from infield–outfield layouts. The implication is that Scottish field systems, so far as we can reconstruct them, were archaic and arrested in their development. The origins of the infield–outfield system have been seen as early, possibly going back to prehistoric times, with the outfield, derived from shifting cultivation, coming first and eventually acquiring a more intensive core of infield.

However, research by Professor Bob Dodgshon has suggested a different interpretation. In many cases the lands belonging to particular Scottish touns are defined by land denominations such as merklands, husbandlands and ploughlands which are known to have originated in early medieval times but which then became fixed and inflexible. It can sometimes be demonstrated that these denominations only refer to the infield area. This suggests that the infield made up the original extent of a toun's cultivated land, as defined in its early charters, and that the outfield represented a later extension into the waste which lay outside the formal framework of early land assessments. Infield may have acquired its intensive character in medieval times as a result of restrictions which prevented touns from expanding their cultivated areas into the waste. The relaxation of restrictions on the expansion of cultivation into the waste, and the consequent creation of outfield, seems to have begun during the fifteenth century but occurred on a much larger scale during the sixteenth century, a period when Scotland's population was growing steadily.

From a farming point of view the creation of outfield made sound sense. Under a medieval infield-only system the livestock would have been driven beyond the head dyke during the summer to keep them away from the growing crops, so the manure that they deposited was wasted. A logical step was to confine the animals into temporary folds at night and then, when they had fertilised plots of land, these could be cultivated. This opportunism, done initially on an irregular basis, may then have been systematised into the more organised outfield farming described above. If this theory and its chronology are correct then the infield–outfield systems which are described in some detail during the later eighteenth century had developed comparatively recently and were far from being static and archaic.

Runrig

Within any toun the pattern of land occupation was a complex one. Farmers rarely held their lands in large, compact blocks. As in the open fields of medieval England holdings were fragmented into a complex pattern of scattered strips and parcels. The township of Funzie on the Shetland island of Fetlar was surveyed in detail in 1799. It had 77ha (189.5a) of arable land split into 459 separate parcels. The Berwickshire village of Coldingham had 596ha (1,473a) of improved land divided into 339 plots owned by 47 different proprietors. These strips were demarcated by baulks or unploughed areas which provided access to the strips and were often used for grazing tethered livestock. Plots were also defined by ploughing ridge and furrow, as will be described in the next section. Each successive ridge might form strips held by different people but sometimes two or three ridges were grouped to form wider blocks of land.

The fragmentation of land within open fields in Scotland is linked to a much misunderstood term: 'runrig'. Runrig involved the intermixture of land belonging to different cultivators. Inevitably this fragmentation required cultivators to co-operate closely in many aspects of farming including the crop rotations they used, ploughing, harvesting, and above all in pasturing their animals so that livestock should not stray into growing crops. There were two kinds of runrig. Proprietary runrig occurred where lands belonging to different landowners were intermingled. This sometimes happened where land was divided between surviving heirs. Normally the eldest son inherited the bulk of the property but where there was no surviving son and more than one daughter it was customary to divide the land equally between them with strict attention to the quality of the land as well as its quantity. This produced intense fragmentation, as both the best and the worst land was shared out between the heiresses.

Fragmented ownership patterns also occurred when tenants were able to convert their short leases to feu ferme tenure which granted the land to them in perpetuity. In the sixteenth century this often happened when ecclesiastical estates disposed of their lands to sitting tenants in order to raise ready cash to pay rapidly rising taxes to the crown. As the tenants' lands were generally already fragmented this produced a complex pattern of ownership, particularly where the number of newly created small proprietors was considerable, as in some of the big feuar touns of the Tweed Valley and the Merse. It was not until well into the eighteenth century that these scattered holdings were consolidated into more compact units.

The other form of runrig occurred when land was owned by one proprietor but was fragmented among his tenants. This arose from the practice of granting holdings as shares in a toun rather than as discrete units. Fragmentation was an inevitable result of attempts to ensure that each tenant received a fair share of the best and the worst land. Originally these shares may have been reallocated every few years or even annually, a practice which seems to have continued longest in the Highlands. A few examples of the redivision of Lowland runrig touns are on record but mostly the shares had become fixed on the ground by the seventeenth century. This is shown by the wording of many leases for fractions of a toun in which the incomer's share is simply defined as those parcels occupied by his predecessor. Tenant runrig could easily be removed by a proprietor by ordering a new division of the lands into consolidated blocks or by waiting until leases of the various shares fell vacant and then amalgamating them into larger units.

We know relatively little about how the shares in runrig farms were allocated though references exist to tenants drawing lots to choose their portions. That such allocation was often done on a systematic basis is suggested by documents and hinted at in place names. Many leases and charters refer to tenants holding the sunny and shadow halves of a farm. Superficially this sounds as if one farmer had a compact block of territory on a south-facing slope and his less fortunate neighbour held land facing northwards, yet this terminology was often applied to farms in situations where the topography does not fit such an interpretation. This appears to be a relic of an ancient practice known as 'sun division' which was first described in detail for medieval Scandinavia and has also been identified in medieval England. Under this system the position of a person's strips in any block of arable land was defined in relation to those of his neighbours by the course of the sun across the sky from east through south to west. To take the simplest case: in a farm divided between two tenants the man whose strips in any field lay towards the east or south would be said to have his strips towards the sun: the sunny half; while the other tenant, whose lands lay towards the west and north, would have his lands away from the sun: the shadow half.

By the sixteenth and seventeenth centuries the terms 'sunny' and 'shadow' occur less frequently in documents but the use of this technique to divide out shares in runrig farms still appears to have been frequent. On the modern map traces of this system appear in place names. The present landscape is dotted with pairs and groups of farms with a common name distinguished by the prefixes 'east' and 'west'. Farms with 'north' and 'south' are far less common. Another frequent pairing is where farms are identified by the prefixes 'over' and 'nether'. In some charters it can be shown that these terms are synonymous with east and west, expressions which themselves referred to sunny and shadow portions in systems of sun division. The frequency of these names suggests that many ferm touns whose lands were allocated in this way were, at some stage, split into two or more units whose names, transferred to modern farmsteads, have perpetuated a memory of the original fragmented and intermingled shares in a system of sun division.

The development of improved rotations, the amalgamation of holdings into larger units, and the enclosure of land rapidly removed the infield–outfield system and runrig in the later eighteenth and early nineteenth centuries, as we shall see in Chapter 6. However, a few stray traces of runrig still survive in the landscape to provide an impression of how arable land throughout Scotland must have looked in earlier times. One notable example is on the island of North Ronaldsay in Orkney. Almost the whole island remained in runrig until 1832 when most of the intermixed strips were exchanged to create consolidated holdings. However, around 80ha (200a) of land at the north end of the island remained in runrig till the 1880s. Even now, although the crofters have had their lands reallocated in compact blocks, they have retained a pattern of unenclosed strip fields producing a patchwork landscape of different crops interspersed with strips under grass on which cattle are tethered to prevent them from damaging the unenclosed crops on either side.

Ridge and furrow

One feature of pre-improvement farming which can often be seen in the modern landscape, often in upland, marginal areas which have not been ploughed during subsequent periods, is cultivation ridges, or ridge and furrow. Cultivation ridges were created by a plough with a fixed mould-board which always turned a furrow slice over in the same direction. In using such a plough it was normal to work outwards, ploughing first in one direction and then back in the other, so that the furrow slice was always turned on to ground that had already been ploughed, and not over untilled soil. To avoid unnecessary waste of time in moving the team from one side of the ploughed area to the other, at the end of each furrow the land was generally ploughed in narrow strips. The result of constantly throwing the furrow slice towards the centre of such a strip was that a ridge was built up with a crest in the centre of the strip and low furrows at the margins.

This makes the formation of ridge and furrow sound accidental but in fact it was done deliberately to assist drainage. Water flowed from the crests of the ridges into the furrows. These were aligned roughly downslope and carried the water into larger field drains. This aspect of ridge and furrow can often be seen today as a vegetation difference. One can frequently find heather, which prefers drier conditions, on the better-drained ridges and moisture-loving grasses and sedges in the wetter furrows. Ploughing ridge and furrow might result in the part of the crop that was sown on the crests of the ridges becoming parched in a dry year, or the grain in the furrows being waterlogged in a wet one. However, such a system provided a way of achieving a basic subsistence yield under a wide range of weather conditions.

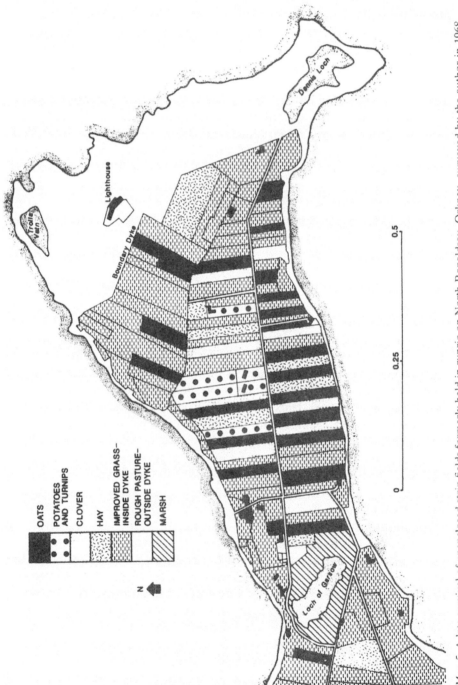

Map 5 A late survival of unenclosed strip fields formerly held in runrig on North Ronaldsay, Orkney, surveyed by the author in 1968.

Figure 13 Curving, irregular, pre-improvement ridge and furrow on a hillside near Douglas in Clydesdale.

Because they were kept in place permanently, pre-improvement cultivation ridges are often broad and high; up to 3 feet from furrow to crest. They are also frequently curved in a reversed S-shape. This is thought to have been due to the difficulty of turning the cumbersome old Scots plough and its team at the end of a furrow. Eight oxen or sometimes more, yoked in pairs, were often used to pull a heavy plough through a stiff clay soil. Turning this team at the end of a furrow was so hard that the ploughman began edging his oxen round into a curve well in advance, producing the characteristic shape.

Ridge and furrow can be seen all over Scotland on improved pasture, golf courses, as at Prestonfield near Edinburgh, or rough moorland. It often stands out best under a low slanting sun in the early morning or late evening when the faint ridges cast shadows, or under a partly melted cover of snow. Not all ridge and furrow dates from pre-improvement times. The technique continued in use until the advent of undersoil drainage in the first half of the nineteenth century. Much marginal land was ploughed up temporarily during the Napoleonic Wars when grain prices were high. Pre-improvement ridges are often found at higher altitudes and those dating from the late eighteenth and early nineteenth centuries are very different in character from earlier ones. The ridges themselves are lower, flatter and often narrower.

The improved ploughs which were developed in the later eighteenth century were less well adapted to throwing up high ridges which, in any case, made the use of the new implements difficult. From the mid-eighteenth century the old high ridges were progressively levelled. Lower ridges were created within the new enclosed fields by ploughing the crests down every couple of years so that the crest of a ridge one year would become a furrow the next. The use of more efficient ploughs and smaller teams of horses allowed cultivation ridges to be ploughed absolutely straight and this is another hallmark of late ridging. The old, high, curving ridges probably survived in some more marginal areas until the end of the eighteenth century. From surface appearance alone it is impossible to decide whether ridges of this type date from the eighteenth century or were created during medieval times although the relationship between areas of cultivation, ridges and other landscape features may provide clues.

So far relatively little effort has been made to plot in detail the visible traces of pre-improvement ridge and furrow and other associated landscape features. This was done recently for part of the Lunan Valley in Angus and it was clear that the crop marks which were mapped showed a complex landscape which had been modified in detail over time in all sorts of ways. Instances were found of trackways overlying ridge and furrow ploughing which was in turn superimposed on even older access ways. Again the scope for detailed fieldwork, especially in conjunction with early estate plans, is considerable.

Cultivation limits and reclamation

In Scotland cultivation limits can be hard to define before the Agricultural Revolution. The most permanent boundary in the landscape was the head dyke which enclosed both the infield and the outfield in many touns. In areas where pasture was abundant and settlement relatively thin, as in many parts of the Highlands, it took the form of a ring-dyke surrounding the settlement, an island of improved land in a sea of waste. This can be clearly seen at the deserted settlement at Rosal in Strathnaver and on many other similar sites. On small low islands, like the northern isles of Orkney the head dyke demarcated not an uphill but a downhill limit, dividing the arable land from the foreshore which was preserved as common grazing. This can be seen best on North Ronaldsay where a substantial stone dyke encloses the island in a continuous circuit of 19 kilometres. Although it did not reach its final form until the nineteenth century it was established at an earlier date.

Old head dykes, usually above the modern limits of improved land, can often be traced as tumbled stone walls or worn turf dykes, sometimes with a contrast in vegetation on either side. Sometimes they emphasise a natural boundary in the landscape, with a marked steepening of the slope above. In other cases the line is more arbitrary, reflecting a balancing of human need against the efforts of further reclamation. Early studies of the head dyke assumed that while temporary intakes of land might be made above it, its position was relatively stable over long periods. Given the changes that occurred in population levels, food prices, living standards, and farming technology during our period this is not entirely likely.

Nevertheless, the altitude of the pre-improvement head dyke in different areas emphasises regional and local variations in environmental conditions and highlights the opportunities which were available to farmers in the past as well as the constraints they faced. In the Outer Hebrides, the Northern Isles and much of the West Highland mainland the limit of improved land is often only 30m (100ft) above sea level, sometimes even lower, reflecting, in a very maritime climate, the degree to which increased rainfall, wind speed and cloudiness with even modest gains in altitude limits the scope for arable farming. On the open moors of Caithness and the rolling hills of Sutherland the head dyke occurs at up to 120m (400ft). In the Grampians, drier and sunnier, it rises to over 300m (1,000ft) at the head of the Dee and the Spey. In the eastern Borders it can be found as high as 365m (1,200ft) though on the more exposed coast of Wigtownshire it drops to 90m (300ft).

Not all land within the head dyke was necessarily improved and temporary outfield plots were sometimes cultivated above it. The head dyke was sometimes extended and the area within its perimeter enlarged. On old estate plans or on the ground it is sometimes possible to trace the line of an older head dyke lying inside the more advanced limits reached during the eighteenth or nineteenth centuries. However, in some areas, notably parts of the Southern Uplands, there does not appear to be a clear head dyke at all.

Although the topic has only been considered in a fragmentary way for particular localities, we have some pointers to the long-term trend of cultivation limits in Scotland between 1500 and the Agricultural Revolution. There is evidence that in medieval times, when climatic conditions were warmer, cultivation was sometimes pushed to limits which would seem impossibly high today. In the Lammermuir Hills between the Lothians and the Merse, and doubtless in other upland areas, traces of ridge and furrow ploughing can be found at altitudes of up to 400 metres. From the fourteenth century wetter, cooler conditions, the dramatic cut in population caused by the Black Death and later epidemics, as well as other influences such as the impact of English invasions, led to some of the highest-lying land being abandoned. Despite this the maps drawn by Timothy Pont at the end of the sixteenth century show that cultivation limits in south-east Scotland were still high by modern standards. This did not necessarily mean that more ground was cultivated overall than in later times. Before the construction of proper roads (see Chapter 8) overland transport of a bulky commodity like grain was expensive and difficult. Every rural community tried to produce the cereals it needed for basic subsistence so that even remote sheep farms high in Border valleys or communities in rocky Highland glens had small patches of arable land. Also, it was often easier to cultivate higher well-drained slopes than lower, more marshy ground, the drainage of which required a lot of expense and labour.

It is harder to generalise about trends in cultivation limits from the sixteenth century onwards because regional variations were considerable. There was a retreat of cultivation in some areas, notably Kintyre during the mid-seventeenth century due to outbreaks of plague. However, during the sixteenth and early seventeenth centuries Scotland's population was growing steadily with an advance of cultivation margins in some districts. In south-west Scotland cultivation limits may have reached their maximum in the late sixteenth century but in western Scotland the most active phase of reclamation occurred some 200 years later. In the Highlands the steady build-up of population during the second half of the eighteenth century caused a general expansion of arable land which continued to the eve of the clearances in the early nineteenth century.

Despite local variations there are indications of a substantial expansion of the arable area in many parts of the Lowlands during the sixteenth and seventeenth centuries. Often this process is indicated by township splitting and the appearance of new settlements in estate rentals. In the Lothians and other parts of central Scotland a major expansion of cultivation occurred in the early seventeenth century with the discovery that lime, when burnt and added to acidic soils, greatly improved crop yields on existing fields and allowed the intake of new land for cultivation.

A series of parish descriptions written in the later 1620s catches this process in action. In areas where a good deal of land was already under cultivation liming encouraged the conversion of outfield to infield and the adoption of more intensive infield rotations. The results of liming were especially impressive at the margins of cultivation such as the plateau below the escarpment of the Moorfoot Hills south of Edinburgh and the moors between the Lothians and north Lanarkshire. Here, liming allowed a considerable intake of new land at altitudes of around 180–220m (600–700ft). Lime was quarried and burnt whenever coal occurred close to limestone and increases in rents, matching the rises in productivity, had been spectacular.

A number of drainage and reclamation schemes were carried out during the seventeenth century. Although modest compared with achievements in the Low Countries or the English fenlands these were nevertheless symptomatic of a growing desire to invest capital and labour in agricultural improvement. A small number of freshwater lochs are known to have been drained from stray references surviving among collections of estate papers. Many other schemes may have gone unrecorded or have yet to be discovered. At Mertoun in Berwickshire Sir Walter Scott of Harden drained a loch and surrounding marshes and converted the land into valuable hay meadow. Sir William Bruce, the architect of Kinross House and other late seventeenth-century classical mansions, reclaimed a good deal of marshy ground around Loch Leven in Fife, turning it into meadow and plantations of woodland.

Reclamation from the sea was also attempted in some places. The coastal lowlands near Alloa were embanked against the sea in the early seventeenth century and another scheme was proposed at Banff in the 1660s to reclaim land at the mouth of the River Deveron below the town. Although this was a failure, renewed attempts during the 1680s were more successful. The most ambitious scheme on record was one for reclaiming Montrose Basin, the huge tidal area behind the burgh of Montrose which connects with the sea via a channel at the south end of the town. In the 1670s work was under way with the intention of reclaiming some 810ha (2,000a) of ground. The burgesses of Montrose opposed the scheme as they feared, probably correctly, that reclamation of the basin would reduce tidal scouring in the channel and cause their harbour to silt up. They must have been pleased when the dyke that neighbouring landowners were having built was destroyed in a storm and the work was abandoned. The remains of their reclamation work, known as Dronner's Dyke, can still be seen at low tide.

Beyond the head dyke: pasture and waste

Over much of Scotland rough pasture was abundant but this did not mean that it was unregulated. It provided a range of resources whose exploitation had to be carefully controlled in the interests of all. As well as grazing, the waste was a source of building materials including turf, clay, bracken, heather, broom and stone. In some areas timber might also be available. In addition the uncultivated land provided peat which, throughout most of Scotland, was the normal fuel of the country people until coal became more widely available with better transport in the later eighteenth century.

Grazing, the collecting of building materials, and the cutting of peat were controlled by estate courts, and the number of animals that any farmer could graze was carefully regulated in proportion to the size of his holding. The different grazing capacities of horses, oxen, cattle, sheep and goats were carefully calculated in making up the allocations. The animals in each township were normally grazed together under the supervision of a common herd. Access from the settlement to the permanent pasture was often by means of a lane or 'loan' leading through the arable land.

Much upland pasture was owned by individual proprietors and grazed in common by their tenants. However, a good deal of rough grazing was held as commonty. This was pasture in shared ownership between two or more landowners and grazed as a common resource by all their respective tenants. The history and extent of commonties in different areas is difficult to reconstruct as details of their location and size are often not well recorded. Detailed surveys survive for some commonties which were divided between their respective proprietors in the eighteenth and nineteenth centuries. Many commonties probably disappeared following less complex and more informal division proceedings, sometimes at much earlier dates.

Many of the commonties which are well documented, and consequently about which we know most, were relatively small; often only a few hundred acres in extent. There was probably more incentive to define carefully these smaller commonties in areas where pasture was in short supply. Many commonties in the Highlands and Southern Uplands were very large. The commonty of Mey in Caithness extended to over 5,665ha (14,000a). Landowners who had shared rights to a commonty guarded them jealously. Such areas could only remain communal resources if they were kept open for grazing; any attempts to plough up and cultivate areas of commonty were usually resisted vigorously because this denied the use of the land to everyone else.

In the Borders large livestock farms had taken over much of the hill pasture. They had developed in some cases from medieval monastic farms and in other areas, such as Ettrick Forest, from forest stedes. The division of much of the upland pasture between these farms made them inaccessible to communities in the surrounding lowlands. In parts of south-east Scotland the arable area had expanded so much by the seventeenth and early eighteenth centuries that many farms were very short of permanent pasture. Sending their livestock to commonties during the summer was the only way in which they could keep their animals in good condition. This explains the survival of commonties like Coldingham Moor in Berwickshire, extending to 2,510ha (6,200a). So crucial was this commonty to the well-being of the livestock in this part of Berwickshire that animals were sent to it from townships several miles away.

During the seventeenth and early eighteenth centuries commonties were seen more and more as barriers to improvement and there was increasing pressure to divide commonties and allocate blocks of land from them to individual proprietors who could have them ploughed and improved. Common pasture belonging to a single proprietor could be improved in this way at any time; it was also possible to divide commonties provided that all interested parties were in agreement. However, it only required one dissenting voice to frustrate an improvement scheme. Early divisions included the commonty of Gladsmuir in East Lothian which was reallocated between the burgh of Haddington and the Earl of Melrose in 1623. Even earlier was the division of the commonty of Inchinnan in Stirlingshire in 1505 between three different owners.

Today the use of peat as a fuel is associated with the more remote areas of the Highlands and Islands but formerly it was the normal fuel throughout Scotland. Peat was still used by many landowners for heating their castles and mansions. On the Abercairney estates in Perthshire in 1696 18 tenants supplied the proprietor with 676 cartloads of peat a year between them as part of their labour services. Even allowing for the carts being fairly small, this gives an indication of how much peat a landowner's household could consume. The main exceptions to the general use of peat were those limited areas where coal outcropped at the surface and was easily worked. In addition some areas were devoid of both peat and coal, such as some of the Northern and Western Isles. There peat was brought in by boat or the inhabitants had to use substitutes like turf or animal dung. In Orkney many of the islanders brought peat by sea from Eday and Hoy. Even in areas where it was relatively abundant timber was usually too valuable to use as a fuel.

Peat occurred abundantly in most upland areas but it had also developed in ill-drained hollows and valley bottoms in the Lowlands. In some places it had built up into extensive domed bogs known as raised mosses. The most extensive of these areas were the estuaries of the Rivers Forth and Tay where a thick covering of peat had developed on top of heavy marine clays, the remains of old estuary mudflats abandoned by the sea.

In many areas reclamation was achieved by removing the peat cover and making 'burntland'. This involved ditching and draining a peat moss to lower the water table, allowing the surface layers to dry out. These were then stripped off, piled into heaps, burnt, and the ashes scattered. A cereal crop sown in the ashes gave a high return compared with normal arable land. Contemporary reports suggest that returns of 10, 15 or even 20 to one were possible on burntland. The process could be repeated year after year as long as the peat moss lasted. When the peat was completely burnt away the buried soil below the moss was often capable of cultivation, with adequate drainage, and the land could be permanently reclaimed. In the Carse of Stirling nibbling away at the fringes of the mosses by means of burntland had reclaimed a good deal of land before the era of large-scale drainage operations in the late eighteenth century. Cultivation of a narrow strip of burntland at the edge of the moss allowed 4–5m (12–15ft) of land to be reclaimed each year, a small improvement whose cumulative effect over long periods could be considerable.

Reclamation by paring and burning was also widespread in the north east and this may help to explain why peat was in short supply in parts of the region by the late seventeenth century. In this and other parts of the Lowlands estate officers supervised the extraction of the remaining peat very carefully. Tenants were restricted in the amount of peat they could cut in order to conserve remaining stocks. Sometimes the cutting of peat, instead of leading to reclamation, could have unforeseen consequences for the landscape. Kilconquhar Loch in eastern Fife, like the Norfolk Broads on a smaller scale, resulted from the flooding of peat cuttings in a former moss.

Shielings

In many pastoral areas of Europe communities practised a system of transhumance whereby livestock, especially cattle, were sent away from the main settlement during the summer to higher or more distant grazings. There they were herded by part of the community who lived in temporary huts, milking the animals and making butter and cheese. The animals were brought back to the main settlement in the autumn. Systems of transhumance can still be found in parts of the Alps and Scandinavia today and were once widespread in the British Isles. In Scotland the summer pastures were known as shieling grounds and the temporary homes which people occupied as shieling huts.

The purpose of sending animals to the summer pastures was twofold. In areas where upland grazing was abundant, it maximised the potential of the high pastures during the few weeks of the year when they were at their best. The livestock were also removed from the risk of damaging the growing crops adjacent to the main settlement, while the pastures near the settlement were preserved for autumn grazing or for cutting as winter fodder. In the Highlands in the eighteenth century, and doubtless at earlier periods too, it was mainly the women and children who went to the shielings. Going to the shielings was an enjoyable social activity, a break from the normal routine of farm and domestic labour. Some of the menfolk went too, often going in advance of the main party to repair the shieling huts. The animals would be taken to the summer pastures in May or June. Depending on the area and its customs the cattle might spend as little as six weeks there or be kept at the shielings until harvest time. The cheese and butter produced at the shieling often formed part of the rent that Highland peasants paid to their landlords, as well as being consumed directly.

Our knowledge of Scottish shielings comes mainly from the Highlands where sending animals to the summer pastures continued until the end of our period. In southern Scotland the custom died out much earlier. In hill areas like the Lammermuirs there are a number of places whose names contain the elements 'shiel' or 'shiels', denoting former shieling sites. These were probably permanently colonised during the twelfth and thirteenth centuries when there was a substantial expansion of population and settlement. In some cases upland areas which had been exploited in this way were granted to monastic houses, who converted the shielings into permanent sheep farms. In some parts of the Borders the use of shielings survived for longer. Some hunting preserves, like Ettrick Forest or parts of Teviotdale and Eskdale, were only opened up for settlement on a large scale in the fifteenth and sixteenth centuries, but it is likely that temporary shielings were already in existence within these forested areas and some of them seem to have continued in use for some time after the initial colonisation. This is suggested by the survival of groups of what appear to be shieling huts beside the Douglas and Mountbenger Burns (NT 274288 and 305263), tributaries of the Yarrow Water. There are also indications that some shieling place names were created at a late date. For instance, the farm of Deloraineshiel must originally have been a shieling of the forest stede of Deloraine in Ettrick. As Deloraine itself was a late fifteenth-century creation, the use of its shieling grounds may have continued into the sixteenth century.

Circular and rectangular buildings which may have been shieling huts have been identified elsewhere in southern Scotland. In the 1920s a number of them, including a group of eleven, were excavated on the bleak moors near Muirkirk in Ayrshire. Pottery from the huts was dated to the sixteenth century. A seventeenth-century reference suggests that shielings continued in use on the moors between Clydesdale and West Lothian until the mid-sixteenth century when they were replaced by permanent farms. By the seventeenth century references to 'shiels' in documents seem to indicate isolated herdsmen's huts rather than groups of dwellings occupied by a substantial number of people, and the custom seems to have continued only in the Highlands.

In the Highlands and Western Isles shielings were ubiquitous until the end of the eighteenth century. The consolidation of holdings to create larger farms and the introduction of commercial sheep farming ended their use in most areas in the early nineteenth century. In Lewis, however, the land away from the coastal fringe was too boggy for sheep to thrive and evictions for sheep farming were few. Smallholding tenants were reorganised into crofting townships but the traditional use of the shieling was maintained in some parts of the island well into the present century. The landscape of Lewis is rich in shieling remains, including primitive huts which may have been occupied during the eighteenth century and substantial cottages built as recently as the 1930s or 1940s. In a sense the tradition still continues. The landscape on either side of the road from Stornoway to Callanish is dotted with small corrugated-iron shacks and summer houses. They are used by the inhabitants of Stornoway in summer as a base from which to cut peat and go fishing, activities which formed part of the life at the shielings in earlier times. Although animals have

Figure 14 A group of shieling huts in central Lewis. The remains of old peat banks can be seen around the huts. The contrast in vegetation between the skinned land close to the huts and the surrounding acid peatlands is prominent.

rarely been pastured on Lewis shielings in the last fifty years there are still people alive today who remember going to the shielings in their childhood.

The remains of shieling huts can be found throughout the Highlands and Islands. On the island of Rhum, the population of which never exceeded around 450, a detailed survey has identified nearly 400 shieling huts. Although remains of such huts are frequently mere tumbled foundations, their sites can often be spotted a considerable distance away by the patches of bright green grass which surround them and contrast with the browns and yellows of the rest of the moorland. This vegetation contrast was produced by the custom of folding the livestock at night in enclosures adjacent to the shieling huts. The dung from the animals enriched the soil, allowing the better grasses to thrive. Even when the shielings were abandoned the contrast in vegetation remained and today sheep still prefer to graze the areas around the ruined huts because of their sweeter grasses. The contrast in vegetation was also due to the prolonged cutting of peat for fuel near the shielings. If you look at the area around groups of shieling huts you will often find old peat banks.

The distance between the shieling huts and the permanent farmsteads varied greatly. In the Western Highlands and Islands, and in northern areas like Caithness and Sutherland, the area of improved land was limited and often took the form of small islands of arable in a sea of permanent pasture. In this kind of country there was much rough grazing at low altitudes close to the settlements and the shielings were often only a short distance away, generally within two or three kilometres of the parent settlement. In areas like Lewis the contrast between farmstead and shieling was one between coast and interior rather than lowland and mountain. The permanent farms were located on the limited areas of fertile land on coastal raised beaches and shell sands while the shielings occupied the peaty centre of the island.

In the eastern Highlands, where settlement in the glens was divided by extensive plateaux and hills, the shielings were often more distant from the permanent settlements. In areas like the Cairngorms and upland Perthshire there was often a considerable contrast in altitude between farm and shieling. The shielings were true mountain grazings with the huts situated at 600m (2,000ft) or more. Where such shielings were relatively distant there was sometimes a second set a short way above the head dyke. The animals were often weak from their long period of wintering with insufficient fodder and needed their strength building up before they could travel to the main shielings. They were driven to the nearer grazings just beyond the head dyke for the first bite of spring grass, to keep them away from the sprouting crops on the arable land. When the growing season began to improve the quality of the mountain pastures the animals were then sent to the higher shieling grounds.

Shieling huts are usually found in groups. The preferred site is often a well-drained knoll adjacent to a stream or a loch. Water was needed for the livestock and for making butter and cheese. One can imagine that fishing for trout and salmon occupied a good deal of leisure time! In many parts of the Highlands two styles of shieling hut can be seen. The older ones are round or oval and very small, often with internal diameters of only 2–3m (7–8ft). Generally only the grass-grown foundations are visible. In most areas only the lower walls of such huts were built of stone, the remainder being of turf. In parts of Lewis, however, some of these older huts were built of stone throughout with lower walls up to six feet thick and a corbelled stone roof in a beehive shape which echoes the style of stonework found on some prehistoric sites in the Highlands and Islands. Beehive shieling huts have also been found elsewhere in the Hebrides, in Sutherland and in Perthshire, so they were evidently once widespread. On Rhum there is a clear chronological progression from beehive structures to larger round huts with attached store chambers and then rectangular buildings. However, the dates at which the various types were in use are uncertain.

The building tradition represented by the beehive huts is an ancient one but the huts themselves need not be very old. Some are known to have continued in use into the nineteenth century although, by that date, new shieling huts were built along more spacious lines. Huts dating from the

Figure 15 Close up of a shieling hut, Airigh na Beiste, west of Stornoway.

later eighteenth or early nineteenth century tend to be rectangular and rather larger. Modern shieling huts in Lewis resemble small cottages with gables, chimneys and fireplaces but their upper walls were still often built of turf. In some areas, notably Skye, the remains of the latest huts stand on top of mounds sometimes 2 metres high. These have been formed by the gradual accumulation of debris, principally turf, from earlier huts. An excavation of one such site in north Skye revealed traces of three superimposed oval huts representing as many major phases of use, and doubtless innumerable minor repairs. In many parts of the Highlands and Islands timber was scarce. The beams that were used for roofing the shieling huts were removed each autumn and taken back to the main settlement. This must have made annual repair of the walls of the huts after each winter a necessity.

Enclosures beside the huts were used for folding livestock but sometimes too for cultivation. The dunging of the ground inside the folds enriched it so much that, provided the shieling was not at too high an altitude, a quick crop of oats might sometimes be taken. Traces of ridge and furrow ploughing or hand-dug lazy beds often indicate that land around shielings was cultivated in this way. In the later eighteenth century, when population was growing throughout the Highlands, there was increasing pressure to convert shielings to semi-permanent farms either by squatters who could not obtain land anywhere else or with the tacit agreement of estate proprietors who could exact a higher rent if land around a shieling was producing crops. The widespread use of the potato may have made this easier.

A distinctive feature of Scottish rural society and the Scottish countryside throughout our period was the extent to which it was dominated by a relatively limited number of large landowners. While small owner occupiers, or 'bonnet lairds', did exist and were a prominent element in some localities they were not as numerous or influential overall as the English yeomen farmers of Tudor and Stuart times. The landscape was parcelled out into estates, some relatively small, some huge. These estates were administered and organised from the landowners' country residences. Whether battlemented castle or classical mansion they are still a prominent feature of the Scottish landscape today. The ways in which their character changed between 1500 and 1800 highlight many of the wider changes in Scottish society and the Scottish landscape; it is to this theme that we turn in our next chapter.

4

From castle to mansion

Scottish society in the sixteenth and seventeenth centuries was, at times, still turbulent and violent. In part this was due to difficult relations with England. Our period opens with the disastrous Scottish defeat at Flodden in 1513. A series of English invasions in the 1540s devasted much of the Lothians and the Borders. Intermittent warfare persisted on the Border until the end of the sixteenth century. After the Union of the Crowns in 1603 international squabbles died away only to surface in a different form in the Civil Wars of the 1640s and Scottish opposition to the Cromwellian regime in the 1650s. The Glorious Revolution of 1688 ushered in the era of Jacobite rebellions, the Stuart cause not being finally crushed until the Battle of Culloden in 1746.

Throughout this period local raiding and feuding was also widespread. Until 1603 this was virtually a way of life for many Border families, by no means always at the expense of the English. In the Highlands the sixteenth century was particularly bad for clan feuding in the vacuum of power created by the collapse of the Lordship of the Isles at the hands of the Scottish crown at the end of the fifteenth century. Although the level of violence in the Highlands diminished during the later seventeenth century there was a resurgence of trouble with the first Jacobite rising in 1689.

Many parts of the Lowlands had become more peaceable by the early seventeenth century but raiding from the Highlands caused people along their margins to take measures to defend their property nearly a century later. The element of violence in early-modern Scottish society has been overemphasised in many popular histories. Recent interpretations have stressed that the history of Scotland at this period was not entirely one of blood and thunder. Towers and castles were status symbols and the martial element in society should not be overstated. Even so, the potential for danger, if not its reality, undoubtedly influenced Scottish landowners. They continued to rely on the protection of castles and fortified houses into the early seventeenth century in much of the Lowlands and the eighteenth century in the Highlands. Whether they lived in a massive baronial castle with curtain walls and gate towers or a smaller tower house the tall stone walls of their fortified homes dominated the landscape, an affirmation in stone of their domination of society.

The Scottish landscape is thickly dotted with castles. Many stand ruined and isolated; others have been remodelled and extended into more spacious mansions. Some stand amid farmsteads, their vaulted basements filled with rusting agricultural machinery, their stonework robbed to build the steadings which surround them. Others are mere grass-grown foundations in isolated valleys. The transition from castle to country house was one of the most important changes in the Scottish landscape between 1500 and 1800. Not only did it mark the transition from medieval towards modern conditions; it also tells us a good deal about how landowners viewed the society in which they lived. These were the homes of the lords and lairds who controlled Scottish society, the centres from which the rest of the landscape was managed and changed.

New fortified houses were built as late as the 1640s. It has been suggested that the Scots continued to build tall, narrow buildings with stone vaults because stone was cheap and widely available while timber for floors and roofs had to be imported and was expensive. There may have been an element of truth in this but a lingering fear of attack and the power of the traditional view of what was appropriate for a gentleman's residence are likely to have been the strongest influences. Compared with their grim medieval predecessors most of the later fortified houses struck a different balance between the need for protection and the desire for more space and greater architectural style. Nevertheless, examples like Coxton in Moray, built in 1644, with a parapet and first-floor entrance reached by a wooden ladder, might easily have dated from two centuries earlier. Fortified houses only began to go out of favour in the Lowlands after the Restoration while conservatism and lack of funds to build new mansions meant that most Scottish proprietors continued to live in them, only slightly modernised and extended in many cases, until much later.

Castles in 1500: the medieval legacy

In 1500 many landed families were still living in castles which had originally been built in the thirteenth century. The continued need for defence and the relative poverty of the country as a result of long wars with England and internal strife during the fourteenth and fifteenth centuries kept many of these medieval castles in active use with only minor modifications.

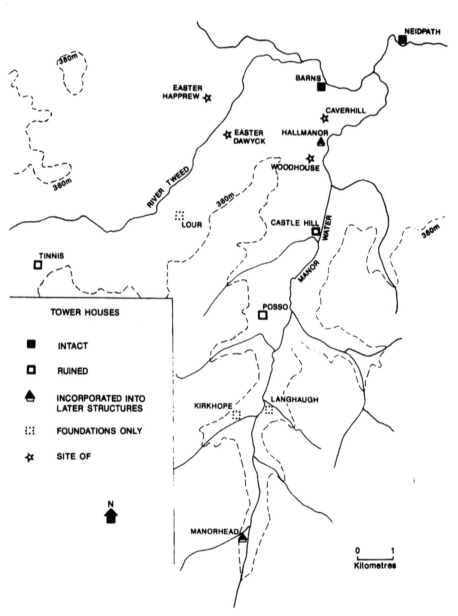

NEIDPATH

380m

BARNS

EASTER
HAPPREW ✦

CAVERHILL ✦

EASTER ✦
DAWYCK

HALLMANOR ▲

380m

WOODHOUSE ✦

RIVER TWEED

380m

LOUR ⠿

CASTLE HILL ☐

MANOR WATER

380m

TINNIS
☐

POSSO
☐

TOWER HOUSES

■   INTACT

☐   RUINED

▲   INCORPORATED INTO
    LATER STRUCTURES

⠿   FOUNDATIONS ONLY

✦   SITE OF

KIRKHOPE ⠿   LANGHAUGH ⠿

N
⬆

MANORHEAD ▲

0   1
Kilometres

Map 6 Sites of tower houses in the Manor Water valley showing the density of their
distribution.

Some early designs continued to serve their owners well for centuries after they were built. In the West Highlands and Islands simple shell keeps, consisting of a massive curtain wall enclosing a courtyard around which were ranged the living quarters and storage facilities, continued in use. Castle Sween (NR 721788) and Dunstaffnage (NM 822344) in Argyll, and Mingary (NM 502631) are examples. Some shell keeps were later strengthened by the addition of a tower house, as at Castle Tiorum beside Loch Moidart (NM 662724). Elsewhere, more developed castles of enclosure with curtain walls, towers and gatehouses, functioned as baronial residences until the end of the sixteenth century. Examples include Caerlaverock on the Solway, Bothwell in Clydesdale, Dirleton and Tantallon in East Lothian, and Kildrummy in Grampian. Few new castles of this kind were built following the Wars of Independence in the late thirteenth and early fourteenth centuries but many older ones which had been damaged by sieges or partly dismantled by the Scots to deny them to the English were reconstructed.

That these castles remained fully functional as strongholds is shown by the remodelling of their defences, like the artillery outworks at Tantallon, or the upgrading of their internal accommodation. At Caerlaverock the facade of Nithsdale's Building, dating from 1634, remains intact, an impressive, symmetrical range tightly squeezed within the curtain walls of the old castle. More spacious accommodation dating from the sixteenth century can be seen at the large clifftop castle of Dunnottar near Stonehaven. Ranges of buildings from the seventeenth and eighteenth centuries can also be seen within the ramparts of West Highland castles such as Mingary.

Castles like these were still a major challenge to besiegers despite the development of artillery. In 1528 James V laid siege to Tantallon Castle but gave up after twenty days of bombardment had proved ineffectual. Castles like Caerlaverock and Hermitage, close to the Border, retained their defensive role throughout the sixteenth century. Wide-mouthed gunports were added to the earlier gatehouse at Caerlaverock as late as 1593. The last period in which many of the great medieval castles of the Lowlands saw action was during the Civil Wars and Cromwellian occupation, following which many were deliberately dismantled. In 1640 the royalist garrison of Caerlaverock surrendered only after a thirteen-week siege. In 1650 Cromwell's army had a tough job overcoming small garrisons at Dirleton and Tantallon. Many Highland castles retained their defensive role well into the eighteenth century.

However, only a few landowners lived in great medieval curtain-wall castles. During the turbulent period following the Wars of Independence such castles were too expensive to build in an impoverished country. A simpler, cheaper solution to the need for defence was developed in the tower house, which became the normal home for the majority of Scottish

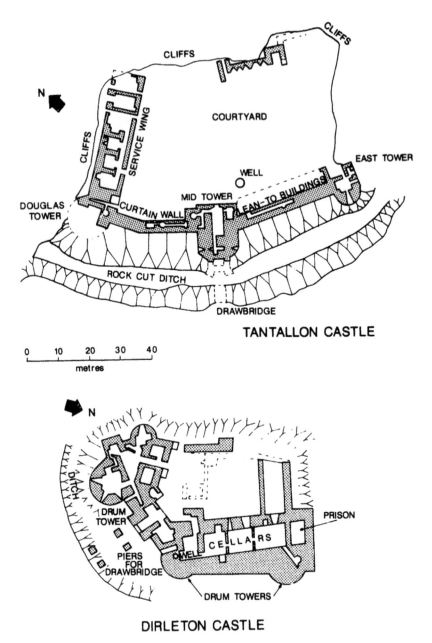

N

CLIFFS

CLIFFS

COURTYARD

CLIFFS

SERVICE WING

WELL

EAST TOWER

MID TOWER

LEAN-TO BUILDINGS

DOUGLAS
TOWER

CURTAIN WALL

ROCK CUT DITCH

DRAWBRIDGE

TANTALLON CASTLE

| 0 | 10 | 20 | 30 | 40 |

metres

N

DRUM
TOWER

DITCH

PRISON

CELLARS

WELL

PIERS
FOR
DRAWBRIDGE

DRUM TOWERS

DIRLETON CASTLE

Map 7 Plans of two Lothian baronial castles which were still formidable in the sixteenth and seventeenth centuries.

landowners down to the later seventeenth century. The number of tower houses built in Scotland has never been calculated but it must have run into thousands. There were over 50 in Tweeddale and more than 100 in Roxburghshire. Although they are a common feature of the modern landscape a considerable number have vanished without trace. In Castleton parish in Liddesdale the Ordnance Survey marks the sites of over twenty tower houses in this former frontier area but there are substantial remains of only one, at Mangerton. The rest were either destroyed during English raids in the sixteenth century or used as quarries for building stone by later farmers.

Tower houses were cheaper to build than curtain-wall castles yet were remarkably effective defensive structures combining maximum security with a modest outlay. At the core of a large medieval castle like Dirleton lay the great hall with private apartments at one end, a kitchen at the other, and storage space in a vaulted undercroft below. A tower house took these elements and stacked them vertically; storage on the ground floor, hall and then private apartments above, within a thick-walled shell which exposed the minimum ground area to attack. This simple but flexible design could be produced at different scales to meet the modest needs of a small laird or the more demanding requirements of a great noble.

Some early towers date from the thirteenth century but most were constructed during two main phases; the fourteenth and early fifteenth centuries, and the late sixteenth and early seventeenth centuries. As they were primarily landowners' homes they were built during periods of prosperity rather than times of war. The start of our period coincides with a phase from around 1480 until after the Reformation of 1560 when relatively few towers were built. Conflict between factions of the nobility in the later fifteenth century, the disastrous defeat at Flodden which removed the flower of a generation of Scotland's aristocracy, the English invasions of the 1540s and then the upheaval of the Reformation combined to create three-quarters of a century during which few landowners had the means, the time or the inclination to build new houses. With the Reformation and the break-up of ecclesiastical estates many small proprietors acquired enough additional lands to be able to afford towers and a new phase of building began.

Tower houses were built to a standard pattern, simple and conservative with limited scope for variation. Early examples like Drum, west of Aberdeen, or the massive baronial tower of Threave in Galloway, were simple squares or rectangles with thick walls rising to three or four storeys and strengthened internally by one or more stone vaults. The main entrance was often on the first floor and the basement storage area frequently had no direct communication with the tower above, save for a small hatch or 'murder hole' in the vault. The entrance was generally protected by an iron grille or 'yett'. The upper floors were reached by twisting turnpike

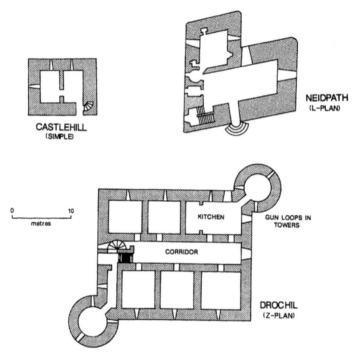

CASTLEHILL
(SIMPLE)

NEIDPATH
(L–PLAN)

0 _____ 10
metres

KITCHEN   GUN LOOPS IN
TOWERS

CORRIDOR

DROCHIL
(Z–PLAN)

Map 8 Some characteristic tower house layouts.

stairs which normally turned to the right so that right-handed attackers trying to force their way up would have their sword arms trapped against the well of the stair while right-handed defenders, cutting downwards, had room to swing their weapons. Above the private rooms there was a parapet walk. The defences of tower houses were generally passive and the walls had few openings. The main way in which attackers could be threatened was from the parapet which usually projected outwards on stone corbels with gaps or machicolations through which missiles could be dropped on anyone attacking the base of the walls.

As so many Scottish towers survive as roofless shells it is sometimes difficult to appreciate that they were primarily homes whose owners were mainly concerned with their families and running their estates. The image of the tower as a home comes out most strongly from examples like Craigievar and Crathes in Aberdeenshire which have been lived in continuously but are little altered. The hall of a tower was frequently used for holding baron courts, the lowest unit of jurisdiction within the Scottish legal system. The rights of landowners with such jurisdictions included 'pit and gallows', the power to imprison and execute criminals. Many towers contain prisons, often in the lowest storey of a wing, accessible only from above, as at Lennoxlove in East Lothian or Comlongon in Dumfriesshire where the prison is built within the thickness of the wall. Although no

Figure 16 The grim outlines of Drum Castle, an early tower house built in the thirteenth century, contrasts with the more spacious seventeenth-century mansion adjoining it (National Trust for Scotland).

sensible proprietor built a tower on a site which could be readily over-looked by attackers, it was often more important to have tower houses located centrally within their owners' estates than to place them in defensive positions that were remote and inaccessible. Towers on isolated outcrops or commanding hilltops are not particularly common. Smailholm, north of Kelso, which stands on a ridge of volcanic rock and is visible for miles, is exceptional.

Nor did towers stand isolated and alone in the landscape. Most were surrounded by stone walls or barmkins enclosing courtyards with the tower on one side and ranges of outbuildings on the others. Recent excavations at Threave Castle in Galloway and the smaller tower of Smailholm in the Merse have shown that these towers had adjoining two-storey hall blocks of which only the foundations now remain. These would have added

Figure 17 Craigievar Castle, Aberdeenshire, completed in the early seventeenth century, represents the culmination of Scottish tower house design, blending the traditional defensive plan with architectural embellishments (National Trust for Scotland).

greatly to the spaciousness and comfort of such fortified houses and may have been more common than has been realised. If, in a sense, the tower was a cheaper version of the medieval keep then the barmkin was a scaled-down curtain wall. Simple barmkins around smaller towers could be defended at need but those surrounding larger towers like Borthwick and Dalhousie near Edinburgh, Newark in Yarrow, or Threave in Galloway were major protective outworks with parapet walks, gatehouses and gun-loops. Barmkins also served as corrals into which livestock could be driven in time of danger. If necessary the outbuildings could be abandoned and the defenders would retreat into the tower. Many barmkins have been removed in later landscaping operations or when a tower was enlarged. Good examples can be seen at Neidpath Castle near Peebles and Red-house near Aberlady; in both cases some of the outbuildings have been preserved within the enclosure.

Tradition and change: the evolution of the tower house c.1560–c.1640

The later sixteenth century witnessed a vigorous phase of tower house building. Some new towers, particularly small ones in the Borders, retained traditional styles and layouts. However, in this final chapter of the story of the fortified house in Scotland the use of old-established forms was combined with new ideas in decoration, design and plan. The desire for protection continued but the demand for greater space, more comfort and more style was increasing. Much of the development in the design of towers at this period reflected attempts to strike a new balance between these seemingly opposite and irreconcilable requirements. There were two ways of achieving more space while retaining a tower house layout; by building bigger towers or by adding wings, still with the emphasis on the vertical rather than the horizontal. The addition of a wing to form an L plan was an early development: it can be seen at Neidpath from the fourteenth century. Nevertheless, this plan became much more common in the sixteenth century. The wing allowed a kitchen or sometimes private quarters to be placed adjacent to the hall. The L-plan had defensive advantages too as the main entrance to the house could be located near the re-entrant angle between the wing and the main block from where it could be covered by gunports. The staircase could be placed in a stair tower in this angle, freeing space within the tower.

A further development in the later sixteenth century was the Z-plan where two round or square towers projected from opposite corners of the main block. This provided more space and a greater flexibility of layout within the tower. One of the best examples is Claypotts Castle on the outskirts of Dundee. Here the defensive advantages of the Z-plan are evident for wide-mouthed gunports in the base of the towers allowed all four walls of the main block to be covered by enfilading fire. Too much should not be made of the Z-plan as a defensive layout. Towers like Claypotts are well equipped with gunloops but in many others their provision was haphazard or almost non-existent. Some smaller towers from this period had no gun loops at all, possibly because their owners were insufficiently wealthy to afford firearms or because they still distrusted them; the rate of fire of a hand gun or small cannon was still painfully slow. The expanded plan was designed primarily for greater comfort. This can be seen in its most developed form at Drochil Castle, north of Peebles, where the main block has become so large that it dwarfs the towers, which are themselves quite substantial.

Not all sixteenth-century towers showed these new influences. Hoddom Castle near Dumfries was built in the 1560s but its massive walls and heavy parapet show that there was a continuing need for defence so close to the Border. Other towers, instead of harking back to earlier centuries, look forward to later country houses by adopting balanced, symmetrical facades, as at Castle Kennedy in Galloway which was built in 1607 and Saltcoats Castle in East Lothian which dates from the late sixteenth century. Barnes Castle near Haddington dates from the 1590s and has an advanced plan for its period. A rectangular main block had square towers projecting from the corners. The barmkin also had square towers at the corners and midway along the walls. The plan seems to have been ornamental rather than defensive but the building was never completed.

The Scottish tower house reached its final phase of development during the first quarter of the seventeenth century. The continuing desire for defence was reflected in the basic tower house plan, in the blankness of the lower storeys and the retention of iron yetts protecting the doorways, but the desire for comfort and a much greater interest in style and decoration can be seen in the upperworks of these new structures. The machicolated parapet and wall walk were abandoned. The placing of gunloops at ground level transferred the defence of a tower from its parapet to its base, freeing the wall-head for ornamental development. In place of the parapet, dormers could be brought forward to the outer face of the wall and turned into gables. Upper windows were made larger and more decorative. The technique of corbelling towers, gables and turrets outwards from the main wall became standard. At Claypotts square upper rooms were projected outwards on top of round towers, producing a very distinctive appearance.

The contrast in style between such towers and earlier ones can sometimes be seen in neighbouring examples, as in the Merse where the fifteenth-century tower of Smailholm is grim and blank walled, more like a prison than a home, while nearby Greenknowe, built in 1581, has more and larger windows, a corbelled stair tower and other embellishments. This phase of development culminated in a group of Aberdeenshire castles which reflect a kind of Indian summer of tower house development in which the primary defensive plan was retained but so embellished as to have become an art form. This group, including Castle Fraser, Craigievar, Crathes and Midmar was the work of the Bell family, local stonemasons who developed their own distinctive style of castle design. The most perfect of the group is generally acknowledged to be Craigievar because it is totally unaltered. In 1610 William Forbes, known to his contemporaries' as 'Danzig Willie', an Aberdeen merchant who had prospered in trade with the Baltic, bought the estate and partly completed castle of Craigievar. The tower was finished by William Bell to Forbes' specification. Craigievar has an L-plan with a square stair tower in the angle between the two blocks. The house is plain up to the fourth floor but from there is crowned by a profusion of corbelled turrets, crow-stepped gables and towers. The building has a slender, well-proportioned appearance and avoids being top-heavy despite the ornamental upperworks.

Bastels in the borders

Many minor lairds and prosperous tenants could not afford tower houses and had to live in simpler semi-fortified houses. In sixteenth-century

Northumberland many small proprietors and wealthier farmers built bastel houses (from the French 'bastille'), two-storey buildings with a vaulted ground floor for sheltering livestock, and a first-floor entrance leading to a single multi-functional room, a poorer version of the tower house's hall, sometimes with a small private apartment at one end. Bastels provided some protection against small-scale raiding. Documentary sources indicate that they were quite common on the Scottish side of the Border during the troubled years of the mid-sixteenth century. The village of Lessudden had sixteen of them in 1544 according to an English source. Even if this term was used loosely to include any stone-built house, remarkably few bastels have been identified in the modern Scottish landscape. One or two have been located in Berwickshire. Fairnington House near Roxburgh, a late seventeenth-century mansion, incorporates a sixteenth-century bastel in one wing. Another may be built into the fabric of the Tontine Hotel in Peebles High Street. Queen Mary's House in Jedburgh is a more impressive example. It is a three-storey rectangular house with a square tower in the middle of one side and a corbelled stair tower in the re-entrant angle between the tower and the main block. It has clear affinities with contemporary tower house design but it has crow-stepped gables rather than a parapet and was altogether a less defensible structure.

At a lower level of sophistication is an interesting group of structures south of Jedburgh among the rolling foothills of the Cheviots. They have been called 'pele houses' but there is no sharp dividing line between them and bastels. They are similar to some of the smaller bastels of Redesdale a short distance across the Border. The best preserved one is at Merv-inslaw (NT 672118), a small rectangular two-storey building with gable ends and a garret. The walls are only 4 feet thick but have few openings. There was no stone vault between ground and first floor but entrances to both apartments were barred by stout inner and outer doors. The house had no fireplace, suggesting that it was only a temporary refuge and foundations of other buildings adjacent to it, set within an enclosure, were probably those of a farmstead.

Until recently no bastels have been identified elsewhere in Scotland. However, fieldwork by members of the Biggar Museum Trust has uncovered a group of them in Upper Clydesdale. The ruins of some had long been known but their grass-grown foundations had been interpreted as those of small tower houses. Other sites had not previously been identified. The excavation of one, known as Windgate House, at the head of a remote valley south of Coulter (NT 016272) showed that it had been a rectangular two-storey structure with a vaulted ground floor. The main entrance was in the down-valley gable at ground-floor level and an internal staircase led to the upper floor. Openings at ground-floor level, if any, had been small but there had been at least one larger window above. Other previously unrecorded bastels have been discovered at the corners

Figure 18 Small but thick walled this modest pele house at Southdean near Jedburgh is a good example of the most modest type of defended house in Scotland.

of fields up small tributaries of the Clyde and at least one near Biggar is still inhabited. These discoveries suggest that bastels were more widespread in the past and may be more common in the landscape than has been supposed.

Courtyard castles and palaces

The medieval curtain-wall castle was not often imitated in later times but some fortified houses which began as simple towers were transformed by the addition of extra wings built around a courtyard on such a large scale that their appearance was changed into something similar. Such extensions were designed to increase domestic comfort, usually by building a more spacious hall than could be contained within the original tower. With a larger hall went better service facilities, kitchens and storage. In layouts of this kind, as at Crichton Castle near Edinburgh (NT 380612), the tower was used increasingly as private accommodation for the proprietor while the new hall provided more ostentatious public space. Crichton, originally a plain fourteenth-century tower, was extended in the fifteenth and six-teenth centuries into a courtyard layout. The exterior is plain and func-tional but inside the courtyard part of the surrounding facade is orna-mented by projecting diamond-shaped blocks of stone, highlighted on a sunny day by a sharp contrast of light and shadow. This decoration is reminiscent of contemporary Italian palaces and was commissioned by the fifth Earl of Bothwell after a visit to Italy. Craigmillar, on the outskirts of Edinburgh, was extended within an imposing curtain wall. Doune Castle in southern Perthshire was originally designed to be a splendid layout with four ranges laid out around a courtyard but only two of them were actually built. The result was nevertheless impressive.

During the early sixteenth century, a period when there was little private castle building, James IV and James V instituted a major rebuilding programme for their royal residences. The new works, influenced by French Renaissance architectural styles, consisted of attractive courtyard dwellings. The royal palace of Linlithgow has a homogeneous Renaissance plan which belies its early origins and complex development. Rebuilding of the early medieval royal castle there took place intermittently over two centuries though the most important work was done for James V. The result was a palace which, although still possessing parapets, gunports and guarded entrances, was primarily domestic in function. It consists of four ranges with corner towers laid out around a square courtyard. The outer facades are rather severe but those facing into the courtyard have large, symmetrically placed windows which let plenty of light and air into the royal apartments. Falkland Palace in Fife preserves the earliest Renaissance facade of its kind in Britain although only the south range and part of the eastern side of the building survive. At Holyrood only the north-west tower remains of James V's alterations. At Stirling the Great Hall was also constructed at this time, large but plain and medieval in style, contrasting with the later palace block and the Chapel Royal, both dating from later in the sixteenth century.

After the death of James V royal works languished and the initiative in developing new architectural styles passed to aristocratic patrons. It became fashionable to attach the term 'palace' to any magnate's dwelling which had grown into a complex of buildings. One example of a castle with an unusually spacious layout was Dunnottar on the clifftops south of Stonehaven. The extensive promontory had plenty of room for domestic buildings laid out in ranges around courtyards and the ruins today resemble those of a small town rather than a castle. The pre-Reformation bishops often had spacious and stylish accommodation too. Spynie, the residence of the Bishop of Moray, is one of the most impressive. It consists of a fourteenth-century castle of enclosure overshadowed by a huge late fifteenth-century tower and was still in use in the later sixteenth century. The fine bishop's palace at Kirkwall dates mostly from the sixteenth century under Bishop Robert Reid but may incorporate the remains of an earlier residence on the same site. The palace has a first-floor hall and ground-floor storage but the addition of a huge five-storey round tower at one end gives it a more martial air.

Orkney has two interesting palaces built by the Stewart earls who, in the late sixteenth and early seventeenth centuries, acted as independent rulers of their remote realm until brought to heel by the Scottish crown. The Earl's Palace at Birsay was built by Robert Stewart in the later sixteenth century. Although badly ruined today, a contemporary plan of the palace survives showing that it had a full courtyard layout with four ranges of buildings and corner towers. The Earl's Palace at Kirkwall was built for Robert's son, Patrick Stewart, who was a true Renaissance ruler, part despot, part patron of the arts. His residence has been described as the finest Renaissance building in Scotland. Dating from the early seventeenth century it is roofless and only two wings survive of what was originally planned to be a full courtyard layout. Even so, the dimensions of the first-floor Great Hall with its large fireplaces and attractive oriel windows are still impressive.

Although it dates from near the end of the seventeenth century Drumlanrig Castle in Nithsdale, the seat of the dukes of Queensberry, can be mentioned here as a late and anachronistic example of the Renaissance courtyard palace tradition. The design of 1679 was based on a much earlier one, probably by the master mason William Wallace who designed Heriot's Hospital in Edinburgh in the early seventeenth century on a similar plan. The design of Drumlanrig echoes earlier courtyard palaces with curtain walls and flanking towers but the detail is classical. As a brave attempt to convert an old form to a new style it does not entirely succeed, but the architect, James Smith, has produced an impressive and dignified building which recalls Tudor country houses in England rather than the new classical mansions which were being built in Scotland by the end of the seventeenth century.

Highland castles in the later seventeenth and early eighteenth centuries

In the Highlands the defensive role of the castle lasted longer than in the Lowlands. Many Highland castles played an important part in the Jacobite rebellions between 1689 and 1746. Their success was largely due to the fact that government and Jacobite forces operating in this area rarely had effective siege artillery. The last major scheme of private castle building in Britain was at Kilchurn, on an island (now a peninsula) in Loch Awe. The original fortress had been a massive five-storey tower house dating from the fifteenth century with an attached barmkin enclosing lower ranges of buildings around a courtyard. In the early 1690s the Earl of Breadalbane, notionally a supporter of William III but also keeping his options open with the exiled Stuarts, proposed the establishment of a Highland militia, 4,000 strong and commanded by himself, to back up the regular army. William wisely rejected the scheme, suspecting that the troops might just as easily be used against him as for him. In the mean time, Breadalbane converted Kilchurn into the centre of his new planned defensive system by adding two four-storey barrack blocks with corner towers, capable of accommodating a large garrison. The castle was never actually used in this role.

While Kilchurn was being extended other West Highland castles were used by Jacobite chiefs as holding points against the government. As late as 1691 MacDonald of Glengarry was improving the outworks around his castle at Invergarry. The MacLeans on the island of Mull had even stronger fortresses. Duart Castle, still the home of the chief of the MacLeans, originated as a small medieval curtain-wall castle on a clifftop site overlooking the Sound of Mull. At a later date a massive tower house was added to the medieval enclosure and new ranges of buildings erected within the curtain wall. A more remote MacLean strongpoint was Cairnburgh Castle at the northern end of the Treshnish Isles west of Mull. Cairnburgh, as well as being one of the most isolated fortifications in Britain, is also one of the strangest. It consists of two small islands with a narrow channel between them. On each island a ring of basalt crags rises up from a rocky foreshore with a level plateau above. On Cairn na Burgh Mor, the largest island, the few places where the cliffs can be scaled have been sealed off by stretches of curtain wall. Cairnburgh Castle was the ultimate natural fortress; it could not be attacked easily from the sea while reefs and shoals made it difficult to put a landing party ashore. On the plateau stand the remains of a two-storey barrack block dating from the late seventeenth or eighteenth century which may have been used by government forces after the MacLeans surrendered the island.

The age of the fortified house in the Highlands lasted well into the eighteenth century. The remoteness and ruggedness of much of the region allowed Jacobite supporters to defy the government almost with impunity. A warning was sounded during the rebellion of 1719, however, when three government warships sailed into Loch Duich and captured the Jacobites' base, Eilean Donan Castle, after a heavy bombardment. Shortly before the Battle of Culloden in 1746 Lord George Murray, the ablest of the Jacobite commanders, besieged a Hanoverian garrison in his father's ancestral home at Blair Castle. Murray's two small field guns made no impression on the castle's thick walls but the defenders were within a few days of being starved into submission when the siege ended. If Kilchurn was the last exercise in private castle building in British history then this was the last proper siege.

Artillery fortifications

Although primitive artillery using gunpowder was first employed in Scotland by English forces early in the fourteenth century it took a long time for the new weapons to influence the design of Scottish castles. Gradually castles were adapted to the threat of artillery attack by strengthening their walls, providing shot holes and platforms for mounting guns, and later by remodelling castle layouts to resist more effectively the new form of attack.

Craignethan Castle in Clydesdale (NS 815463) was one of the first castles designed from the outset to be proof against artillery. It was built for Sir James Hamilton of Finnart, a natural son and favourite of James V, in the 1530s. Hamilton had seen the latest style of fortifications in Italy and incorporated some of these ideas into his new castle. The westerly side of Craignethan is the most exposed to attack and it is in this direction that the defences are concentrated. First comes an outer curtain wall enclosing a courtyard and pierced with 22 gunloops. This leads to a 9m (30ft)-wide ditch beyond which is an inner curtain wall with even more shot holes. In the bottom of the ditch is a concealed caponier, a covered passage with loopholes from which small-arms fire could rake the ditch. Lastly you reach the central tower, one of the biggest in Scotland, low and squat with a western wall 5m (16ft) thick, designed to resist a protracted bombardment.

Craignethan was one of only a few private residences in Britain designed from the outset to incorporate artillery defences. Henceforth artillery fortifications on this scale were the prerogative of royal castles and government forts. New fortified houses in Scotland continued to incorporate gun loops but within essentially traditional designs. In some medieval castles earthworks for mounting artillery were added during the sixteenth and seventeenth centuries; at Tantallon two generations of artillery outworks can be seen. The massive rock cut ditch and inner rampart with a traverse and gun tower protecting the entrance were probably in existence at the time of the siege of 1528 and may well have helped to make the bombardment ineffectual by soaking up the fire of the besiegers. Beyond these are a triangular-shaped earthwork known as a ravelin, and an outer ditch, probably dating from the seventeenth century.

So far artillery defences had only involved modifications of traditional castle design but the English invasions of the 1540s gave rise to a completely new type of fort based on the angled bastion which had been developed in Italy during the 1530s. After the spectacular victory over the Scots at Pinkie in 1547 the English decided to establish permanent garrisons on Scottish soil rather than maintain a large army in the field. A number of strongpoints were built, incorporating the new ideas of fortification. The largest was at Haddington where the entire town was surrounded by earth and timber ramparts with bastions at the angles. There is no trace of these defences today. At Eyemouth a narrow peninsula overlooking the harbour was defended by building across its neck a curtain wall with bastions, parts of which are still visible. Dunglass, south of Dunbar, formed a base for the English forces from which men and supplies were sent forward to Haddington. The inland side of the camp was defended by a little bastioned fort whose lines are still clearly visible. It is misleadingly named 'French Camp' on the Ordnance Survey map. At Aberlady the old castle of Luffness is surrounded by a series of ditches which may be the remains of a fort raised by French troops who were supporting the Scots against the English invaders.

The Jacobite rising of 1714 led to the Hanoverian government establishing a number of new military posts in the Highlands. The first four were authorised in 1717. They had similar plans, comprising two sets of barracks built on either side of a central courtyard whose other sides were protected by walls loopholed for musketry. One was built at Inversnaid, east of Loch Lomond. Another was established at Kiliwhimin near the south end of Loch Ness. At Inversnaid parts of the ruined barrack blocks form the outbuildings of a farm, while only a fragment remains of Kiliwhimin.

The other two posts are in better condition. Ruthven Barracks in the Spey valley near Kingussie occupies a commanding knoll which may be partly artificial and which had been the site of a castle from medieval times. Although the barracks are roofless the walls are intact and the remains present a very different appearance from traditional Scottish fortifications. Towers at two of the corners which might seem to have been designed to provide enfilading fire along the walls actually served as a brewhouse and bakehouse. A stable block was added at the rear of the barracks to accommodate the horses of a troop of dragoons who patrolled the military road through Speyside. The barracks hardly look capable of resisting a serious attack but in 1745 Ruthven was successfully defended by a sergeant and a dozen men against a force of 300 clansmen. Bernera is similar to Ruthven except that the barrack blocks are double ones. They were built to command one of the main ferry crossings to Skye at Kylerhea but because they stand in the middle of the flat coastal plain the buildings look more like a misplaced mansion than a fortress.

In 1690 General Mackay rebuilt Cromwell's old fort at Inverlochy, renaming it Fort William, and also established a strongpoint based on the medieval castle at Inverness. In the 1720s their defences were upgraded, and the base at Inverness became known as Fort George. The barracks at Kiliwhimin were replaced by a new bastioned strongpoint, Fort Augustus, which was finished shortly before the Jacobite rebellion of 1745. These three forts had not been designed to resist a determined attack by an enemy equipped with artillery and during the 1745 rebellion they fared badly. Fort William held out, though with some difficulty, but Fort Augustus surrendered after a lucky shot exploded its magazine. The defenders of Fort George capitulated when its attackers threatened to explode mines beneath the walls. Both forts were partly demolished by the Jacobites. Despite this, Fort Augustus was rebuilt and continued in use into the nineteenth century. It was eventually sold to the Benedictine order and parts of its fabric have been incorporated into the abbey and school which occupy the site today, a curious change of roles. Fort William also outlasted its usefulness and ended up housing navvies before being demolished to make way for a railway station. Nor is there anything to see of the fort at Inverness; the 'castle' which stands on the site today is a nineteenth-century imitation.

After the 1745 rebellion the government, having decided that a new fort was needed at the northern end of the Great Glen in case of future trouble from the Jacobite clans, opted for a new site as the existing one at Inverness was cramped and awkward. Their choice was a peninsula projecting into the Moray Firth east of Inverness which was more secure and could easily be supplied by sea. The original Great Glen forts had been built cheaply and had proved inadequate. This time the government built the strongest possible fortress using the most advanced technology of the day. The new Fort George is the best example in Britain of an eighteenth-century artillery fortification. Commenced in 1747 it was not completed until 1769, by which time all threats of another Jacobite rising had vanished.

The defences of Fort George were concentrated on the landward side, facing the Highlands, and their scale is still impressive today. First of all there is a huge V-shaped outwork or ravelin surrounded by a ditch, designed to keep attackers well back from the main curtain wall. The area of the ravelin alone is greater than that of many medieval castles. Behind the ravelin is a great ditch spanned by a single bridge leading to the main gate piercing the thick curtain wall. The gate is flanked by bastions from which a withering crossfire could be poured on attackers. Inside the fort are barrack blocks designed to accommodate up to 2,500 troops. The buildings, like the defences, have not been substantially altered and their simple Georgian style is dignified and sober. Emergency barracks, proof against plunging mortar fire, were built in casements under the ramparts. Fort George remained an army base until modern times but once it was clear that there was no further threat from the Highlands its role was reversed. It was turned into a coastal fort protecting the Beauly Firth against the French during the Napoleonic Wars.

The first undefended mansions

Although tower houses were being built as late as the 1640s, the need for defence was steadily decreasing. Tastes in architecture, and the lifestyles which accompanied them, were changing. There was some overlap between old and new architectural styles even within the same region. In the early 1640s, when Sir Alexander Innes was having his anachronistic tower house built at Coxton in Moray (NJ 262607), only a few miles away another member of the same family was moving into Innes House (NJ 278649), an elegant L-plan mansion with no traces of fortification and

only a hint of the old castellated style. One of the last lairds' houses to
be built with specifically defensive features was Leslie Castle in Grampian
(NJ 599248), completed in 1661 yet fitted with several gun loops, a vaulted
basement and with iron grilles over the windows.

Despite the weight of tradition, increasing contact between Scotland
and England, as well as with France and the Low Countries, was generating new ideas about what the home of a Scottish noble or laird should
be like. In the decades following the Restoration of Charles II in 1660,
the old fortresses rapidly went out of fashion. Even so, old traditions died
slowly. This was partly because of the considerable cost of building a
totally new mansion in a country which was still comparatively poor. Few
landed estates could generate sufficient surplus capital for their owners to
emulate the great nobles of England or the Continent by building totally
new country mansions.

A compromise adopted by many landowners in the later seventeenth
century was to remodel and extend their existing towers. Sometimes this
simply involved building a new, more spacious wing alongside an existing
battlemented tower. This can be seen in the Duke of Lauderdale's residence at Lennoxlove in East Lothian (NT515721). The contrast is even
more stark and uncompromising at Drum in Grampian (NJ 796005) where
thirteenth-century tower and seventeenth-century mansion stand side by
side. In other cases greater effort was made to combine old and new in a
more integrated scheme. The Scottish practice of facing exterior walls
with harling or roughcast allowed different styles of stonework to be
hidden under a uniform coat. Sometimes what appears from the exterior
to be entirely late seventeenth- or early eighteenth-century in design can
be shown, by inspection of the interior, to be a composite work with a
medieval tower at the core. One of the grandest of these transitional
houses, part castle part mansion, is Traquair House near Innerleithen.
The original three-storey tower forms one end of the present main block.
Extensions were added in the mid-sixteenth and seventeenth centuries to
a height of four storeys and the tower was raised to match. In the late
seventeenth century a courtyard flanked by two service wings was added
in front. Later modifications tried to impose as much symmetry as possible
on a complex and composite design. Traquair is a delightful blend of old
and new architectural ideas.

It is a mistake to assume that there was no tradition of building undefended mansions in Scotland before the early seventeenth century. A number
of medieval hall-houses are known in Scotland, including a group in the
Western Highlands. They were rectangular buildings with first-floor halls
and ground-floor storage areas. Although most known examples have
been dated to the thirteenth century a number of them continued in use
into the seventeenth century. Undefended mansions were also associated
with monasteries. The Abbot's House at Arbroath Abbey, dating from

Figure 19 Traquair House, near Innerleithen, originally a fortified house, later extended into a mansion but preserving much of its original character.

around 1500 is a good example. At Provan Hall, now within the suburbs of Glasgow, stands a small sixteenth-century two-storey house with crow-stepped gables and a circular stair tower protruding from one angle. It faces on to a walled courtyard and another range of buildings was added on the opposite side of the courtyard during the eighteenth century. The hall may originally have served as a hunting lodge. The arrangement of non-defended buildings around a high walled courtyard which, like a barmkin, could be defended at need, can also be seen from Orkney and Shetland where protection from the wind probably also influenced the design. Langskaill House on Gairsay in Orkney (HY 434219), built in the mid-seventeenth century, has three ranges of buildings laid out around a courtyard. The gateway on the fourth side is flanked by gunloops. Skaill House on the west mainland of Orkney (HY234186) is a more developed and rambling version of the same plan.

Nevertheless, although undefended mansions did not develop completely from scratch in the seventeenth century, a distinct group of new mansions can be seen in the Lothians. Their location is significant: they were close to the capital in the most peaceful part of Scotland. Moreover the owners of many of them were successful Edinburgh lawyers and merchants. Such men were perhaps less bound by tradition, less concerned with the status symbol of a battlemented tower, than old established landowners.

The typical seventeenth-century laird's house was built on an L-plan

Figure 20 Hamilton House, Preston, East Lothian, dating from the early seventeenth century, has design features recalling earlier fortified houses.

with a stair tower in the re-entrant angle. The main block and wing were only one room deep with the family accommodation on the first floor, service and storage facilities below. The plan was derived almost directly from contemporary tower houses and, like them, it could be adapted to different scales to suit the wealth and pretensions of the owners. Two good examples of this type of house stand almost opposite each other in the centre of the East Lothian village of Preston. Hamilton House was built in 1626 for an Edinburgh advocate. It consists of a main block with two wings framing a small courtyard. The original entrance is in a curious semi-hexagonal tower in the angle between the main block and the west wing. Nearby is Northfield House, built for a wealthy Edinburgh merchant. Its steeply pitched roof with attic dormers and corbelled corner turrets recalls the main block at Traquair and it seems to be an older building, perhaps sixteenth-century in date, which has been remodelled. Like Hamilton House the original entrance was in a tower set in the angle between the main block and a wing.

    If the continuation of the castellated tradition in such houses seems backward-looking it should be remembered that many Tudor country houses in England used plans and architectural details derived from earlier fortresses. The architect's job of designing houses had not yet become separate from the mason's task of building them and this is reflected in the continuing use of characteristically Scottish designs. The main blocks of these houses were still one room deep with all the apartments interconnecting. Only slowly were symmetrical facades, double-pile plans two or more rooms deep, and central scale and platt staircases adopted.

The early use of features derived from England can be seen at Winton House in East Lothian (NT438695). Built in the 1620s, with classical ornamentation, it has tall twisted chimney stacks recalling Elizabethan and Jacobean mansions south of the Border. By the early eighteenth century a new style of smaller country house was beginning to appear with unified and symmetrical facades, two storeys in height, sometimes with a sunk basement. The facade was laid out around a central doorway with a scale and platt staircase replacing the old turnpike stair. Two East Lothian houses demonstrate this transition. Pilmuir House (NT 486695) was built in 1624. The original entrance was in a central wing housing a stair tower, with a separate corbelled-out stair tower giving access to the upper floors. In the early eighteenth century the house was remodelled; the original rear of the building was made into a new front with a symmetrical facade and central entrance approached by a flight of steps. The two faces of Pilmuir reflect different centuries, one looking backwards to the fortified house, the other forwards to the Georgian mansion. Bankton House near Prestonpans, dating from the early eighteenth century, has a similar symmetrical facade with a classical pediment above the main entrance and curving, Dutch-style gables above. By the mid-eighteenth century the Georgian mansion had reached a standardised design which, scaled down, served admirably as a manse or the home of a prosperous farmer or, with an extra storey added and wings or side pavilions, as a sizeable country mansion.

The classical country house

The first true classical country houses, using designs developed from those of Andrea Palladio in Italy, via the work of English architects like Inigo Jones, Vanbrugh and Wren, began to appear in Scotland in the later seventeenth century. Their first exponent was Sir William Bruce (c.1630–1710) the younger son of a Fife laird who became a successful Restoration politician and courtier. Architecture was only one of his many interests. Much of Bruce's early work involved remodelling existing houses, including his own at Balcaskie in Fife (NO 524035). He undertook several commissions for the Duke of Lauderdale, Charles II's Secretary of State for Scotland. His most important work for Lauderdale was the remodelling of Thirlestane Castle near Lauder into a symmetrical layout. Bruce's masterpiece was Kinross House, built for himself between 1675 and 1693, the first completely classical mansion in Scotland and an enormous advance in country house design. It has a double-pile plan, two rooms deep, like contemporary English houses, but much of the detail is

French in style. It has two main storeys over a basement, and an attic floor whose windows are almost concealed above a heavy cornice. Kinross House is a confident and self-assured design. The gardens around the house were laid out at the same time as the house as part of an integrated plan, something unheard of in Scotland and not even common in England at this time.

Bruce's largest mansion, again a completely new design, was Hopetoun House west of Edinburgh, built between 1699 and 1702. The Hopetoun family had made a fortune from the lead mines at Leadhills (Chapter 9) and the first earl commissioned a design which was based on the most up-to-date houses south of the Border. It consisted of a central main block with side pavilions linked by screen walls to the main building. In 1721 the Earl employed William Adam to enlarge the house on a scale which was grander than anything yet seen in Scotland. Using Bruce's central block as a starting point, Adam remodelled and extended the house producing the imposing facade which can be seen today with concave walls linking two large side pavilions to the extended main block of the house. In detail the two periods of work by two different architects sometimes fail to match but the overall effect was a splendid and impressive house which set a new standard in elegance and spaciousness for Scottish landowning families.

Despite the magnificence of Hopetoun only a few new country houses were built in Scotland during the later seventeenth and the first half of the eighteenth century. There was simply not enough money available and most landowners continued to adapt and extend their old fortified houses. Bruce's classical tradition was continued by architects like James Smith who remodelled the huge rambling mansion of Dalkeith Palace into a more unified layout. James Smith was also responsible for building the anachronistic Drumlanrig Castle but his design for Yester House in East Lothian was very different, a plain and severe classical mansion. William Adam, who died in 1748, was the last architect to have a distinctly Scottish classical style. From the later eighteenth century Scottish and English architects worked increasingly on either side of the Border. William Adam, the son of a Kirkcaldy builder, had been an apprentice of Bruce. His achievements have been eclipsed by those of his famous sons but in his day his work was extremely influential.

Duff House on the outskirts of Banff is one of William Adam's grandest and most distinctive houses, a medieval castle with Baroque detail which imitates Vanbrugh's style. It was built between 1730 and 1739 for Lord Braco, by all accounts an overbearing and unpleasant patron who was determined to impress, if not overawe, his contemporaries. Duff House is a high and dominating building, rich with Baroque detail, with a central classical pediment. The main block is flanked and overtopped by two towers which rise high above the facade. The design has a very strong vertical element in contrast to the horizontal layout of the classic Palladian mansions of the period. The intended matching side pavilions for the house were never built due to a dispute between Adam and Lord Braco over costs. So bitter was Braco over the disagreement that he refused to live in the house when the main block was completed. William Adam also built in a plainer, more severe style, as at House of Dun in Angus, dating from 1730. Here the giant triumphal arch-style entrance is out of scale with the rest of the building. Adam was sometimes so determined to achieve effect that he forgot some of the basic rules of proportion. Haddo House near Tarves in Grampian is a more restrained Palladian mansion with a main block linked to two side pavilions by curved wings.

The great age of country house building began at the close of our period as agriculture became more profitable generating more capital that could be diverted into house building. Although a number of architects worked in Scotland at this period some of the most impressive work was done by William Adam's sons, John and especially Robert. John Adam's designs ranged from the homely and warm as at Moffat House (NT 083053) to the large and plain as at Moy House in Moray (NO 015589). Robert Adam could also build in a fairly simple, unadorned style, as with Lauderdale House, a country mansion in an urban setting, dominating the main street of Dunbar, or Letterfourie in Moray (NJ 448626), an unusually tall house, improved by its setting among fine gardens. Robert Adam's work also includes grander, more severe mansions like Kirkdale House in Galloway (NX 515533).

Towards the end of the eighteenth century the Gothic style of country house began to develop, involving a return to the motifs of medieval Europe rather than ancient Greece or Rome. In a sense the Scots baronial style had never entirely disappeared so that there was not a great gap between its survival and revival. From the late tower houses of the 1620s one can trace the Scots baronial style through many of the early seventeenth-century mansions that succeeded them, in late seventeenth-century country houses like Drumlanrig in some of William Adam's eighteenth-century mansions like Duff House, and in new 'castles' like Inveraray. The earliest Gothic Revival country houses designed by the Adam family generally had only a thin veneer of medievalism on what was basically a classical country house plan. Robert Adam's achievements in this style included Mellerstain and Wedderburn in Berwickshire as well as Seton House in East Lothian. His crowning achievement in this style was, however, at Culzean on the Ayrshire coast. Culzean is one of Scotland's greatest country houses, designed in Adam's mature castellated style and memorable for its restored Adam interiors as well as the exterior. The existing castle was remodelled in the 1760s and 1770s by the ninth and tenth earls of Cassillis but it was from 1777 when Robert Adam was called in to redesign the house, that it acquired its present form. Part of

Figure 21 Haddo House, Grampian, completed in 1735, is one of William Adam's best-known Scottish versions of a traditional Palladian mansion (National Trust for Scotland).

Figure 22 Mellerstain House near Lauder, rebuilt by William and Robert Adam in the mid-eighteenth century, preserves some of the most attractive internal decorations in Scotland.

Figure 23 Culzean Castle, remodelled by Robert Adam from 1777, represents the culmination of his 'castle style' of country mansion.

the extensions from the 1760s were demolished to make room for a big drum tower housing the first-floor saloon, right on the edge of the cliffs.

New houses in the Highlands

The advent of improved houses in the Highlands was delayed into the mid-eighteenth century. More substantial houses for minor lairds and tacksmen, who sublet portions of an estate from the clan chiefs, began to appear earliest in the south-west Highlands where the second duke of Argyll was introducing far-reaching changes in the tenurial structure of his estates with an eye to increasing their commercial potential. A number of these still survive. They had two storeys and an attic, with facades which were roughly symmetrical around a central entrance. Inside, the plan was a simple one with two rooms on each floor divided by a central staircase. The original block of Glencaple House, dating from around 1740, is one of the best-preserved examples. Achlian, on the shores of Loch Awe (NN 121242) is another. Towards the end of the eighteenth century these small, simple dwellings began to be replaced by a more conventional type of small Georgian house, slate roofed, well pro-portioned and symmetrical, which was used for farmsteads in the more prosperous parts of Argyllshire and for many small landowners' homes. These houses are identical with contemporary ones in the Lowlands and were built largely by Lowland masons, as there was insufficient local expertise in many areas.

In the middle of the eighteenth century the classical country house also made its appearance in the Highlands. Early examples were built by cadet branches of the Campbell family. Airds House in Argyllshire (NM 909449), dating from 1738, is one of the finest and best preserved, with a classical facade and curving screen walls linking the main block to side pavilions enclosing a central courtyard. The introduction of houses of this type was even more of a revolution than in the Lowlands because there was no gradual transition here from fortified house to classical mansion. The abruptness of the contrast can be seen at Breachacha in Coll. Beside the fifteenth-century tower house and barmkin stands the mansion that replaced it in 1750. Built for the MacLean laird of Coll, it is a plain three-storey block linked to two side pavilions, a simple rendering of the classical country house in a remote and wild setting. The design was embellished during the nineteenth century by adding some rather crude and clumsy Scots baronial-style battlements and turrets. Johnson and Boswell stayed here in 1773 on their Highland tour. Johnson, with a highly romantic notion of what was appropriate for a Highland chief, dismissed it as 'a tradesman's box'. Boswell, better able to appreciate the revolution in living standards that it represented, described it as 'a neat ·new built gentleman's house'.

The dramatic change in the circumstances of Highland landowners during the second half of the eighteenth century, with increasing commercialisation and greater incomes, is shown at Lochbuie in Mull. The old Lochbuie House, built in 1752, was one of the simple two-up-two-down laird's houses described earlier. Johnson and Boswell stayed here too and Johnson was unimpressed with the poor standards of furnishing and facilities. He would have had little complaint about the house which succeeded it a generation later. Old Lochbuie House now forms part of the outbuildings of a fine three-storey classical mansion erected around 1790.

One Highland mansion which deserves detailed consideration on account of its early date and its importance in Scottish country house design is Inveraray Castle. The third duke of Argyll succeeded to the estate of his elder brother in 1743 at the age of 61. A lawyer and politician, he had wide-ranging intellectual interests which included architecture. Although he had not visited the seat of the Campbells at Inveraray for nearly thirty years he immediately began planning to improve it. Having established that the old castle was semi-ruined and unfit for habitation he engaged Roger Morris, an English architect, to design a new house.

As Morris could not spend much time in such a remote location as Inverary, William Adam was engaged as supervisor of the project. The design of the new Inveraray Castle was a curious one, echoing the past in some respects but in advance of its time in others. It consisted of a nearly square building with round towers projecting boldly from the corners. In the centre, instead of a small open courtyard, rose a tall central tower with clerestory windows lighting a high hall below. Although the interior layout was classical in concept the outer appearance was Gothic, the first time the style had been attempted on so grand a scale. In the nineteenth century the appearance of the house was altered by putting conical caps on the towers, removing the battlements from the main block, and building on an extra attic storey which diminishes the impact of the central tower but fortunately the basic design was not interfered with. The effect has been described, rather cruelly, as a vast toy fort but there was no denying its distinctiveness.

The main phase of building lasted from 1744 until the death of the third duke in 1760. The scale of the undertaking was immense, for the logistics of building a huge house in what was, in the mid-eighteenth century, a remote and inaccessible area, were daunting. Although much of the stone was obtained locally, skilled workers and much of the other building materials had to be imported, often from a considerable distance. Sadly, the building was still unfinished when the duke died in 1760 and he never occupied it. The fourth duke was not greatly interested in Inveraray and there was a hiatus in building activity for a decade. The house was eventually finished in the last quarter of the century under the fifth duke.

Inveraray was a striking achievement. As a precursor of Gothic style it influenced the design of country houses not only within Scotland but in England too. When William Adam died in 1748 he was succeeded in the task of supervising the building of the castle by his eldest son John but the younger Robert Adam also visited Inveraray and a good deal of the inspiration for his later castle style, seen at Culzean and Mellarstain, seems to have been derived from it. Later Highland mansions by other architects who had visited Inveraray or families who were connected with the dukes of Argyll, also echo Inveraray's style; Taymouth Castle, home of the earls of Breadalbane is an example.

In any Scottish community today the two oldest surviving buildings are likely to be the castle and the parish kirk. In these more secular times it can be difficult to appreciate the central role that the church played in the lives of our ancestors. The church influenced the landscape in many ways; directly through its networks of parish churches, chapels and religous houses, less directly as a major landowner and political force. During our period the nature and role of the church in Scotland changed drastically. In our next chapter we look at the impact of these changes on the landscape.

5

The church in the landscape

The church was a central element in the lives of most of the population of Scotland throughout our period but its organisation and role changed drastically between 1500 and 1800. In 1500 Scotland was a Catholic country, still closely tied to Rome. The fifteenth century has often been seen as a period of decline in the Scottish church leading inexorably to its demise at the Reformation in 1560. Certainly the system was subject to gross abuses, as the reformers were quick to point out. However, the basic institutions of the church, and the expression of these in the landscape from abbey and cathedral to parish church and chapel, were more healthy than has sometimes been admitted, within the constraints of a relatively poor country, large parts of which had been devastated by English invasions during the fourteenth and fifteenth centuries.

Following the Reformation much of the structure of the old church was allowed to decay. The new, austere faith concentrated on the religious community of the parish. The new form of worship produced changes in the internal layout of parish kirks but for over a century after the Reformation the structure of the church remained in a state of flux and conditions were not propitious for building new places of worship. It was not until after 1690, when the Church of Scotland was finally confirmed as Presbyterian, following long periods of episcopacy, that much new church building was undertaken. This chapter looks at various aspects of the church in the Scottish landscape beginning with the early sixteenth century, then considering the changes which occurred at the Reformation and finally tracing their effects through the seventeenth and eighteenth centuries.

Religious houses and cathedrals

The reformers in the mid-sixteenth century made scathing attacks on the laxity and worldliness of the monks, friars and nuns in Scotland's religious houses. Some of them had been the subject of critical reports as early as the fourteenth century. During the late fifteenth and early sixteenth centuries morale in the monasteries cannot have been improved by the widespread practice of appointing secular clergy as abbots or even laymen as 'commendators' (literally 'protectors'). However, the picture of a system in decline has probably been overdrawn. Although their members may have been less scrupulous in their devotions in some cases than in earlier times the monastic houses were far from moribund; indeed they exibited greater vitality than they had for much of the fifteenth century. Some smaller abbeys, such as Saddell in Kintyre, were in difficulties and were suppressed before the Reformation but life continued within the cloisters of most abbeys, priories and nunneries much as it had done. There were even a few new foundations such as the Trinitarian priory of the Cross Kirk at Peebles (1474). The various orders of friars were still active, particularly the Observantine branch of the Franciscans who established a number of new houses in the late fifteenth and early sixteenth centuries including one at Jedburgh which has recently been excavated.

Elsewhere the continuation of monastic life into the sixteenth century is reflected in stone by programmes of rebuilding and improvement, in some cases following destruction by invading English armies. This work was undertaken despite the deteriorating financial position of most abbeys which were alienating their lands in order to meet rapidly rising royal taxation. At Cambuskenneth near Stirling a major restoration programme was followed by a rededication of the abbey in 1521. At Jedburgh, which had been burnt by the English in 1464, the south presbytery chapel, transepts and crossing tower were rebuilt in the late fifteenth and early sixteenth centuries. At Scone an extensive scheme of repairs was under way while work was continuing on the abbeys of Kelso and Newbattle on the eve of the Reformation. At Melrose Abbey work had been going on intermittently since the abbey was burnt by the English in 1385. The parts of the abbey church which date from the original twelfth-century Cistercian building are plain, almost severe, in design but the rebuilt eastern end is ornate and elaborate. It has huge windows with delicate tracery and a wealth of carving including such grotesque gargoyles as a pig playing a set of bagpipes. The master mason responsible for some of the best work is known to have come from England, and the presence of French craftsmanship can also be detected. In architectural, if not spiritual, terms Melrose in the late fifteenth and early sixteenth centuries was no backwater; it was in the mainstream of European developments.

In south-east Scotland the English invasions between 1544 and 1549,

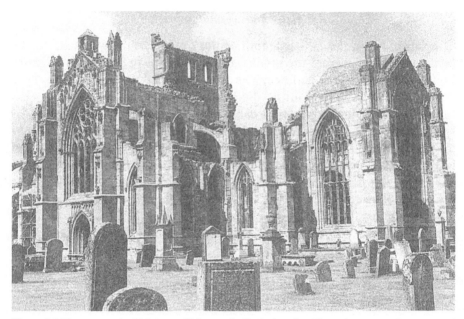

Figure 24 The east end of Melrose Abbey, rebuilt during the fifteenth century, has some of the most delicate and lavishly ornamented late-medieval church architecture in Scotland.

rather than internal decay, caused the demise of most religious houses. Hardly an abbey, priory, friary or nunnery escaped severe damage while religious houses around the Firth of Tay such as Balmerino Abbey (NO 359248) and the nunnery at Elcho (NO 163209) were burnt by landing parties from the English fleet. The great Border abbeys suffered especially seriously. Although there was little time for recovery before the Reformation it is significant that rebuilding was under way at many sites by 1559.

The subsequent history of Scotland's religious houses is one of neglect and sometimes of deliberate destruction. Contrary to popular belief there was no universal demolition of monasteries by angry Protestant mobs though the abbey of Scone was severely damaged during the earliest phase of the Reformation. The wrath of the reformers was directed at the urban friaries, many of which were wrecked. This may have been because of their greater accessibility to the urban rioters who precipitated the Reformation and because the nobility had less interest in protecting the friaries. Elsewhere the interiors of abbey churches were merely stripped of their statues, rood screens and other idolatrous symbols. An act of the Privy Council ordering the removal of places and monuments of idolatry encouraged some destruction, particularly in the west where the abbey of Paisley was burnt and those at Kilwinning (NS 303432) and Crossraguel (NS 275083) damaged. All that remains at Kilwinning is the gable wall of one of the transepts of the church. In other areas where local magnates adhered to the old faith monastic houses were spared for a time. In Galloway Lord Maxwell protected the abbeys of Dundrennan (NX 749475) and Sweetheart (NX 965662). In most monasteries the existing monks were allowed to continue in residence until gradually they died out but in time the processes of decay and demolition were inevitable.

From the 1530s the abbeys had come increasingly into the hands of laymen and this process was merely hastened by the Reformation. At Melrose the commendator's house, possibly adapted from an earlier abbot's residence, can be seen adjoining the monastery. In the decades following the Reformation, as the numbers of resident monks dwindled, the claustral ranges of many abbeys began to be plundered of their stone. At Beauly Priory Lord Ruthven stripped the lead off the roofs in 1572. Abbeys adjacent to large towns suffered particularly. Cambuskenneth Abbey served as a convenient stone quarry for the masons of Stirling and several buildings in the old town including Mar's Work and Cowane's Hospital are built from the remains of the monastery. All that remains above foundation level today is the solid and sturdy late thirteenth-century free-standing bell tower which adjoined the monastic church. At Arbroath much of the older part of the town is built with stone taken from the abbey. Those monastic houses which survived most intact were often more remote and inaccessible like the Augustinian house on Inchcolm, an island in the Firth of Forth. Here the fine state of preservation of the buildings around the cloister as well as the church itself gives a good impression of the appearance of a medieval religious house. On the more remote island of Iona the buildings of the abbey, although ruined, were in a sufficiently good state of preservation to permit full-scale renovation during the present century so that the abbey still flourishes as a religious community. Another medieval abbey which has been restored is Pluscarden in Moray, still a Benedictine house, with a skilfully rebuilt church and cloister and a well-preserved original precinct wall.

A rural setting was not always a protection from destruction though. At Canonbie, close to the Border, the Augustinian priory lay within the Debateable Land, so Henry VIII had tried to have it suppressed in 1544 during the dissolution of the English monasteries. Whether this had any effect or whether its demise was the result of the Scottish reformers, nothing remained on the site by 1620 and only a few place names like 'Canonbie' itself mark its former existence. Monastic churches themselves often continued in use as parish kirks. Even here preservation was not automatic. Sir Walter Scott of Branxholm removed so much of the stonework of the church at Melrose Abbey that when in 1618 the local community decided to refurbish the nave for use as a parish kirk they had virtually to rebuild it. The problem with many abbey churches was that with their marked divisions into nave and chancel, aisle and transept, they were structurally unsuited to the new open form of congregational worship favoured by the reformers. As a result it was often only the nave of an abbey church which continued in use while little effort was made to maintain or repair the remainder of the structure.

The Border abbeys are still magnificent even in ruin. Each has its own distinctive character. At Melrose the fifteenth-century eastern end of the church, with its large traceried windows and fine carvings, is the most impressive aspect of the ruined abbey. Although the claustral buildings have been reduced to their foundations their layout is still clear and one can admire the engineering skill of the canal which brought water to the abbey from the Tweed. Dryburgh Abbey has been described as Scotland's most picturesque medieval site, close to the river Tweed and overhung with trees. Here it is the church which has fared worst while the claustral buildings, particularly the east range, are better preserved. At Jedburgh the abbey church, largely complete though roofless, still dominates the main street of the burgh. The domestic buildings of the abbey, sited on a series of terraces falling steeply to the Jed Water, have recently been excavated. At Kelso only fragments remain of the fine Romanesque abbey church.

In the west Crossraguel, near Maybole, is a good example of a small Cluniac abbey, in ruins, but with parts fairly intact including some of the domestic buildings. The abbey was largely rebuilt in the fifteenth century with the fine tower house, gatehouse and doocot being added in the sixteenth. The tower was possibly built to accommodate the young Earl of Cassillis who lived here for a number of years under the guardianship of the abbot. In Galloway, Sweetheart Abbey, overlooking the estuary of the Nith, was founded in 1273 by Lady Devorgilla in memory of her husband, John Balliol. In the difficult period after Flodden the monks put themselves under the protection of Robert, Lord Maxwell, the warden of the Scottish west march. The Maxwells received substantial grants of land from the abbey in return. At the Reformation the influence of the Maxwells helped to protect Sweetheart, and the last abbot remained until 1587. Various parts of the abbey church and its buildings including the former refectory were used as the parish church into the late nineteenth century. In 1779 the ruins were bought by a group of local people to prevent further destruction and, while the buildings around the cloister have mostly been levelled, the church, though roofless, is largely complete. The boundary wall enclosing the monastic precincts, constructed from massive roughly squared granite boulders, is still visible to the north of the abbey, perhaps the best of its kind in Scotland. Galloway's other Cistercian houses, Dundrennan and Glenluce (NX 185586), have not fared so well and are badly ruined.

Monastic houses were rarer in the Highlands and Islands but some examples can be seen in attractive settings. Saddell Abbey (NR 784320) has only a few fragments left but Ardchattan Priory (NM 971349) was largely rebuilt in the late fifteenth and early sixteenth centuries. The south range of the conventual buildings was converted into a private house after the Reformation and although the house was enlarged and remodelled in the nineteenth century it still has the original monastic refectory at its core, with the ruins of the church, parts of which were used for worship until 1732, close by. At Iona as well as the rebuilt abbey there is also an interesting ruined nunnery. Scotland had relatively few nunneries. They were less well endowed than most monasteries, with unostentatious build- ings which have left little trace in the landscape. At Iona the church and complex of buildings grouped around the cloister give a good impression of what one of these communities was like.

Although many of Scotland's medieval cathedrals were located in or adjacent to large towns, as at Aberdeen, Glasgow and St Andrews, several of them were sited in smaller centres such as Dunkeld, Dunblane and Whithorn in settings which were almost rural. Like the abbey churches they survived the Reformation with varying degrees of success; some, like Fortrose, falling almost totally into ruin, others continuing to be used by the local community. At Dornoch the cathedral was heavily restored in the nineteenth century. It had succumbed not to the zeal of the reformers but to the depredations of a raiding party of Clan MacKay who burnt it in 1570. It remained roofless until 1616 when the choir and transepts were reroofed to serve as the parish church. Opposite the restored cathedral part of the bishop's palace survives as a hotel. The cathedral of Dunblane has likewise been restored but much of Dunkeld is in ruins. At Whithorn, the site of an early Christian church and a place of pilgrimage during medieval times, the cathedral was a monastic one. The roofless nave of the original church still survives though the new church, built in 1822, overlies the cloisters of the former monastery.

In the centre of the seemingly isolated island of Lismore stands the remains of Scotland's smallest and most remote medieval cathedral, which was the seat of the bishopric of Argyll. The nave has been altered and cut down in height to serve as the parish church for the island. Beyond its western end the foundations of the choir and tower of the former cathedral are still visible. The building stands within a circle of field boundaries which may delimit the perimeter of an early Christian monas- tery. Several kilometres away towards the south end of the island are the ruins of Achadun Castle (NM 803393), a fortified courtyard dwelling which served as the bishop's palace into the late fifteenth or early sixteenth century. Situated on a rocky knoll with sheer cliffs on the seaward side, the castle has fine views across Loch Linnhe to Mull and Morvern.

Collegiate churches

As the reputations of the monasteries and friaries declined, wealthy laymen began to channel their endowments to the church in different directions. During the fifteenth and early sixteenth centuries it became fashionable for landowners to found non-monastic churches in which groups or 'colleges' of secular priests headed by a provost held services with more ceremony than was possible in an ordinary parish church, saying masses for the souls of the founders and their families. Such collegiate churches had greater architectural pretensions than ordinary parish kirks. Many of them had cruciform plans with central towers and a number contain the tombs of their founders. In the second half of the fifteenth century at least eleven were established and during the first half of the sixteenth century another thirteen. Many were in the Lothians but others were widely scattered including St Mary's at Cullen and St Duthac's at Tain. The continuing vitality of the collegiate movement is shown by St Mary's at Biggar, the last great church to be built in Scotland before the Reformation. An impressive cruciform church with an apsidal east end and a tower over the crossing, it was founded in 1546 by Malcolm, Lord Fleming, and work on it was still continuing at the Reformation. Collegiate churches fared better than monastic ones after the Reformation. Many already served as parish churches and their smaller size made them more easily adaptable to the new forms of worship than the great abbey churches and cathedrals.

Some collegiate churches developed from earlier private chapels, as at

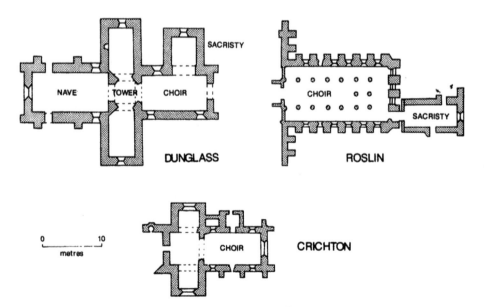

Map 9 Some examples of the plans of collegiate churches.

Dalkeith, others from existing parish churches. Although these private churches were sometimes lavishly endowed by their founders, in many cases the cost of construction proved to be higher than expected and the buildings were never completed. Either the financial resources of the families were insufficient or the Reformation intervened to halt construction. In several cases the choir and sometimes the transepts of a church were built but the nave was never added, as at Crichton, Roslin and Seton.

The church at Dunglass (NT 768719) is a good example of a completed collegiate foundation which survived destruction during the English invasions of the 1540s. Following the Reformation it was converted into a barn and stable. One gable was broken open to allow access for carts, and rows of holes in the vaulting show where timber floors were inserted. Nevertheless, Dunglass is still largely intact, an attractive church though severe and plain in appearance. It has a cruciform plan with a low tower over the crossing. Sir Alexander Seton of Dunglass received permission to establish a collegiate church here in 1450 but there may have been an earlier private chapel on the site.

The church at Dunglass was built more or less at one period but Seton, west of Prestonpans (NT 419751), is more composite. The nave was either never completed or was demolished after the Reformation when the church went out of use. What survive are the choir, transepts and tower of a church whose plan was similar to Dunglass but whose architecture is more ornate, with a fine polygonal apse end. The first phase of construction dates from the 1430s but successive generations of Setons extended and embellished the building. The transepts and tower were added as late as the 1540s. Unlike Dunglass, which is rather dark inside, Seton is light and airy, the large windows having preserved much of their tracery. The foundations of the living quarters of the priests who officiated at the church can be seen nearby.

One of the finest collegiate churches in Scotland, Lincluden near Dumfries, is reasonably well preserved, though roofless. As well as the choir, the south transept and part of the nave, Lincluden is unusual in that some of the domestic buildings which accommodated the provost and priests, dating from the fifteenth and early sixteenth centuries, still survive with a formal knot garden incorporating an early medieval motte. Lincluden was founded by Archibald, third earl of Douglas on the site of a Benedictine nunnery. Douglas had the house suppressed in 1389 complaining that due to the nuns' sloth and neglect the buildings were not being maintained and that the sisters spent more time bringing up their daughters(!) than attending to their devotions. His allegations were accepted and the new church was raised on the foundations of the nunnery though building was probably done mainly in the time of the fourth earl who died in 1424. Lincluden contains the magnificently carved tomb of Princess Margaret,

Figure 25 Roslin Chapel, the most architecturally accomplished and distinctive of Scottish late-medieval collegiate churches.

daughter of King Robert III and wife of the fourth earl. Another ruined but interesting collegiate foundation in western Scotland is Castle Semple (NS375601), established in the grounds of the castle by Lord Sempill in 1504. After his death at Flodden in 1513 the plain rectangular church was embellished by adding a three-sided Gothic apse and a fine burial monument to its founder.

The most glorious product of the Scottish collegiate movement is Roslin Chapel south of Edinburgh. Standing near the castle of the Sinclairs, the chapel is remarkable for the riot of Gothic carving that covers every part, interior and exterior, an exuberance which contrasts markedly with the severe and plain style of most late-medieval Scottish architecture. The interior is particularly impressive; the stone-vaulted roof is encrusted with sculpture to the point of eccentricity. Most fantastic of all is the celebrated 'Prentice Pillar', one of the internal columns, which is carved almost grotesquely with designs that spiral round the column. Tradition has it that the pillar was carved by a talented apprentice during his master's absence, and that the older craftsman, on his return, killed the lad out of envy! A more prosaic explanation is that the name of the pillar derives from the Prentys family, skilled English sculptors with no recorded contact with Scotland but who might, possibly, have been called in to work on the chapel. The vocabulary of Scottish architectural historians tends to run out of control when they describe Roslin for the building is in a class of its own. Founded by William St Clair, Earl of Caithness and Orkney, on the site of an earlier chapel, it was under construction by 1446. Like Seton, the church lacks a nave: only the choir and parts of the east walls of the transepts were built.

Sanctuary and pilgrimage

In medieval Scotland all parts of a church were considered to offer a degree of sanctuary and this often included the churchyard and the area around it. In practice the actual right of sanctuary was often ineffectual and readily violated. However, some places were granted special rights of sanctuary by the crown. These could include substantial areas of land within which fugitives could seek the King's peace. The functioning of this 'right of girth' as it was known usually depended on the presence of a religious house to shelter and feed refugees but was sometimes bestowed on royal lands and residences too. In most cases the right of sanctuary ended at the Reformation.

The extent of the designated area of sanctuary was indicated by boundary markers or crosses. At Torphicen in West Lothian there was a preceptory of the Knights of St John with a right of sanctuary. There had been a church here from the end of the twelfth century with a cruciform plan and a central tower. During the fifteenth century the transepts and tower were rebuilt in a fortress-like style which echoes contemporary towerhouse design. The nave and choir of the original church, together with the domestic buildings of the knights, have vanished but the transepts and tower were preserved for use as a courthouse by a local landowner. A stone inscribed with a cross stands in the churchyard marking the centre of the sanctuary area. The perimeter of the area, which had a radius of about 1½km (1 mile) was defined by a series of boundary stones, some of which still survive and are marked on the Ordnance Survey map as 'refuge stones'.

The best surviving sanctuary cross stands near the ancient monastic site at Dull in Perthshire (NN 806492). The only royal sanctuary to remain in being after 1560 was at Holyrood Abbey in Edinburgh. The area of the sanctuary included Arthur's Seat and Salisbury Crags. A girth cross stood at the entrance to the sanctuary area at the foot of the Canongate and a series of letter Ss carved into the causeway of Horse Wynd at the foot of the Canongate still marks the boundary. Elsewhere round the perimeter of the park the original sanctuary wall is still visible in places.

A number of pilgrimage sites continued to attract visitors, and royal patronage, into the sixteenth century. Among the most popular were the shrines at Tain and Whithorn. James IV, who was killed at Flodden in 1513, was a regular visitor to these and to other shrines such as Kilwinning and the shrine of St Adrian on the Isle of May. In 1536 James V made a pilgrimage on foot from Stirling Castle to the chapel of Our Lady of

Loretto near Musselburgh. The Cross Kirk at Peebles was a place of pilgrimage dedicated to St Nicholas and pilgrimages continued to be made here into the early seventeenth century. The cult stemmed from the discovery on the site in the twelfth century of an ancient cross (possibly of early Christian origin) supposedly inscribed with the name of St Nicholas. When the church was converted into a Trinitarian priory in the fifteenth century the rebuilt church was specifically designed to incorporate the shrine and relics.

Whitekirk in East Lothian was also an important venue for pilgrims. Tales of miraculous cures from a holy well at Whitekirk began to spread in the early fourteenth century. By the following century large numbers of people were visiting the site: one source claims that in 1413 15,653 people came to Whitekirk. James I placed it under his personal protection and had a set of pilgrims' hostels built to accommodate visitors. In 1434 the church was visited by Aeneas Sylvius, the future Pope Pius II, who walked barefoot to the shrine without making allowances for the severity of the Scottish climate. He suffered from rheumatism for the rest of his life as a consequence. James IV also visited Whitekirk but in 1537 James V granted the hostels to his favourite, Oliver Sinclair, who demolished them and built a tower house with the stones. The remains of the tower are now incorporated into the teind (tithe) barn that stands beside the largely fifteenth-century church. The church survived the English invasions of the 1540s but was substantially renovated following arson by a group of suffragettes early this century! No trace now remains of the original holy well at Whitekirk; it supposedly dried up in the nineteenth century as a result of agricultural drainage operations.

Parish kirks before the Reformation

In England many parish churches, built in late Anglo-Saxon times or soon after the Norman Conquest, evolved gradually over the centuries, their additional aisles, chapels and monuments mirroring the growing size and prosperity of the communities they served. The tendency was to modify existing churches rather than to abandon them and build new ones. In Scotland conditions were different. The legacy of medieval parish kirks was a poorer one than south of the Border even before the Reformation. Throughout Lowland Scotland during the twelfth century a network of parishes had been laid out and new stone churches built to serve many of them. The fourteenth and fifteenth centuries were not favourable times for church building, though. The devastating series of wars with England and internal dissention channelled energy into the construction of castles rather than churches, and the appropriation of the revenues of a great many parishes by religious houses severely limited funds for maintaining the fabric of parish churches. Some 85 per cent of parishes had their revenues appropriated by some religious body, whether abbey or cathedral, bishopric or collegiate church. The parochial system became the most impoverished element in the Scottish church.

Late-medieval Scottish parish churches were usually plain rectangular boxes without aisles or transepts, often without a tower, a simple wooden rood screen being the only division between nave and chancel. In the Highlands late-medieval church architecture was even simpler than in the Lowlands. Parish kirks were merely small rectangular buildings of rubble masonry whose austerity suggests continuity from ascetic early Celtic monasticism. Even on the fringes of the Highlands churches could be simple structures. St Mary's church at Grandtully (NN 886506) looks more like a farm steading from the outside with its lime-washed rubble walls and long, low irregular roofline. It is thought to date from the early sixteenth century. Inside it has a painted timber vault for part of its length with the rest of the building open to the rafters.

In the Highlands, with widely scattered population and large parishes, there were many small dependent chapels with associated burial grounds serving outlying communities. Today these are often so badly ruined, so simply built, and so poorly recorded as to defy accurate dating. Often only grass-grown foundations and a scatter of headstones within a tumbled enclosure wall are all that remains, sometimes only a cross and a name in antique script on the map. Examples include Caibeal Catriona (NR 643113) and Ardnacross (NR 764266) in Kintyre but a glance at a large-scale map of any part of the West Highlands will reveal others.

Although many late-medieval Scottish churches were architecturally unpretentious their interiors were more highly decorated than is often realised. In north-east Scotland a number of kirks have ornate sacrament houses with late-Gothic decoration. These were designed to keep the consecrated elements of the mass and good examples can be seen at Deskford (NJ 508616)(1551) and Kinkell (NJ 785190) (1524). Pre-Reformation Scottish churches also contained some fine monuments. The practice of burying notable people – mainly the nobility, lairds and the clergy – within Scottish churches and erecting memorials to them continued until the Reformation and although much damage was caused to such monuments in the later sixteenth and seventeenth centuries some fine examples escaped the sledgehammers of the reformers. At Rodel in Harris (NG 047831) the south wall of the cruciform medieval church, the most ambitious architecturally in the Western Isles, has a magnificent tomb built for Alexander MacLeod of Dunvegan in 1528. A Lowland counterpart can be seen at Douglas (NS 836310). Here the church, which was embellished by the powerful Douglas family, contains a fine sequence of their family tombs. Local landowners sometimes financed their own burial aisles in pre-Reformation churches like the tall example at Arbuthnot church (NO

801746) built by Sir Robert Arbuthnot at the end of the fifteenth century which resembles a tower house as much as an appendage to a church.

Parish kirks after the Reformation

The Scottish Reformation caused a major shake-up in the structure and operation of the Scottish church which in many cases led to the merging and reorganisation of parishes leaving many old, abandoned kirks to fall into ruin. In other cases new churches were built in more convenient locations within a parish and the old ones left to decay. Examples include the church whose foundations can be seen on the island of Inchcailleach in Loch Lomond (NS 411907) which, until the seventeenth century, served as the parish church of Buchanan but was replaced by one in a more convenient location. The church on Eilean Munde, an island in Loch Leven near the mouth of Glencoe (NN 083592), was abandoned in 1673 when two parishes were merged, although it continued to be used as a burial place. In East Lothian the parishes of Whitekirk and Tyninghame were merged in 1761 and the old church at Tyninghame was largely demolished. Enough fragments remain to show that it had been a magnificent gem of Norman architecture.

In England the Reformation was marked, at parish level, by continuity in tradition rather than a break with the past. In Scotland the Reformation led to more profound changes in the nature of worship, which had a marked effect on the internal layout of most Scottish parish churches. The reformers condemned the division of medieval churches into compartments; nave and choir, aisles and transepts. They wanted single-chambered open buildings in which the congregation could see their minister clearly, hear his sermons and take part in the celebration of communion. Stress was placed on the preaching of the Word rather than administering the sacrament and this was emphasised by the dominance of the pulpit, sometimes a great three-decker affair like the one at Dyke in Moray (NH 990584). Pulpits were resited in the centre of the south wall with the pews facing them from all directions and churches became open rectangular boxes with unencumbered views from end to end. It was often easy to adapt the interiors of small medieval parish churches but the larger monastic and cathedral churches were less well suited in size and structure to the new form of worship and often only the nave or choir was maintained for parish worship.

Mistaking art for idolatry, the reformers purged churches of statues, ornaments, carved woodwork, organs, stained glass and wall paintings. Few parish kirks have retained more than vestiges of their pre-Reformation furnishings. Plain whitewashed interiors or grey stone walls replaced the colourful medieval wall paintings giving a bare, austere appearance to many churches which would have surprised the original builders. In one important respect the interiors of post-Reformation churches were more class-conscious than their predecessors. A feature of many new or converted churches was a separate gallery or 'laird's loft' for the local landowning family, reflecting the fact that the patronage of parish churches was now in lay hands. In the church at Abercorn near Queensferry (NT 081791) the loft for the earls of Hopetoun has an adjoining retiring room where the family could relax and take meals between services! At Bowden (NT 554301) there is also a retiring room behind the laird's loft, and a private burial aisle below, a layout which occurs in other churches built after 1560.

To draw people in to the revitalised church the reformers placed great emphasis on the parish community but this social concern was not reflected in the provision of many new places of worship. This was due partly to lack of funds and partly to unsettled political conditions. The later sixteenth and early seventeenth centuries were not propitious times for church building. Landowners, who were responsible for looking after the fabric of parish kirks, were often slow to part with cash for maintenance or reconstruction. As a result many parish churches were in a poor state of repair in the seventeenth and eighteenth centuries while new churches were often modest and utilitarian in appearance with simple belfries taking the place of more expensive towers. One visitor to Scotland, remarking on the semi-ruinous state of so many of the churches he saw, wrote that 'in many parts of Scotland the Lord still seems to be worshipped in a stable'.

Nevertheless some new churches were erected. One of the earliest was at Burntisland, where a new kirk was built in 1592. Burntisland had grown considerably during the sixteenth century and the new church was designed to house the enlarged congregation and express the community's growing prosperity. The plan is an unusual one, unparalleled elsewhere in Scotland and possibly based on a Dutch design. The church is square with a central tower and a wooden gallery on each wall facing a pulpit set in the south-west angle.

Many new churches in the seventeenth century were simple rectangular structures following the late-medieval Scottish tradition in their Gothic architecture as well as their plans. Many are plain and austere but at their best they have a simplicity which is characteristically Scottish. A particularly attractive example is the church at Lyne, near Peebles (NT 191405). Built with funds provided by Lord Hay in the early 1640s, it stands on a prominent hillock, framed by mature trees, and is a simple rectangle with a small belfry in place of a tower. The original oak pulpit and Lord Hay's canopied pew still survive. Another interesting church stands in the hamlet of Durisdeer among the Nithsdale hills (NS 893037). The surprisingly large size of the church for so small a community is explained by the patronage of the Queensberry family from nearby

Figure 26 The parish church of Lyne near Peebles, built during the 1640s, is a good example of a simple yet attractive post-Reformation kirk.

Drumlanrig Castle. Inside the church, which was built in 1699, there is a fine monument to the second duke of Queensberry erected in 1713.

A number of new post-Reformation churches adopted a T-plan, the wing housing the laird's loft and burial aisle balanced by a tower on the opposite side of the building. The harled and whitewashed church at Gifford (NT 535681) dating from 1710, is a good example. A few seventeenth-century churches were cruciform in plan like Sir William Bruce's one at Lauder (1673). A simple rectangular plan with a gable belfry at one end and a porch in the south wall of an otherwise plain exterior was widely used. By the later eighteenth century the availability of larger beams of imported timber allowed roofs with a greater span to be built and many wider-bodied churches were constructed. Another distinctive late eighteenth-century plan was the 'hall church' with galleries running along both side walls and one end wall, as at Inveraray (1794).

In the later eighteenth century various dissenting groups began to build their own churches. A good example can be seen at Blairlogie near Stirling (NS829969). The church was built in 1761 as a result of the secession of part of the congregation of the parish and bears a commemorative inscription. The Catholic church also enjoyed a revival in Scotland at the end of the eighteenth century. Its rising fortunes are reflected by two churches in Moray, a stronghold of the old faith under the Catholic Gordons. At Tynet near Fochabers (NJ 378612) St Ninian's church, built in 1755, is a

Figure 27 Soutra Aisle, the only surviving fragment of the medieval hospice of Soutra, lying between Edinburgh and the Border Abbeys on the line of Dere Street. The excavated foundations of other buildings belonging to the hospice can be seen in the foreground.

long, low, simple building which from a distance could easily be mistaken for a row of farm cottages. However, a short distance away at Preshome (NJ 409614) is St Gregory's church, built only a generation later but much bolder and more ostentatious in appearance.

The reformers did not permit burial within churches themselves. This explains the paucity of post-sixteenth-century burial monuments in Scottish kirks. However, some notable figures continued to be commemorated in monuments, like the marble one to the Earl of Seafield, one of the leading figures behind the Union of 1707, in the church of St Mary's in Cullen. Local landowning families were permitted to add separate chapels or burial aisles to existing churches or to create them from parts of old abandoned kirks. Sometimes this preserved parts of an early church which would otherwise have been demolished. The fine Norman doorway at Edrom church in Berwickshire (NT 827558) survives only because it was made into a burial vault. Some fragments of religious houses were also preserved in this way. On the bleak moors of Soutra separating the Lothians from Lauderdale, close to the line of the Roman Dere Street, stands a low, windswept building roofed with heavy stone slabs. Soutra Aisle is all that remains of a hospice for pilgrims and travellers founded in the twelfth century along this important routeway between Edinburgh and the Border. After the Reformation it was too remote to be of service as a parish church. Most of the fabric was removed to build enclosure walls and farmsteads during the nineteenth century but part of the church was appropriated as a burial vault for a local landowning family and was left intact. At Largs the Skelmorlie Aisle is all that remains of the old kirk. The aisle was added to the church in 1636 but the remainder of the building was demolished in 1802. The elaborate Renaissance monument within the aisle, one of the finest of its kind in Scotland and Dutch in inspiration, takes the form of a triumphal arch over a burial vault containing the lead coffins of Sir Robert Montgomery of Skelmorlie and his wife.

The more secular role of post-Reformation churches is sometimes visible. Each parish had a kirk session, a body of lay elders responsible for maintaining religious and moral discipline in the community. Many churches have fixed to their exterior walls sets of jougs, or iron neck bands, by which offenders could be secured. At Greenlaw in Berwickshire the link between kirk and law was even stronger: the sturdy-looking tower of the church was actually built in 1712 as a prison. A courthouse, now demolished, stood on the far side of the tower from the church giving rise to the local rhyme about Greenlaw: 'Here's the kirk and here's the law, Hell's hole atween the twa.' The importance of teinds (tithes) in maintaining parish clergy after the Reformation is reflected by the survival of teind barns adjacent to some churches. A solid example with crow-stepped gables rebuilt in the eighteenth century can be seen near the church at Foulden in Berwickshire (NT 931557). Another example, incorporating the remains of an earlier tower house, stands above the church at Whitekirk in East Lothian (NT 597816).

Churchyards and tombstones

Scottish churchyards, although only a minor element in the landscape, are a fascinating study. Before the Reformation landowners and other prominent persons were buried and commemorated inside churches while ordinary people interred in the churchyard did not have prominent grave markers. Churchyards were open and were often used for holding markets and fairs, for sports and for archery practice. Some crosses within churchyards are actually mercat crosses rather than religious symbols, as at Dallas (NJ 121518) and Duffus (NJ 175686) in Moray or Kincardine O'Neill (NO 592996), an important market centre at a crossing of the Dee upstream from Aberdeen. Sunday markets continued to be held in the churchyard here until 1692. Even then it was the timing of the markets rather than their location which was the cause of offence. In other places weekday markets continued to be held in churchyards into the eighteenth century although by this period the erection of headstones and other types of churchyard monument must have interfered increasingly with such activities.

In the West Highlands a vigorous tradition of late-medieval monumental sculpture continued into the sixteenth century. Consisting principally of upright crosses and recumbent slabs carved with effigies of warriors and churchmen, they are sometimes still found in the open but in many church-yards have been collected together and taken indoors for safe keeping. Good collections can be seen at Kilmory (NR 702751), Kilberry (NR 709642) and Saddell (NR 784320) in Argyll and at the priory on Oronsay, a small island near Colonsay where some thirty slabs have been brought into the former prior's house. Although there is a superficial resemblance to the style of early Christian crosses carved in the same region there was no direct continuity between the two traditions of sculpture. Particular local schools of carving have been identified at Iona, Saddell Abbey, Oronsay Priory and around Loch Awe, the crosses and slabs produced in each district being distinguished by subtle differences in the style and motifs used. The distribution of this tradition of sculpture coincides closely with the sphere of influence of the Lords of the Isles who were patrons of the abbeys at Iona and Saddell. The main flowering of the tradition occurred in the fifteenth century before the Lordship was forfeited to the crown in 1493 and the main source of local patronage was removed. Sculpture continued at Oronsay in the sixteenth century for a more local market.

Once ordinary families began to acquire specific plots in churchyards they started to mark them with head and footstones and these were increasingly ornamented to become memorials to the dead. Few tomb-stones have survived from the late sixteenth century although from early collections of epitaphs it is known that many once existed. However, many old churchyards have some seventeenth-century stones and a wider selection from the eighteenth century. Their range of style and decoration is considerable. There are upright headstones, recumbent slabs, table tombs where the slab is raised on four legs, and chest tombs where the sides of table tombs have been filled in with vertical slabs. Decoration tends to dwell on the emblems of mortality such as the skull and crossbones or the hourglass, a grim warning to those still living. In many cases the tools of a person's trade are also depicted. Sometimes these are easy to identify, like the scissors of the tailor or the hammer of the smith. In other cases they are less obvious, like the square and compass of the mason or the mill rind, the piece of metal supporting the upper millstone, for a miller. The standard of carving on earlier tombstones is often crude but striking. As the eighteenth century progressed the decoration became more refined, sometimes very elaborate. In some cases the style and standard of decoration hints at particularly accomplished groups of masons operating over a local area. At Tranent, for example, the churchyard contains an especially fine collection with some very ornate table tombs.

In the West Highlands the pre-Reformation tradition of stone sculpture continued with some distinctive and attractive tombstones from the

Figure 28 An ornately decorated table tomb in the churchyard at Tranent.

seventeenth and eighteenth centuries. Churchyards in Argyll contain many fine examples decorated with galleys and ships in full sail or ploughs drawn by teams or two or four horses. In the burial ground of Eilean Munde (NN 083592) is a striking tombstone to Duncan MacKenzie, a local tenant, depicting him in the act of cutting down a mounted dragoon at the battle of Prestonpans in 1745. Other sites mark the burial places of incomers to the Highlands, like the small graveyard adjoining the ruins of the government fort at Inversnaid (NO 349098), east of Loch Lomond, where a number of headstones commemorate soldiers from the garrison who died on active service at this remote outpost.

In the later eighteenth and early nineteenth centuries the activities of 'resurrectionists' or body-snatchers, who dug up freshly buried corpses to sell to the urban medical schools, led to a careful watch being kept over churchyards, particularly around Aberdeen, Edinburgh and Glasgow. Mort houses were built in some churchyards, as at Udny near Aberdeen, in which coffins were locked for up to three months until they were no longer fit for sale. Special watch houses can be seen at the gates of churchyards like Newton Mearns outside Glasgow and Glencorse, Pencaitland and Spott near Edinburgh. Another means of thwarting the body-snatchers was to encase newly buried coffins with mortsafes, iron outer coffins or grids, sometimes topped by a massive stone slab. The mortsafes could be dug up some months later when the body was no longer at risk, and reused. Three mortsafes can be seen in the churchyard at Logierait in Perthshire (NN 958521), including one designed to encase a child's coffin, and four at Cluny in Aberdeenshire (NJ 684125).

The break-up of eccelesiastical estates with the Reformation and their transfer to lay hands had a major impact on rural society and was a significant force behind changes in agriculture during the later sixteenth and early seventeenth centuries. However, the story of agricultural improvement in Scotland has often been couched in terms of complete stagnation until the middle of the eighteenth century followed by a rapid 'Agricultural Revolution'. Recent interpretations suggest that this is simplistic and misleading. In our next chapter we look at the ways in which the landscape of the Lowlands changed under the impact of agricultural improvement not only in the later eighteenth century but in earlier times too.

6

The landscape of improvement: the Lowlands

The pace of agriculture, and the face of the countryside in Scotland changed only slowly during the sixteenth and seventeenth centuries. The Scottish farmer of 1500 would have found little that was radically new in the landscape of 1700. Most of the changes that occurred were ones of degree rather than kind. Nevertheless, the later seventeenth and early eighteenth centuries witnessed the first hesitant stirrings of improvement. From the 1760s the rate of change accelerated rapidly and the last four decades of the eighteenth century saw the landscape of many parts of the Lowlands totally transformed. The chronology varies from one district to another. In progressive areas like the Lothians improvement began earlier – from the 1730s – and had been largely completed by the 1790s. In more remote areas like the north east large-scale changes did not begin till the 1770s and 1780s.

The period from the 1760s to the end of the Napoleonic Wars was labelled the Agricultural Revolution by an earlier generation of writers on Scottish economic history. In recent years ideas have changed and there has been considerable debate regarding whether there really was an 'Agricultural Revolution' at all in eighteenth-century Scotland. New research has lengthened the timescale involved, stressing the importance of hitherto unnoticed changes in the seventeenth and early eighteenth centuries and also emphasising that a considerable amount of improvement was still left to do in the nineteenth century.

There is no doubt that the tremendous increase in the output of descriptive writing about Scottish agriculture and the economy in general that occurred towards the end of the eighteenth century tends to focus attention on this period as the most significant phase of change in the Lowland countryside. These works include various theoretical books on agricultural improvements by Scottish writers, surveys of the work actually achieved such as Alexander Wight's tours through Scotland in 1778, the Board of Agriculture county reports and that marvellous cornucopia of information from the 1790s, the Statistical Account of Scotland. Nevertheless, while it is acknowledged that the processes of economic, social and landscape change were more complex, more regionally varied in their chronology, and more protracted than has sometimes been claimed there is no doubt that the eighteenth century, particularly its last four decades, saw major changes in the Scottish countryside.

Mansion and policy

In one sense, agricultural improvement began with the decline of the tower house. In Chapter 4 we saw how in many parts of Scotland the need for defence declined from the early seventeenth century. After the Restoration it was fashionable to extend and remodel fortified houses into larger, more comfortable mansions and to build new, undefended country houses. Hand in hand went a desire to improve the settings of such houses.

Before the seventeenth century most Scottish castles and towers had been surrounded by walled gardens, enclosures and small plantations of trees. A great many had home farms with their attendant kailyards and paddocks adjacent to them. In the later sixteenth and early seventeenth centuries more elaborate gardens were laid out around some Scottish castles. A good example can be seen at Aberdour in Fife where a formal walled garden was laid out for the fourth Earl of Morton in the 1560s or 1570s. It comprised a series of terraces on a sloping site to the south of the castle along with a doocot and orchard. Edzell Castle has the most attractive and best preserved of these early walled gardens. Dating from 1604 it has sets of decorative sculptured panels set into its walls, a summer house and doocot. Other gardens have survived less completely but are nevertheless interesting. From the battlements of Stirling Castle you can look down on the King's Knot, the centrepiece of an elaborate formal garden with parterres (formal flower beds) and a ditched enclosure containing an octagonal mound. The design of the King's Knot has clearly been influenced by contemporary English garden design but its date is uncertain. Some writers have suggested that it was laid out for Charles I in the 1620s but others suspect that elements of it at least were created nearly a century before, for James V. The remains of what has been a fine terraced garden can be seen on the steep slopes below Neidpath Castle near Peebles. A short distance away at Posso on Manor Water (NT 200332) some curious earthworks beside the ruined tower appear to be the remains of an ornamental garden thought to date from 1649.

The trend for enclosed formal gardens continued into the later seventeenth century. The best example is Pitmedden in Aberdeenshire.

Figure 29 Pitmedden Gardens, Grampian, laid out by Sir Alexander Seton in the later seventeenth century, is one of the few surviving examples of an early formal garden in Scotland (National Trust for Scotland).

Alexander Seton, Lord Pitmedden, was removed from his position as a law lord due to his opposition to James VII's Catholicism. He retired from public life and concentrated his efforts on improving his estate, particularly the garden. Its four great parterres, bordered by box hedges, contain designs which are believed to have been modelled on the gardens of Holyrood Palace in Edinburgh, one of which bears the Seton coat of arms.

Deer parks were not particularly common in Scotland and in the seventeenth century the term 'park' meant any enclosure. 'Policies' were the assemblage of enclosed parks, ornamental gardens and planting surrounding a country house. During the later seventeenth century landowners began to increase the scale of their landscaping activities by enlarging their policies, enclosing them into a series of parks, and planting larger blocks of trees. The fashion seems to have spread from estates around Edinburgh in the 1620s and became general throughout the Lowlands from the 1660s. It was encouraged by an act passed by the Scottish

Parliament in 1661 which offered tax relief on land enclosed in this way. Both the new-style country houses and their policies were manifestations of the same desire to enhance estates and so closely were the two related in the minds of contemporaries that rebuilding a house and laying out more extensive policies were rarely done in isolation. This can be seen in the diary of the Earl of Strathmore in which he describes the landscaping work which he did around Glamis and Castle Lyon in Angus in the later seventeenth century. As well as rebuilding the castles he had considerable site alterations made; quarrying away rocky outcrops, draining and infilling marshy hollows, levelling ground, and removing old irregular plantations.

Scottish gardens continued to be formal in plan for most of the eighteenth century, even when more relaxed, informal styles had become popular in England. The great English landscape gardeners like Capability Brown and Humphry Repton had little influence north of the Border. Modelled on Versailles, Scottish gardens were laid out with elaborately patterned parterres, long straight avenues through woodland, and water features. One of the best examples in its day was at Drumlanrig in Dumfriesshire where the gardens were created in the late seventeenth century.

Sometimes the mains or home farm was enclosed at the same time and proprietors began to experiment with new agricultural techniques. Some residences like Gordon Castle had deer parks adjoining them but well-fed cattle, sheep and horses grazing in neat enclosures also enhanced the setting of a landowner's residence. Several Scottish landowners imported better-quality English and Irish livestock and started breeding them with the aim of building up their own prime herds. Some also tried new crops, at first tentatively on small plots in the kitchen garden and then as part of new rotations in their parks.

Although these enclosed policies were only small islands of improvement in a sea of open-field cultivation and were created for amenity value rather than economic motives they were nevertheless a start. One of the first large parks, at Lennoxlove in East Lothian, may have been built as a joke. The story is that it was constructed in 1681 by the Duke of Lauderdale for a visit to Scotland by the Duke of York, later James VII and II. On a previous trip to Scotland James had claimed that there were not 400 acres enclosed in the entire country. Lauderdale, determined to prove him wrong, had 400 acres surrounded by a stone wall, whose outline can still be traced today!

During the same period the second earl of Tweeddale was already creating more extensive policies a few miles away at Yester to ornament a new house which was never started in his lifetime. A description of the Yester estate, written about 1720, claimed that the perimeter of the plantations was eight miles in circumference and protected a million trees. That this was no great exaggeration is indicated by John Adair's map of East Lothian, drawn in the 1690s, in which the policies at Yester are huge compared with others in the county. Such work had its economic as well as its aesthetic side, as is confirmed by the Earl of Strathmore's comment that at Castle Lyon he had planted trees around the house whose value, when mature, would be equivalent to the current rental value of the entire estate.

Another noted early improver in East Lothian was the sixth earl of Haddington. At Tyninghame in the first years of the eighteenth century he began to enclose land and lay out plantations on sandy coastal soils which his neighbours considered too poor to improve. He placed shelter belts around his new enclosed parks to protect them from the salt sea winds and also planted larger blocks of woodland. The 400-acre Binning Wood was the most celebrated, as it contained many beech trees which at that time were rare north of the Border. Such woods were not merely ornamental: they were big business. The Earl of Haddington received a useful income from the thinnings, and when the trees were mature a woodworking industry grew up at Tyninghame where the estate's water-powered sawmill can still be seen. The Earl was also one of the first Scottish landowners to experiment with fallowing his arable land and trying new crops like clover and sown grasses, to the ridicule of less progressive neighbours who couldn't see the sense of sowing grass on land that could produce a crop of oats.

The transformation to larger-scale commercially oriented enclosure came first in Galloway with the stimulus of the cattle trade. The growth of the English market after the Restoration encouraged Galloway land-owners to expand cattle production. Some of them built large parks adjoining their castles in which cattle could be fattened and improved by cross-breeding with larger Irish animals. A pioneer in these developments was Sir David Dunbar. At Baldoon near Wigtown he had a park built which could winter 1,000 cattle. A contemporary description estimates its dimensions as 4 × 2.5km (2½ x 1½ miles). His practice was to buy lean animals from his tenants in summer, winter them in the park and send them to England, suitably fattened, the following autumn. Dunbar's cross-bred animals fetched three or four times the price of normal lean Scottish beasts.

Although Dunbar's park is the best-known example other Galloway landowners, like the earls of Cassillis at Castle Kennedy near Stranraer, were enclosing on a similar scale. The trade continued to prosper in the years after the Union. By 1724 land was being taken from leasehold tenants and enclosed into cattle parks under the landowners' direct management on such a scale that it sparked off the so-called Levellers' Revolt of 1724–5. Bands of people went round the countryside throwing down the walls and wrecking the enclosures, the only example of large-scale anti-enclosure riots known from Lowland Scotland. The authorities reacted promptly to the trouble, which soon ceased, but the real motives behind

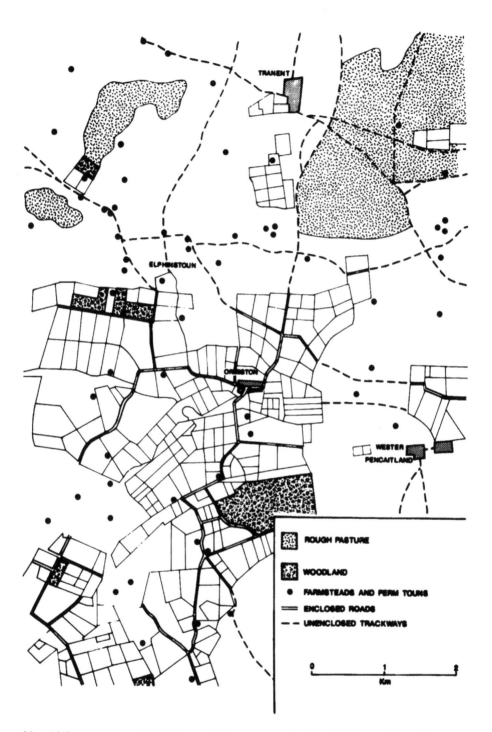

Map 10 Part of the early landscape of improvement in East Lothian redrawn from the Military Survey of 1747–55. The enclosed fields on the Cockburn of Ormiston estates contrast with the open field country further north around Tranent.

the protest, the people involved and how they were organised is still unclear.

The rate of improvement during the first half of the eighteenth century was gradual. Prices for agricultural produce were low so that profits for reinvestment were marginal. Many landowners like Sir John Clerk of Penicuik or George Dundas of Dundas, who had small but fertile estates outside Edinburgh, proceeded slowly and cautiously instituting changes year by year which were small in scale individually but significant in their cumulative effect over a lifetime.

Improving the policies around country houses and even enclosing the mains was all very well but the overall impact of this work on the Scottish landscape was limited. A start was needed on improving standards of farming throughout each estate. The tenants were too impoverished and too conservative to undertake improvements themselves so the initiative had to come from their landlords. One of the first Scottish landowners to set about remodelling his entire estate was John Cockburn of Ormiston. He was an ardent Anglophile, a supporter of the Union of 1707 who sat as a member for Haddington in the new Westminster Parliament. Contact with England had made him painfully aware of the shortcomings of Scottish agriculture. He wanted to drag Scotland into the modern world and when he succeeded his father in 1714 he resolved to introduce improved English farming methods on to his estates. He began by granting long leases on favourable terms to his tenants if they agreed to begin enclosing their farms with hedges and ditches. Starting with four farms on relatively poor soils, he had the steadings on his estates remodelled along more efficient lines. He also rebuilt the village of Ormiston and founded an agricultural society there for local landowners and tenants who were interested in meeting and discussing improved methods of farming. Cockburn tried to initiate change for social as much as economic motives and in his enthusiasm he overreached himself and went bankrupt. However, his work had attracted widespread interest: other landowners had started sending their best tenants to Ormiston to learn the new techniques that Cockburn had introduced and the best of his own farmers went on to make names for themselves as improvers.

Dividing the commonties

A major disadvantage of the old system of farming was the lack of winter fodder from the arable land. This meant that large areas had to be maintained as permanent pasture. As was mentioned in Chapter 3, many lowland areas had extensive tracts of land tied up as commonties, areas of rough grazing in shared ownership between two or more proprietors and grazed in common by the livestock of their tenants and cottars. With the development of new rotations incorporating sown grasses, legumes and especially turnips, which could be fed to cattle in enclosed courts and to sheep in the fields, much more winter fodder was available from the arable land. The sight of flocks of sheep feeding on turnips in the fields during winter and in the process dunging the land ready for the next crop is still a common one and epitomises the Agricultural Revolution in Scotland. With more winter fodder from the arable land there was increasing pressure to divide up the commonties between the various proprietors who had rights over them. Sometimes the land involved was high-lying and only fit for pasture. In such cases division only involved the enclosure of large blocks of the former commonties by new boundary walls. However, many commonties included large areas of land which were improvable and could be converted to arable.

Divisions of commonty could always be arranged provided that all the landowners concerned were agreeable, and a number are known dating from the seventeenth and even the sixteenth centuries. Legislation passed by the Scottish Parliament in 1695 allowed any landowner with rights to a commonty to compel a division to be made even if the co-owners were apathetic or opposed to the idea. The date at which commonties were divided under this legislation varied. Some were removed in the early eighteenth century, others not for another hundred years. A lot depended on the potential value of the land after division and the degree of difficulty in arranging a settlement acceptable to all the parties involved.

Most of the largest commonties, like the 2,500ha (6,200a) of Coldingham Moor, were broken up in the later eighteenth century. The commonty of Hassendean near Hawick was divided between 1761 and 1763. The land surveyors who carried out the division drew up an initial survey of the commonty and then apportioned it out in blocks among the various proprietors. Their central baseline from which the survey was laid out became a main road leading between a group of newly built farms.

Reclaiming moss and muir

In Chapter 3 we mentioned that the pre-improvement farming landscape contained a lot of unreclaimed waste land in addition to commonties, much of it low-lying and marshy. As grain and livestock prices rose it became more economically worth while to reclaim such land. In addition, many improving landowners saw it as a kind of duty to bring such underused land into cultivation. One of the most extensive reclamation schemes was in the valley of the River Forth above Stirling. In the mid-eighteenth century this was a backward and remote area. Most of the broad, flat valley floor, an area of around 10,000ha (25,000a), was covered with a thick layer of peat. The Forth had been an estuary during the period of high sea levels following the last glaciation. As the sea retreated a woodland cover developed but this was killed off by wetter climatic conditions during later prehistoric times. The wetter conditions encouraged a layer of peat to build up to a depth of 6–7 metres. Below this were rich marine clays or carselands, the former mudflats of the buried estuary, which offered good prospects for arable farming if the peat could be removed and the land drained. Settlement had long shunned this area, clinging to the well-drained slopes above the peat mosses. Small-scale reclamation by individual farmers had nibbled away at the margins of the peat over the centuries but a more systematic and large-scale approach was needed to transform what contemporaries saw as a dreary and unproductive wasteland. An impression of its original character can still be gained from unreclaimed portions of peatlands which survive today, notably Flanders Moss (NN 6298).

In 1767 Lord Kames began to undertake systematic planned reclamation on his estate at Blairdrummond. He started by granting tenants long leases to 10-acre plots of peat moss, charging no rent for the first seven years and only gradually increasing the rent thereafter. Remission of rent was designed to compensate the tenants for the labour involved, particularly in the early years when they would receive little return for their work. By 1775 he had 25 smallholders at work. As plots were allocated on areas of deeper and deeper peat the rent-free period was extended to 19 years. When Lord Kames died in 1782, 52 small farmers were settled on the mosslands. His son continued the reclamation scheme so that by 1790 115 crofts had been leased.

The established farmers on the edges of the peat mosses looked down on their new neighbours, literally and figuratively, giving them the scathing title of 'moss lairds'. But although the labour of reclamation was considerable the value of the new land was high while the crofters made money during the early years by selling for fuel the peat which they were carving up. By the early years of the nineteenth century over 485ha (1,200a) of moss had been cleared and 1,000 people were living on the reclaimed land. Neighbouring landowners followed Kames' example and undertook reclamation schemes of their own. The smallholdings were laid out in strips running back at right angles from the main access roads alongside which the steadings were built, like Hebridean crofting townships. The surrounding farmers soon changed their tune and became eager to buy out the smallholders to extend their own farms. Many of the crofters sold out at considerable profit and some went to Canada to undertake fresh pioneering work.

As farm amalgamation proceeded the strip-like pattern of crofts disappeared and gave way to large enclosed fields. The first moss cottages were simple turf-walled structures but by the end of the eighteenth century these were being replaced by more substantial steadings of brick made from the local carse clays. The method of reclamation involved cutting deep channels through the peat down to the underlying clay. These channels drained into the River Forth and great chunks of peat were cut away and tipped into the ditches to float down to the estuary of the Firth of Forth, a source of complaint for the local fishermen whose nets they fouled. In order to obtain a sufficient head of water in the channels for floating the peat away Lord Kames had a 9m (30ft) diameter water-wheel erected at Mill of Torr near Blairdrummond in 1787. This lifted water from the River Teith into a canal which fed into the system of ditches. The main channel from the water-wheel can still be seen crossing the A84 at NN 731980.

Reclamation of foreshore land also took place in areas like the upper part of the Firth of Forth around Alloa and Airth, although less land was involved and the process is less well recorded. Embankments along rivers like the Dee, Don, Findhorn and Spey reduced the risk of flooding and allowed the expansion of arable farming and improved pasture where there had previously been only rank grasses. In some cases this expansion was over-enthusiastic and river defences proved too expensive to maintain. An example can be seen in the Spey marshes near Insh above Aviemore where drained and cultivated land was left to revert to reed swamp.

In some parts of the Lowlands there was an extensive intake of new land from moorland and waste at the margins of cultivation. In north-east Scotland many proprietors allowed crofters to settle on and reclaim land, charging them low rents until the land was improved. In this area the crofts were carefully integrated into the rest of the farming system and supplied a reservoir of labour for use on the larger farms.

New field patterns

Enclosure was the most obvious, and for many people the most fundamental, aspect of agricultural change at this period. The first peak of activity occurred during the 1760s and the main one at the very end of the eighteenth century and the early years of the nineteenth. Although during the first half of the eighteenth century most improvements had been financed by landowners, tenant farmers played an increasingly important part in providing the money and labour to enclose the land as they accumulated capital and became more commercialised in their outlook. Unlike England, where the enclosure of remaining open-field arable land required a separate act of Parliament for each parish, in Scotland the process of amalgamating the fragmented and intermixed strips and blocks of land was mostly done easily and rapidly by landowners on their own estates. Lands lying runrig between different tenants could simply be reallocated by landowners into compact blocks. Holdings on multiple-tenant farms could be both consolidated and amalgamated by landowners simply waiting until the leases for the various shares fell due and then refusing to renew them, gradually merging the holdings into larger and larger units.

A slow process of amalgamation had been taking place in many parts of eastern Scotland from the seventeenth century. As a result of this many townships, instead of having half a dozen small tenants all scratching a bare living, already had one or two larger holdings worked by tenants using hired labour.

This kind of amalgamation had also occurred in parts of the Borders. On the Buccleuch estates, covering thousands of acres in Roxburgh, Selkirk and Dumfriesshire, 60 per cent of upland farms had already been converted into large, single-tenant holdings, many of them over 1,000 acres in extent, by the opening of the eighteenth century. However, such farms still needed to keep much of their more fertile bottom land under crop because of the difficulty of buying in grain for subsistence needs from the surrounding lowlands. Thus much of the land that would have provided meadow and winter pasture was tied up as arable and the size of the flocks that could be wintered on these farms was greatly reduced. From the 1780s the introduction of sown grasses and turnips provided extra winter fodder from the arable land. As transport improved and grain supplies from the lowlands were assured it was possible for these farms to turn their arable land over to producing animal feed, allowing them to increase the size of their flocks and to specialise wholeheartedly in commercial sheep production.

Where different proprietors, rather than their tenants, had lands intermixed consolidation into compact blocks was more difficult. However, another act passed by the Scottish Parliament in 1695 provided a straightforward means of dividing such lands out of runrig. Some of the most troublesome cases were the large townships on former monastic lands where many sitting tenants had been granted their holdings in perpetuity and the old, highly complicated pattern of intermingled strips had fossilised. For instance, the runrig lands around the village of Eyemouth, which were divided in 1764, extended to 370ha (920a) broken into over 600 parcels. Many divisions were arranged by private agreement without involving the courts and the disappearance of both tenant and proprietary runrig has left little documentary evidence. Other cases were more contentious, like the division of the runrigs of Tranent, extending to about 200ha (500a). Here part of the lands were shared between twenty-six smallholders and the rest was owned by the York Buildings Company, which had acquired them as part of the estates of the Earl of Winton when they were forfeited and sold after the rebellion of 1715. Disputes between the Company and the smallholders dragged out the proceedings for more than a decade.

The process of change from the old landscape to the new can often be studied by looking at estate plans, particularly where 'before and after' surveys were carried out. There was often an important element of continuity in the location of farmsteads and the alignments of roads and access ways but in many cases the new landscape of regular enclosed fields was laid out with little reference to the pre-improvement countryside. Sometimes enthusiasm for order and rationality went too far and an over-rigid geometric pattern of fields was laid out by the theodolites of the land surveyors with scant regard for variations in topography, drainage and soil conditions. Early enclosures immediately around country houses were often square and on the small side. Later fields on tenanted holdings were larger. Fields were often smaller on heavier clays – from 6–12ha (15–30a), and from 12–20ha (30–50a) on lighter soils.

The enclosures were bounded by open ditches in low-lying areas like the carselands of the River Forth. Elsewhere hedges, usually of quick-growing hawthorn, were planted although these are rare in the northern Lowlands. Throughout the uplands where hedges would not thrive and in many lowland areas too the drystone dyke was the normal field barrier. Walls built with mortared stone were usually restricted to the boundary walls of estate policies, which remain a characteristic feature of the Low-land countryside. Hedges took some years to form an effective barrier to animals but drystone walls were fully stockproof as soon as they were finished. In an age when labour was relatively cheap and everyone seemed infected with tremendous enthusiasm for promoting change as rapidly as possible, this may help to account for the popularity of stone walls.

Walls also provided a means of using up the large quantities of stones that were being cleared from the glacial tills which formed the subsoil over much of the Lowlands. The removal of stones from the cultivated land had been an ongoing process from the earliest cultivation but it was intensified now with the development of lighter, more expensive ploughs. In some areas where stones were particularly numerous consumption dykes far thicker than normal were built. In Aberdeenshire many dykes are wider than they need to be, for this reason. The most famous consumption dyke, at Kingswells, just outside Aberdeen (NJ 862069), dates from the mid-nineteenth century showing how long the process of stone clear-ance continued. In some areas stones were piled into clearance cairns in the middle of fields rather than dumped around their edges. Good exam-ples can be seen above the Yarrow Water near Broadmeadows (NT 408308) and on the northern slopes of White Meldon (NT 210440) near Peebles.

Drystone walls, like their counterparts in northern England, were gener-ally built with two outer faces, bonded together by courses of through stones, with a core of packed rubble protected by a layer of capstones. There were some distinctive regional variations on this structure. The Galloway dyke was built like a normal stone wall in its lower half but above this had a single layer of large stones fitted together so that substantial gaps were left between them. These gaps, supposedly, acted as a deterrent to livestock and stopped them from trying to jump over the wall. The

Galloway hedge was a stone wall built along a slope with a hedge rooted on the uphill side but trained through the base of the wall to grow on the downhill side of the dyke. Examples of both types of boundary can still be seen throughout Galloway.

The appearance of walls varied depending on whether the stones that made them up had been taken out of the till, in which case they tended to be more rounded, or extracted from small quarries, which gave them a fresher, more angular appearance. Walls in lowland areas were frequently made of 'field stones' thrown up by cultivation while the builders of upland march or boundary dykes often opened up small quarries on the hillsides specially for wall construction. If you follow march dykes over the hillsides you can often find the small, overgrown quarry faces. The appearance of walls also varied depending on the type of stone used in their construction but there has been little attempt, compared with the north of England, to examine regional and local differences in dyke construction. These drystone dykes, a prominent feature of upland and lowland areas alike, represented a tremendous investment of time and labour in their construction. Writers on improvement often commented that hedges, though they took some years to become established, became better barriers as they aged provided that they were properly maintained. Stone walls, on the other hand, were never better than when they were first finished and tended to deteriorate with age. This is often evident today as the expense of maintaining the thousands of miles of dykes is often prohibitive while the necessary skills to do so are also frequently lacking. The result is that many crumbling dykes have been replaced or reinforced with post and barbed-wire fences.

The new farmsteads

The new landscape of improvement was organised around farmsteads of improved design. The scale of the change in rural building that occurred from the last quarter of the eighteenth century is so great that a comparison with the 'Great Rebuilding' of Tudor and Stuart England is not inappropriate. By the end of the eighteenth century the houses of more prosperous farmers were being built to designs derived from the homes of ministers or small lairds. They were often of two storeys, sometimes three, with symmetrical facades. Outbuildings changed more slowly and were still frequently built of unmortared stone. Estate mains were often designed as prestige buildings and were highly ornamented. Proprietors were increasingly willing to allow tenants the remission of a year's rent at the start of a lease to allow them to erect better steadings.

The appearance of the new farmsteads depended on the size and nature of the farm. Farms tended to be larger in the more arable-oriented east of Scotland. In the Lothians and the Merse, where the new mixed arable

Figure 30 This solidly built farmstead near Annan is a good example of the improved farmhouses which were built throughout the Lowlands in the late eighteenth and early nineteenth centuries. Note the chimney for a steam-driven threshing machine on the left.

and livestock farms were among the largest in Scotland, steadings were correspondingly big. Their outbuildings were grouped around courtyards to minimise movement and increase efficiency. The stackyard, where the corn was stored before threshing, lay outside the courtyard to the west of the barn so that the sheaves got plenty of air and did not rot. Inside the courtyard cattle could be fed during the winter. A line of cart sheds faced into the yard, the number of arches being a good measure of the size of the farm. Above them were granaries, and the threshing barn was built on at right-angles at the rear. On many later eighteenth-century farms the outbuildings were ranged around three sides of a courtyard in a U-shape with the fourth side open or delimited by a wall. A later development was to fill in this fourth side by an additional range of buildings, pierced by a high-arched entrance gateway. During the nineteenth century more complex plans with two enclosed courts developed. At first the farmhouse formed part of the new ensemble of buildings but the dunghill at the door no longer fitted with farmers' new social image. As their wealth and pretensions increased, their farmhouses were increasingly built apart from the rest of the steading.

In areas where farms were smaller, such as the north east, and in the dairying areas of the western Lowlands where the storage requirements of farms were more modest, U-shaped courtyards or simple L-shaped blocks of outbuildings continued in use. Farmhouses were more often built with only one storey and attic dormers. Ellisland Farm near Dumfries (NX 929839), built for Robert Burns during his brief tenancy from 1788 until 1791, is a good example of a small late eighteenth-century farmstead on a holding of only 70ha (170a).

In many areas only a few of the first generation of improved steadings from the later eighteenth century have survived. Most were replaced in the mid-nineteenth century by larger, more palatial farmsteads designed on even more rational and efficient lines. Some good examples of eighteenth-century outbuildings survive on estate mains such as North Mains of Ballindarg (NO 406513) from 1761 and Pitmuies House (NO 567497) from 1770, both in Angus. The Glamis estate in Angus provides several good examples of this early phase of rebuilding. These and other late eighteenth-century farmsteads were built by local masons using local materials and styles but their replacements were architect-designed, often from widely circulated pattern books. The walls of the new steadings were usually rubble masonry using local sandstone or whinstone. Brick was not widely used except in clay areas like the Carse of Gowrie and the Carse of Stirling. In areas like Angus, where local supplies were available, slate provided a suitable covering for both farmhouse and outbuildings. In Fife and the Lothians, where there was no good roofing stone, imported slate was used for the farmhouse but the outbuildings were roofed with pantiles, which were cheaper.

The improvement of farm workers' accommodation lagged behind that for farmers and their animals. Even at the end of the eighteenth century cottars and farm workers in many areas were still living in single-roomed hovels with turf walls and thatched roofs. Conditions for farm workers did not improve significantly in many areas until the mid-nineteenth century. Gradually, in the more advanced areas, these huts were giving way to decently built cottages with solid stone walls and pantiled roofs. In areas like the Lothians and the Merse where it was normal to employ married farm workers, rows of farm workers' cottages standing adjacent to the farmsteads which they served are a prominent feature in the landscape, although many date from the nineteenth rather than the later eighteenth century. In other districts, however, notably Angus and the north east, the custom was to employ unmarried farm servants who lived together, often in spartan and squalid conditions, in bothies which formed part of the steading.

In areas like the Lothians, where improvement had started early, the transformation of the countryside had proceeded a long way by the early years of the nineteenth century. Even here the process was far from complete. The landscape continued to be modified during the nineteenth century, particularly during the mid-century period of 'high farming' when landlord and farmer alike were prepared to sink a substantial proportion of their profits into improvements like underdraining, steam threshing

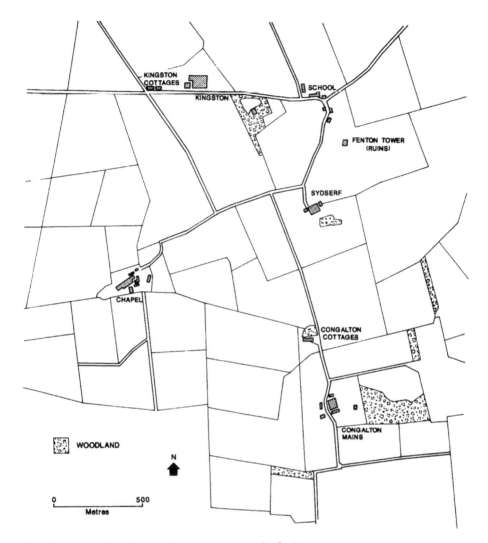

Map 11 A typical landscape of improvement in the Lothians.

machines and the embellishment of their farmsteads in a variety of architectural styles. In such areas the half-century after 1760, spanned by a single working lifetime, saw the total transformation of the landscape. Although large-scale mechanisation, modern farm buildings like silos, and changes such as field enlargement have altered this landscape in recent years the basic features of the Lowland countryside today are still those of the Agricultural Revolution.

The end product of the efforts of the improvers – not only the landowners but also the farmers and the labourers – was a highly efficient and rationally laid out landscape. William Cobbett, the celebrated English writer on agriculture and rural life, visited the Lothians in the early nineteenth century and was impressed by what he saw. A century earlier landowners from this area had brought English farmers north to demonstrate improved techniques to their tenants. By the time of Cobbett's visit English proprietors were starting to bring Scottish farmers south for similar reasons! Cobbett described the countryside as 'land as fine as it is possible to be. . . . Everything is abundant here except people who have been studiously swept from the land.' Indeed the farmlands of eastern Scotland do sometimes look empty because of the lack of isolated houses and cottages between the farmsteads but Cobbett was mistaken in thinking that the landscape had been depopulated. The big new farmsteads and their attendant cottages often held as many people as a small village elsewhere. In addition, many people had settled in the new planned villages.

The threshing machine

The Agricultural Revolution in Lowland Scotland was a triumph of improved organisation and innovation but few new mechanical inventions were involved. One, however, had an influence on the landscape: the threshing machine. Threshing corn by hand with a flail to separate the grain from the straw was a labour-intensive operation throughout the winter months. There had been many attempts to devise suitable machinery to make the process cheaper and quicker, but the machines had proved insufficiently robust or had damaged the grain in the process. The first practical threshing machine was constructed by Andrew Meikle, the best known of a distinguished family of East Lothian millwrights and engineers. His first machine was made in 1786 for a farmer near Clackmannan and the second installed at Phantassie near East Linton. The success of his machine was immediate and it was adopted rapidly in the arable areas of south-eastern Scotland. By 1794 there were already sixty-one threshing machines in the Carse of Gowrie alone. They did not become established in many northern parts of Scotland until the early nineteenth century.

Meikle's threshing machine could be driven by a variety of power sources. The most common method was horse power with two, four or sometimes six horses walking in a continuous circle. Sometimes these horse mills, horse gins or horse gangs were open, especially on smaller farms. On larger farms they were housed within a circular or polygonal building. Circular ones are more common in Angus, Kincardine and Perthshire where local slate was available. In Fife and the Lothians the use of large pantiles encouraged polygonal roofs. Their sides were generally open to give the horses as much ventilation as possible and they were frequently placed on the north side of the barn to help to keep the animals cool. These buildings are still common throughout eastern Scotland; they have

Figure 31 At Shortrigg, near Hoddom, two sources of power for a threshing machine stand side by side. The late eighteenth-century windmill was replaced by the circular horse-gang.

often been adapted as storehouses and their open sides have sometimes been filled in.

Horse-driven threshing machines were cheap to build but made exhausting work for the animals and prevented them from being used elsewhere on the farm when threshing was in progress. Farmers soon began to experiment with other sources of power. Water power was an obvious alternative. A water-driven threshing machine was not necessarily any more expensive than a horse-driven one but not every farm had access to a convenient stream. A good example can be seen at Blairbuie in Galloway (NX 362420). On farms where the water-wheel has long been dismantled traces of the dam and lade often survive to indicate that a water-driven threshing machine was once in use.

Windmill-driven threshing machines were also built, though in smaller numbers. They were twice as expensive as horse- or water-driven machines. Only larger farms could afford them and not every farm was sited so as to make maximum use of wind power. Windmills were also prone to damage by sudden squalls, though the resourceful Meikle invented a system by which the sails could be taken in quickly by means of a rope operated from within the mill. A fine example can be seen at Shortrigg near Hoddom in Dumfriesshire (NY 162744) where the late eighteenth-century windmill was later supplemented by a horse gang. In

Orkney, where the wind is ever-present, smaller windmill-driven threshing machines were introduced in the nineteenth century. They had six triangular sails attached to low drystone towers. The application of steam power to threshing machines was an early nineteenth-century phenomenon. The first steam-driven threshing machine in East Lothian was installed in 1803 but they only became common in the 1820s and 1830s in those parts of the Lowlands which had ready access to coal, and were only economic on larger arable farms. The steadings of farms with steam engines could be distinguished from a distance by the tall brick chimneys rising above their outbuildings, giving them the appearance of factories which, in many respects, they were.

Planned villages

The improving movement of the later eighteenth century introduced another new element into the Scottish settlement pattern which is still prominent today: the planned estate village. Over 300 were established throughout Scotland during the later eighteenth and early nineteenth centuries. Some became quite large. New Pitsligo, founded by Sir William Forbes in 1787, had a population of over 2,000 a century later. However, many of these villages have shrunk since the nineteenth century as a result of rural depopulation; very few failed entirely, although many did not grow as large as was originally hoped. At New Leeds in Aberdeenshire the landowner clearly had unreasonable expectations for his creation! The aims behind foundation of these villages varied. Some were designed to accommodate estate workers, others to provide sources of employment in services and trades, especially in textile manufacture, for people who had been moved off the land as a result of changes in agriculture. From the landowner's point of view such villages not only absorbed surplus population: they also increased his rentals. This could be done by establishing the villages on land that had hitherto been poor and unproductive. At the same time such settlements provided a useful local market for estate produce. Other planned villages were associated with specific industries: quarrying, mining, but especially textiles and fishing.

Although exhibiting tremendous variety in detail these villages have a number of common features. They were generally either totally new settlements or existing ones transferred to an adjacent site. They also had regular, geometric street plans. At their most basic these might be single straight main streets with rows of buildings on one or both sides. The textile settlement of Douglastown in Angus or Port Logan in Wigtownshire are good examples of the simplest kind of village layout. More sophisticated layouts incorporated a cross street meeting in a central square, or streets intersecting at right angles to form a grid pattern. Central squares

Figure 32 Newcastleton, laid out as a textile-weaving centre for the Duke of Buccleuch in the later eighteenth century, was the largest planned estate village in the Borders.

were sometimes very large, as at Newcastleton in Liddesdale, Lumsden in Aberdeenshire or Grantown on Spey.

Housing standards in planned villages were usually carefully controlled either by using architect-designed specifications for every house or, at the very least, by applying a standardised set of building regulations to which individual developers had to conform. Two-storey houses were generally considered to give a village a more prosperous and attractive appearance but many settlements were built with mainly one-storey cottages. The village plan often included an area of land lotted into smallholdings on which the inhabitants could grow vegetables, potatoes or oats, sometimes with enough land to graze a cow. These lotted lands often took the form of regular strips running back at right angles to the street frontage.

The combination of standardised plans and detailed building specifications, plus the fact that the villages were mostly created within a fairly short period, gives them a uniformity lacking in English villages which have grown organically over several centuries. At the worst this can make Scottish estate villages dour and drab but when done well, particularly in combination with a good choice of site, they make an attractive and distinctive contribution to the landscape.

The first true planned villages date from the early eighteenth century although a good case can be made for including one or two like Gifford, which were established at the end of the seventeenth century. As we have seen, Scotland already had a tradition of small, planned rural settlements

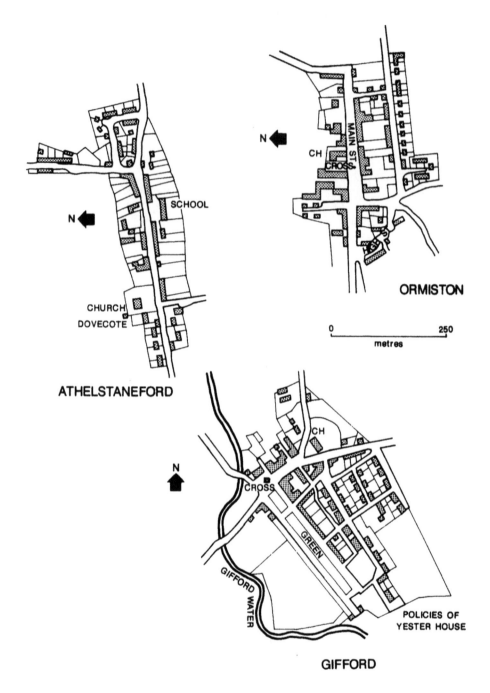

Map 12 Some examples of planned village layouts.

and there was hardly a pause between the foundation of burghs of barony and the first planned villages. The aims behind settlement foundation changed slightly, though. Burghs of barony were designed as trading centres while planned villages often emphasised rural industry. The number of planned villages increased greatly from the 1750s and village foundation continued briskly into the early nineteenth century. However, the rapidly increasing concentration of industries like textile manufacture in the towns brought an end to the planned village movement by removing the *raison d'être* of most of them while the coming of the railways killed off their role as market centres.

Although the status of most planned villages is clear there are sometimes problems of definition. In south-east Scotland, where villages were already a feature of the settlement pattern several existing villages were improved and redeveloped without changing their site or layout. In villages like East Saltoun the rows of plain, single-storey cottages with classical ornamentation around the doors, similar to the improved cottages for farm workers which were being built adjacent to new farmsteads in the area, are an indication of considerable investment by the local landowner. At Dirleton there is an interesting contrast between simple cottages of this type dating from the later eighteenth century and more ornate two-storey ones decorated in the picturesque style, from a generation or two later. Elsewhere existing kirk touns like Glamis and Monymusk were modified and extended in a similar way.

Although they are widely spread throughout Scotland, with the exception of the Northern Isles, planned villages are more densely clustered in certain areas, notably the north east where there are nearly 100, Angus and Lowland Perthshire and Galloway. Many new villages were created by landowners expanding their policies to include the sites of existing settlements, combined with a desire to smarten up the appearance of communities close to the gates of their mansions. A good, if early, example is Gifford in East Lothian. At the end of the seventeenth century the Earl of Tweeddale had the old village of Bothans removed in order to extend the policies around Yester House preparatory to rebuilding the mansion itself. The village was moved to a new site at the gates of the park and the modern settlement of Gifford was the result. Most of the houses and cottages in the village are eighteenth- and nineteenth-century replacements of the original ones but the plan of the settlement, and the new church built in 1710, remain unchanged.

The pattern of village development can often be related to groups of landowners who, as relations or friends, borrowed ideas and plans from each other. For instance the Earl of Findlater established New Keith in 1750 on a stretch of moor near the existing straggling market centre of Keith. Around 1755 his neighbour the Earl of Fife founded Newmill 3km (1.5 miles) to the north. The plan of New Keith was used by Sir Archibald

Figure 33 Cuminestown, Grampian, built for Joseph Cumine of Auchry from 1763, retains its regular grid plan of streets and many of its original single-storey weavers' cottages (Dr D. G. Lockhart).

Grant of Monymusk for his settlement of Archiestown. Grant then went on to design Cuminestown with a similar plan for his friend Joseph Cumine of Auchry, and the village of New Byth for another friend William Urquhart, who was also friendly with Cumine whose brother-in-law, Lord Gardenstone, founded Laurencekirk. Many early village developers were members of policy-making bodies including the Commissioners for Forfeited Estates and the Board of Trustees for Manufactures.

John Cockburn's village of Ormiston is usually taken as the settlement that started the planned village movement. In the 1730s Cockburn, who had been improving his estate for some years, decided to remodel Ormiston along the lines of an English village. He brought in an English land surveyor to lay out the settlement and its surrounding fields. The result can still be seen in Ormiston's wide, tree-lined street, broad enough for markets to be held and closed off at either end by right-angled bends in the road. The houses were mainly built by their occupiers with Cockburn providing the materials but he stipulated that the dwellings should be of high quality with two storeys, mortared stone and slate roofs, at a time when single-storey thatched cottages were the norm.

Later in the eighteenth century other landowners who were redesigning their villages did so to a more rigidly set plan and had all the buildings constructed at their own expense to ensure uniformity. Tyninghame is the classic example of a village where development was tightly controlled in this way by the proprietor. The cottages, school and village hall were all architect-designed to a uniform pattern. Athelstaneford, a few kilometres from Tyninghame, provides an interesting contrast for here the development of each plot was left in the hands of the individual occupier rather than the estate. The Kinlochs of Gilmerton leased a series of plots at moderate rents to people who would build good-quality houses to replace what the minister called the 'small, dirty, dark hovels' that made up the existing village. Each householder received enough ground for a garden plus a share of arable land big enough for growing oats or potatoes or, if kept under grass, for grazing a cow. Each smallholder built his own dwelling with only a general set of guidelines; the cottages are mostly single-storeyed with pantile roofs and rubble walls in a pleasant vernacular style with each house differing in detail from its neighbour.

Early textile villages in the north-east were linked with the linen industry and sometimes with woollen manufacture. Archiestown was founded around 1760 as a community of weavers by Sir Achibald Grant of Monymusk. Its main street widens into a large, tree-lined square and the village has preserved its original plan well with several of the original weavers' cottages surviving. Cuminestown Strichen and New Leeds were established as linen-making centres while at Keith there was also a woollen mill. Villages were often associated with lintmills, waulkmills and bleachfields. Other planned settlements towards the end of the eighteenth century were developed as cotton-weaving centres; Houston in Renfrewshire and Dalbeattie in Galloway are good examples. Laurencekirk in Kincardineshire was laid out by Lord Gardenstone from 1768 using a plan derived from an estate village in Ireland and by 1793 had a population of over 500. Handloom linen weaving was the mainstay of its economy but there was also a linen spinning mill and a bleachfield. Luthermuir once housed over 200 weavers and is sadly shrunken today but some of the early clay-walled cottages survive and a lone handloom weaver, the last of his kind in Scotland, continued making linen here into the late 1970s.

In the 1790s the Duke of Buccleuch developed Newcastleton in Liddesdale on an ambitious scale as a weaving centre. It has a central square with two smaller ones along the main axis of the settlement and cross streets running at right angles to the main thoroughfare. Like many Scottish planned villages it has a rather dour appearance which is increased by the way that the houses front directly on to the pavement without any gardens. This is a common feature not only of planned villages but also of earlier baronial burghs like Stonehouse in Clydesdale. This layout was adopted because landowners feared that if the cottagers, who were often smallholders, were given any space before their front doors they would use it as a site for their dunghills, ruining the appearance of the model settlement.

Fishing villages often depended on the provision of a pier or harbour by a proprietor. Sometimes they developed from earlier communities. At Cullen the original royal burgh stood between the castle and the mouth of the Cullen burn. Some time before the eighteenth century the settlement had moved to the high ground east of Cullen House. A separate fisher toun grew up by the shore from the seventeenth century onwards but in 1811 Seafield, a totally new settlement, was laid out further inland above the fisher toun.

The Highlands were affected by major social and economic changes between 1500 and 1800 just as were the Lowlands. However, the very different conditions which obtained there produced important contrasts in both the chronology and nature of such changes compared with the Lowlands. This in turn influenced the way in which the landscapes of the Highlands developed; we now turn northwards and westwards to examine the processes which were involved and their effects on the countryside.

7

The landscape of improvement: the Highlands

The modern landscape of the Scottish Highlands is one of the most distinctive in Britain. Looking at the peaty wastes of Rannoch Moor, the peaks of Sutherland rising abruptly from bleak lochan-studded plateaux, or the rugged mountains of Glencoe and Torridon, it can sometimes be difficult to remember that they are part of the same country as the regular, efficiently planned landscapes of improvement in the Lothians. At their wildest, in the far north west, the Highlands might well seem like another planet rather than a different country.

The appearance of the Highlands clearly owes much to its distinctive geology and climate, and particularly to the ice ages which have produced the features of glacial erosion and deposition that are so prominent today. Nevertheless this is an area which was settled by man from early times and where human activities have been crucial in shaping the modern landscape. Down to the seventeenth century the rural settlement pattern and economy of the region differed in degree rather than kind from those of the Lowlands, albeit adapted to a much harsher environment. During the eighteenth century, however, the paths of landscape change in the Highlands and Lowlands began to diverge. In part this was due to the more limited economic potential of the Highlands but political and social factors were also at work.

The history of the Highlands in the first half of the eighteenth century is often viewed through a romantic haze of of tartans, bagpipes and bonnie princes which obscures the reality of a traditional and conservative society under stress and on the brink of far-reaching changes. The second half of the century saw the initiation of these changes against a background of growing population pressure in certain areas. Various schemes were implemented which tried to reconcile the economic development of an environmentally marginal area with the maintenance of a large and growing population on the land. By the end of the century it was clear that these objectives were irreconcilable and many Highland landowners had come to realise that if they wished to avoid ruin they would have to opt for the commercial development of their lands regardless of the effects on the inhabitants. Over much of the Highlands this involved moving and resettling the population. The reasons for this, and the timing of the changes, varied from one district to another within the Highlands. In the south and east agricultural improvement was conducted on a model derived from the adjoining Lowlands. Changes began earlier and were more gradual, giving society more time to adapt. In the northern and Western Highlands change was often delayed until the late eighteenth or early nineteenth century. In this area the most significant trend was the widespread introduction of commercial sheep farming, leading to the so-called 'Highland Clearances', one of the most emotive terms in Highland folk-history.

In the northern and Western Highlands the combination of a rising population and its redistribution within estates from the interior glens to coastal areas in order to make way for sheep farming was a major factor in creating the crofting system which still dominates the landscape of these areas today. Visitors to the Highlands sometimes think that the crofting system is an ancient and traditional one. In one sense this is true. Holdings in the Highlands had been small for centuries, providing only a bare subsistence for their occupiers. Crofting continued this tradition and fossilised a pattern of smallholdings which are an anachronism in the modern landscape. But although crofting incorporates elements of the old Highland system of farming, its basic features in many areas, particularly the ways in which the townships are laid out, are more recent than the steam engine and the cotton mill. The ruler-straight patterns of crofting townships in Lewis or Caithness reflect the rigid geometry of the age of the improvers rather than the less regular landscape of earlier centuries. This chapter traces the ways in which the landscapes of the Highlands evolved during the eighteenth century and examines the political, economic and social forces which underlay these changes.

The political dimension

To appreciate fully the context of landscape change in the Highlands in the eighteenth century some mention must be made of the distinctiveness of the region's society and the political implications of this. Until the mid-eighteenth century the Highlands were remote and rarely visited by outsiders, preserving an archaic, clan-based society which had no parallel in western Europe. The combination of remoteness and rugged terrain along with what outsiders viewed as an alien culture and language meant that this area, covering half of Scotland, was only loosely integrated into the rest of Britain. For centuries Scottish monarchs had been able to exert only intermittent and uncertain political control over the Highlands.

Even after the Union of 1707 the distinctiveness of the Highlands would not have mattered so much had it been expressed purely in terms of an underdeveloped economy and backward society. The main resource which the region produced that was in demand south of the Border was live cattle and the trade in this was secure enough without any necessity for external interference in this strange and savage area. However, the adherence of some clan chiefs to the cause of the deposed Stuarts after the Glorious Revolution of 1688 brought the Highlands into the centre stage of British and European politics. Jacobite rebellions in 1689, 1715 and 1719 either began in or were confined to the Highlands. The reason for this was simple: the military basis on which the clan system was organised meant that this was the only part of Britain where an irregular army of trained fighting men could be raised quickly.

The Hanoverian government made some efforts, after the rebellions of 1715 and 1719, to open up the Highlands to outside influences and to police the region more effectively by means of military roads and forts (see Chapters 4 and 8). These measures were limited in their impact but this did not seem to matter greatly as the Jacobite threat appeared to have diminished during the 1720s and 1730s. The complacency of the authorities was shattered by the near success of the Jacobite rebellion of 1745, which shook the Hanoverian regime all the more because it was so unexpected. Prince Charles Edward Stuart, landing in the West Highlands with only a handful of followers, raised a small but highly mobile army from the minority of clans whose chiefs were still sympathetic to the Stuart cause. After defeating the government forces at Prestonpans and gaining control of most of Scotland the army, augmented by forces raised mainly from north-eastern Scotland, invaded England. Moving swiftly and outmanoeuvring their opponents, the Jacobites reached Derby, a few days' march from London, before they withdrew. The last phase of the rebellion was fought around and among the eastern Highlands. Badly led and starving, the Jacobite army was devastatingly defeated at Culloden near Inverness on a cold spring day in 1746. Highland society and the Highland landscape had been changing before Culloden and would have continued to change if the '45 rebellion had never occurred. Nevertheless, the rising had made the British government aware of the need to bring the Highlands under proper control and it greatly increased the degree of official involvement in the region.

Highland society and the landscape of clanship

It is also necessary to understand something of the nature of traditional Highland society in order to appreciate how this influenced the landscape. It is a truism to say that Highland society was based on the clan but despite all that has been written about Highland clans we know remarkably little about how they functioned. Notionally clans were bodies of people related by blood and descended from a common ancestor. They possessed a surname deriving from that ancestor and inhabited a specific clan territory. Clans were ruled in an authoritarian but patriarchal way by their chiefs. They formed an aristocracy that was close knit and exclusive, vitually closed to outsiders and unique in Europe. There has been a tendency to idealise the Highland clans. The strength of kinship links and bonds of mutual obligation within clan society should not disguise the fact that the system was based on, and helped to perpetuate, gross social inequalities.

Various branches of the chiefs' families provided a kind of gentry or middle class known as tacksmen. In economic terms the tacksmen acted as middlemen, being prominent as merchants and creditors in a society which had no other mercantile class. In military terms they were a kind of hereditary officer group. They leased large blocks of clan territory which they then sublet to individual clansmen, saving the chiefs the trouble of collecting rents themselves.

Although the larger chiefs and even the most prosperous tacksmen might live in some style in castles and fortified houses many were accommodated far more modestly. MacIain, chief of the Glencoe branch of the MacDonalds, a small but notorious clan, was living in a simple undefended stone house at the time of the infamous Massacre of Glencoe in 1692. Most tacksmen lived in still meaner houses and the contrast between their lack of material possessions and their pride in their aristocratic lineage struck many visitors to the Highlands in the early eighteenth century as strange.

The emphasis on the military basis of the clan meant that Highland chiefs tried to maintain as many people as possible on their territories in order to maximise their fighting force. This in turn produced poverty and led to periodic famine. Of the ordinary clansmen, a fair proportion were tenants at will holding their land from the chief via tacksmen on a year to year basis by verbal agreement rather than by written lease. There was also a substantial class of cottars or sub-tenants whose landholdings were even smaller. The gradations within the lower ranks of Highland society varied from one area to another and are far from clear but a large percentage of the population probably had only a small stake in the land. The smallness of the clansmen's plots did not diminish their strong attachment to their land.

The basic features of agriculture and settlement in the Highlands had much in common with the Lowlands. Arable farming was organised on infield–outfield lines and the tenants' lands were divided runrig with a system of periodic reallocation of shares continuing in many areas into the eighteenth century. Oats and bere were almost the only cereals, with a little rye in some areas and small plots of flax grown for domestic use. In coastal areas infields were manured with seaweed as well as the usual dung and turf. Highland farms were generally composed of small areas of arable and valley-bottom meadow and huge expanses of upland pasture. On an estate like Barrisdale in Knoydart only 32ha (80a) out of 5,260ha (13,000a) was in cultivation. Settlement took the form of scattered touns held by several joint tenants. There were fewer large nucleations like the kirk touns of the Lowlands. In some areas larger farms worked by more substantial tenants with the aid of cottar labour had emerged. But, although the differences in farming systems between Highland and Low-land were of degree rather than kind they were nevertheless important. In such a rugged and often inhospitable environment the best land, and the settlement that accompanied it, was scattered in discontinuous strips and pockets along the coast and through the major glens, separated by wide expanses of moor and mountain. This isolation of one district from another helped to foster inter-clan rivalries.

In an area which was pre-eminently suited to livestock rearing and not at all favourable to crop production it is curious that the basis of diet for the ordinary clansman was oatmeal rather than meat and dairy produce. In some well-favoured areas with deeper soils and lower rainfall arable land was more extensive. Such districts included the bottoms of the major glens and the fringing lowland strip from Inverness north to Caithness. Over much of the Highlands the arable land was fragmented in tiny blocks and parcels among the boulder-strewn slopes. Where the ground was more level the land was cultivated using light ploughs drawn by up to four small horses. Elsewhere cultivation by spade or cas chrom, a heavy foot-plough, was normal, especially in the north-west Highlands. Associated with this hand cultivation was the creation of lazy beds to give deeper, better-drained soils in limited areas. On a sloping piece of land steep-sided ridges of earth, peat and seaweed manure were dug with deep ditches between. This improved the drainage and deepened the soil on the beds. Lazy beds can be considered as a form of ridge and furrow (Chapter 3) adapted to hand cultivation. The ridges are much more accentuated and sinuous than those produced by ordinary ploughing. Lazy beds can still be seen in use today but large areas of abandoned lazy-bed cultivation surround most existing and abandoned settlements in the north-west Highlands and Islands. These date mainly from the period of population build-up in the later eighteenth and early nineteenth centuries when potatoes, rather than cereals, were the main crop. They are a striking testimony to the one resource which the area possessed in abundance at this time: human labour.

Over the Highlands as a whole in the first half of the eighteenth century most families had only around 1.2–1.6ha (3–4a) of cultivated land to sustain them. This figure fell even further later in the century as population began to grow and the average may have been as low as 1ha (2.5a) per family. Many families had even less. In Assynt 300 families occupied 120ha (300a) of arable land. Although pasture was abundant, winter fodder was in even shorter supply than in the Lowlands due to the lack of meadow land and the fact that in many areas livestock were not grazed on the stubble after harvest. There was often no stubble to graze for the crop was pulled out by the root rather than cut with a sickle.

Some parts of the Highlands were more fertile, with greater expanses of arable land, and produced a surplus of grain in most years for those areas where cultivation was more difficult. Caithness, Easter Ross, Lewis, Tiree, the valleys of the Spey and Dee, and parts of Highland Perthshire were among these areas. Other districts had a perennial deficit of grain: Shetland produced only about a third of the cereals that its inhabitants needed, importing them mainly from neighbouring Orkney and Caithness. In areas deficient in grain the sale of cattle by the tenants provided them with cash not only to pay for their rents but to buy in small quantities of oatmeal.

The early eighteenth century: the beginnings of change

It is easily forgotten that Highland society, if seemingly archaic to outsiders, was far from static particularly in the late seventeenth and early eighteenth centuries. What transformed it, and the Highland landscape, was the increasing penetration of commercial influences from outside. The old justification for the economic system – its support of military power and a stable social system – was beginning to be less important. As Highland landowners were drawn into the wider world of British society and politics they needed more money to sustain an increasingly expensive lifestyle at court and abroad. However, their rents were paid largely in services – including the military service of their clansmen – and in kind. Increasingly they needed money. They began to look at their estates from a more commercial viewpoint.

Many developments in the Highlands at this time demonstrate this. The rise of the cattle trade allowed many chiefs to commute their rents in kind into money payments. Away from the arable areas three-quarters of the rents on most Highland estates were being paid in money by the mid-eighteenth century. The sale of cattle by ordinary tenants provided them with cash to pay these money rents. In this subsistence-oriented area, paradoxically, ordinary clansmen were often more involved in the market than many Lowland tenants who still paid rents mainly in produce and left their landlords to market it. But Highland tenants entered the market unwillingly as an adjunct to a bare subsistence and most of the profits of the cattle trade went to the chiefs and tacksmen rather than to the ordinary farmer.

Early in the eighteenth century some landowners and tacksmen began to specialise in large-scale cattle raising for the droving trade, a move which paralleled the activities of some Galloway proprietors (Chapter 6). The result was a substantial increase in rent in some areas, such as Skye, Glenelg and Harris. The activities of these early cattle barons showed that income (for a fortunate minority at least) could be substantially increased by switching from the traditional system of mixed farming to specialised livestock rearing, a foretaste of future developments.

Improvement along Lowland lines, emphasising farm amalgamation, enclosure and improvements in arable production, began first in the southern and eastern Highlands. Early changes in farm structures and tenancy conditions were notable on the estates of the dukes of Argyll in the southwest Highlands. From the late seventeenth century the House of Argyll had been trying to draw their West Highland empire more closely into the mainstream of British life with a series of social and economic reforms. This policy has been viewed as far-sighted by Campbell apologists, but there is little indication that before the work of the fifth duke of Argyll in the later eighteenth century the Campbells viewed improvement in any terms other than as a means of beautifying their seat at Inveraray and its policies. The aim of their reforms was to increase rents to finance their lifestyle as British (rather than Highland) landed magnates, and later to subsidise their grandiose building projects. Their lands were allocated less and less on the basis of kinship and more on the ability of tenants to pay higher rents. On their estates in Tiree rents doubled between 1703 and 1736.

With more commercial attitudes to estate exploitation some Highland landlords were beginning to consider their tacksmen as unnecessary intermediaries who were rack-renting the tenants and creaming off a sizable proportion of their surplus. Again the Campbells led the way. In 1737 the second duke of Argyll had his estates in Mull, Morvern and Tiree surveyed and concluded that the tacksmen there had outlived their usefulness. Land was leased direct to tenants on long leases. The scheme failed in the short term as the tenants were less convinced of the value of the scheme than the duke. In particular the introduction of competitive bidding for holdings led to unrealistic rents being offered. The phasing out of the tacksmen was one of the most important social effects of these changes on the Argyll estates and elsewhere. The tacksmen's military role was removed after 1746 and many of them found it hard to adjust to the new commercial ethos which was pervading the Highlands. They were among the earliest emigrants in many areas, leaving the ordinary clansmen without leaders or spokesmen.

The early eighteenth-century Lowland approach to improvement – starting with the mansion and its policies and working outwards – was transferred to the Highlands and can best be seen on the great estates like those of the Duke of Atholl at Blair Atholl and Dunkeld, the earls of Breadalbane at Taymouth, and the dukes of Argyll at Inveraray. The building of Inveraray Castle has been described in Chapter 4. At the same time the policies were being improved with the addition of bridges, buildings for the home farm, a new water-mill, a doocot and a hilltop folly. New estate roads and miles of enclosure walls were built during the 1750s as work on the castle progressed. Elsewhere throughout the Highlands similar features can be seen on a smaller scale where country houses are surrounded by a nucleus of enclosed and planted policies, often with an adjacent mains or home farm enclosed with a pattern of regular fields.

Planned villages

A feature of the settlement pattern of the Highlands was the virtually total lack of towns and even villages. The pre-improvement Lowlands had a range of nucleated settlements from village-sized burghs of barony to large towns. In the Highlands even villages were rare. Inverness, the largest town in the north, was a Lowland town on the Highland periphery. Other market centres like Dunkeld were located along the Highland/Lowland boundary and were frequented by Highlanders bringing cattle and horses to exchange for meal. Within the Highlands there were only a handful of minor centres like Inveraray, Fort William and Stornoway. There was general agreement that the Highlands needed more villages and towns to act as centres of trade and industry and also to function as civilising agents which would wean the Highlanders away from their indolent and unproductive habits by teaching them the discipline of regular work.

The third duke of Argyll's building programme also involved the creation at Inveraray of one of the earliest and finest planned settlements in the Highlands, one whose architectural distinction has been little affected by modern development. The small burgh of Inveraray stood close to the old castle when the third duke inherited the estate. The town was not quite the collection of squalid hovels described by some contemporary travellers. Sketches made in 1746 show that it had some solid two-storey houses with mortared stone walls and slate roofs. These were the town houses of Campbell lairds and the homes of lawyers at this important legal centre where the Sheriff and Justiciary courts for Argyllshire were held. Nevertheless, most of the houses in Inveraray were simple thatched cottages and the settlement had evolved gradually with a haphazard layout.

Figure 34 The planned village of Bowmore, Islay, focusing on its distinctive round church, was one of many new communities created in the Highlands in the late eighteenth and early nineteenth centuries (Dr D. G. Lockhart).

The duke determined to rebuild the settlement further away from the new castle on a promontory from where it could be viewed to advantage. Building began in the 1750s with a new Palladian-style town house and a large inn. These two buildings, along what is now Front Street, still dominate the view of Inveraray from the castle.

Work on the settlement was halted by the death of the third duke and little was done under his successor. Only with the accession of the fifth duke in 1761 did building resume. Various plans for the settlement had been prepared. The one which eventually emerged on the ground was simple yet effective. A main street ran across the promontory with a short cross street in the centre and, parallel to this, Front Street running along the shore. The dignified three-storey tenements and two-storey houses in the main street focus on a central church while the town house, inn and other buildings on Front Street were unified into a single facade by a linking arcade. The little town has not changed much since then and the fifth duke's scheme still has the power to impress.

Few Highland landowners had the resources for development possessed by the dukes of Argyll but several others were involved in the creation of planned settlements. The Campbells of Shawfield on Islay began to lay out Bowmore from 1768. Here, as at Inveraray, the aim was to move an existing settlement away from the vicinity of a new mansion. A conventional grid plan was used for Bowmore with the main street running back from the pier and focusing on an impressive circular church.

A number of large planned villages were established in the Grampians. Grantown on Spey is probably the best known. Highest of all was Tomintoul, on a plateau at an altitude of 330m (1,100ft). Designed to function as an industrial centre as well as a market for agricultural produce, Tomintoul got under way from 1785. Industry failed to develop and hopes to turn the settlement into a spa also failed so that Tomintoul remained heavily dependent on agriculture. Nevertheless it continued to flourish and its regular grid plan and large central square are still striking.

Forestry

In an area in which land was the principal, almost the only, source of income in the early eighteenth century, many Highland proprietors began seeking other means of increasing their incomes. Some of the industrial developments in the Highlands at this time including iron smelting, quarrying and lead mining will be considered in Chapter 9. These demonstrated a more flexible approach to economic development. The start of large-scale commercial forestry was another indication of this. The extent of Highland woodlands had been steadily reduced over the previous few centuries by normal exploitation for timber, by burning to deny shelter to wolves and outlaws, both of which persisted into the eighteenth century, and to provide charcoal for iron smelting. Nevertheless, there were still extensive areas of the old Caledonian pine forests in both the eastern and Western Highlands as well as some deciduous woodland, mainly oak birch and alder, in the south west.

The commercial exploitation of Highland forests had been hindered by their inaccessibility in earlier times. In the seventeenth century there had been some felling of pine trees for ships' masts in parts of the Western Highlands like Ardgour and around Loch Arkaig where the timber could easily be shipped out. Some timber from Rannoch, upper Deeside and Speyside had been floated down to Perth, Aberdeen and the Moray Firth respectively but only on a small scale. In the eighteenth century the clear-felling of pine trees and the coppicing of deciduous woodland became more common, the peak of activity coming during the Napoleonic Wars. The coppicing of woods to provide charcoal for the iron industry is discussed in Chapter 9 but trees were also coppiced to produce bark for tanning.

The Black Wood of Rannoch on the south side of Loch Rannoch had been exploited commercially in the early eighteenth century with rather crude sawmills. They formed part of the estate of the Robertsons which was taken over and managed by the Commissioners for the Annexed Forfeited Estates after the rebellion of 1745. They put forestry on a sounder footing with more efficient water-driven sawmills, and schemes for extensive replanting within areas protected from the depredations of grazing animals by dykes and fences.

The most extensive pine forests were probably those on Speyside. The commissioners for the Scottish navy had bought timber from Abernethy in the 1630s and floated it down the Spey but large-scale forestry did not develop for another century. In 1728 the York Buildings Company bought 60,000 trees in the Forest of Abernethy from Sir James Grant of Grant. They cleared away some of the worst obstructions in the river bed of the Spey during periods when the river was low by building fires against rock barriers and then dousing them with water to make them crack. This allowed timber to be floated to the mouth of the Spey with greater ease.

The woods of Glen More and Rothiemurchus further upstream were not developed until later in the century. In order to extract the timber the levels of several lochs were artificially raised and sluice gates fitted. This allowed controlled floods of water to be released to help carry the logs down to the Spey if normal streamflow was inadequate. In 1783 the Duke of Gordon sold timber in Glenmore Forest to two merchants from Hull. Between then and 1805 large areas of the forest were felled. Formerly the timber had been steered down the Spey in small rafts guided by coracles but by the later eighteenth century large rafts of 60–80 trees were being constructed. The timber was sent to Hull and the Thames for naval use but a thriving shipbuilding industry also developed at Garmouth on the Moray Firth. The pine forests of Glen More and Rothiemurchus appear to have regenerated prolifically after this period of felling and many of the mature pines which you can see today date from this time. During the nineteenth century, however, large areas of forest were opened up to sheep and deer whose grazing prevented the regeneration of new seedlings, providing problems for modern conservationists and foresters.

Today the largest remnants of these native pine forests are still on Speyside. The Black Wood of Rannoch is also extensive and there are some significant areas left in upper Deeside. Elsewhere in the Highlands the surviving pine woods are only small fragments or have been substantially altered by later planting. Rothiemurchus is perhaps the most extensive, attractive and least altered area of forest. It contains pure stands of pine rising to nearly 30m (90ft) but also scattered birch, rowan and alder trees. The characteristic ground flora consists of heather and bilberry giving way to grass and bracken where grazing has been heavier, with cotton sedge and sphagnum moss in wetter hollows. The woods have a distinct fauna too which includes red squirrels, pine martens, capercaillies, black grouse, ptarmigan and crested tits. A nature trail around Loch an Eilean near Aviemore provides a good introduction to these pine woods while the Landmark Centre at Carrbridge has an exhibition on the ecology of the Speyside forests.

Highland forestry in the eighteenth century was not entirely a story of

Figure 35 Traditional Highland pine forests like these at Rothiemurchus on Speyside were increasingly exploited commercially during the eighteenth century.

indiscriminate logging. In some areas extensive afforestation was under-taken. Larch trees were being planted as early as 1737 on the Atholl estates. Later in the century the fourth duke of Atholl, the 'planting duke', was responsible for the afforestation of extensive areas around Dunkeld and Blair. By the time of his death in 1830 it was estimated that he had overseen the planting of 14 million larches.

New problems, new directions: kelp and fishing

The most fundamental background influence which shaped the Highland landscape during the second half of the eighteenth century was the rapid rise of population. The causes of population growth have been debated; undoubtedly the diminution of inter-clan violence was one factor. The spread of inoculation against smallpox was an unquantifiable but possibly significant influence. Increased income from the cattle trade, fishing and towards the end of the eighteenth century from kelp also encouraged demographic growth. In the second half of the eighteenth century the spread of the potato allowed more people to be supported from a given area of land. The timing of the start of this population increase is also unclear. Some historians have detected signs of land hunger in the closing years of the seventeenth century in districts like Rannoch. Others consider that significant population growth was confined to the second half of the eighteenth century, overwhelmingly within its last two decades.

Between 1755 and 1801 the population of the Highlands as a whole rose by around 20 per cent. This was not excessive in comparison with popu-lation growth in the Lowlands or England. However, this overall figure hides distinctive regional variations. In the southern and eastern Highlands the populations of many parishes barely increased at all. On the other hand the rise was much greater in the north-west Highlands. This can be seen in the landscape in the swollen size of the settlements that were deserted with the clearances and in the huge expanse of lazy beds around them. It is also evident in the extension of cultivation around shielings and the conversion of many of them into permanently occupied farms.

In many parishes on the north-west mainland the scale of population increase was around 60 per cent and in the Outer Hebrides 75 per cent or even 100 per cent. The result was an increasing pressure on the means of subsistence. The amount of cultivable land available per family, already small, was further diminished. The proportion of cottars, who had only tiny plots of land, increased. Cultivation spread into even less favourable areas; on to river haughs where periodic flooding was a risk and on to steeper and more boulder-strewn hillsides. Population growth was rapidly outstripping resources and this was reflected by falling yields due to the over-intensive cultivation of the best land and rising labour inputs in relation to returns as more and more marginal land was brought into cultivation. The problem was staved off rather than solved by the spread of the potato from the 1730s although it only became a widespread staple foodstuff in the last two decades of the century.

As the pressure of population on limited resources grew, it became clear by the 1780s that the traditional economic system in the Highlands was on the verge of crisis and that only drastic change would prevent serious recurrent famines. Various pundits had their own pet solutions to the problem. For some it was agricultural improvement; for others the development of industries like fishing, textile manufacture or kelp production. The problem was that these economic 'experts' consistently exaggerated the resource potential of the Highlands and underestimated the problems of development. They failed to realise the tremendous range of environmental, economic and social conditions within the Highlands and did not appreciate that solutions which might work in one district were not universal panaceas.

In the north-western Highlands disaster was staved off, yet at the same time made more inevitable, by the development of the kelp industry. Kelp, or seaweed, could be burnt to produce a vegetable alkali which was an essential ingredient in the manufacture of glass and soap, and for bleaching linen. These industries used imported wood ash from North America and the Baltic, and especially barilla from Spain, produced by burning salt-rich maritime plants. Barilla was of higher quality than kelp but more expensive. Kelp was burnt in Scotland from the late seventeenth century but for a long time it could not compete with low-priced imports. It was introduced to Orkney in 1722 to serve the bleaching industry in Dundee, and to North Uist in 1735. From the 1750s kelp was produced in several parts of the Hebrides and the western mainland. However, the industry really took off from the 1780s as prices began to rise and then doubled or even trebled during the Napoleonic Wars when imports of barilla were interrupted. The greatest centres of kelp production were the Outer Hebrides, Orkney, Skye, Mull, and parts of the north-west mainland.

Superficially kelp seemed to be an ideal industry for this area. Seaweed was a self-renewing resource whose yield was more consistent than that of crops or livestock. Kelp required no capital, no equipment and no skill to produce. Only large amounts of labour were required and this the region had in abundance. As many as 10,000 families were dependent upon kelp at the peak of production. The seaweed was cut from rocky shores in summer; in some cases rocks were actually dumped on sandy stretches of the coastline to encourage seaweed to grow. The work of collecting the kelp was laborious, uncomfortable and wet. It took 20 tons of seaweed to produce one ton of kelp, some 400,000 tons being gathered each year. The seaweed was then dried on foundations of boulders, traces of which can still be found, and burnt in simple kilns, remains of which are still common on the foreshores of the main kelp-producing areas. The kilns were simply shallow pits surrounded by stones. In Orkney the kilns were round and about 5 feet in diameter but in the Hebrides they were rectangular, up to 7m (24ft) long. After the seaweed had been burnt a coagulated mass was left in the bottom of the kiln and it was this that was sent southwards for the chemical industry. The landlords virtually monopolised the trade and creamed off the bulk of the profits. The income they made from kelp was double that from their land rents on many estates at the height of the boom.

In order to guarantee a labour force for collecting and burning the kelp many landowners encouraged excessive subdivision of land within existing townships and sometimes laid out new ones. In these settlements the amount of land leased to the tenants was too small to allow them to make a living from agriculture alone and rents were set at a high level reflecting not so much the productivity of the land but the wages derived from kelp. These were the first crofting townships. Kelp and agriculture did not mix well though. Collecting and burning the seaweed monopolised the labour force during summer, the time when work was most needed on the land. In addition, the practice of using seaweed as a manure, which had produced some respectable crop yields in the past, was forbidden by landowners as all the seaweed was required for making kelp.

The kelp boom was short lived: 1815 brought peace and with it the renewed import of barilla. Within a few years protective tariffs which had helped to make kelp competitive were reduced or withdrawn. Prices fell and the industry declined rapidly during the 1820s leaving a population with insufficient land and a desperate need to bolster their incomes from other sources. By postponing the need for estate reorganisation for more than a generation and encouraging continued population growth the kelp industry had stored up problems for West Highland landlords and heartbreak for their tenants.

Another activity on which hopes for development in the West Highlands were pinned was fishing. In Shetland, where it had long been traditional, fishing did provide an important and successful alternative to farming. There the haaf or deep-sea fishing for cod and ling had encouraged landowners to subdivide small farms into three or four crofts and let them to part-time fishermen, a process which has left a permanent mark on the Shetland landscape. As with the kelp industry, fishing occupied most of the male labour force during the summer months, work on the crofts being done by the women and children. In the West Highlands, however, the inhabitants took to fishing reluctantly, with a lack of skill and capital which restricted their efforts to inshore fishing from small boats while large vessels from the Clyde and east-coast ports took the bulk of the catch. Bounties were payable for the construction of fishing boats but this encouraged the financing of large decked vessels or busses by merchants from the Lowlands rather than local crofter-fishermen. The Highlanders were perhaps right in their caution for although the herring fishing was good in the 1780s and early 1790s the shoals began to appear less regularly in the Minch after that time and the industry became markedly less profitable for local men. In the Outer Hebrides white fishing for cod and ling provided a more dependable source of income than the erratic shoals of herring.

In 1786 the British Fisheries Society was incorporated as a semi-philanthropic group whose main aim was to encourage the development of fishing in the Highlands by laying out new villages. By 1787 they had decided on three sites for development: Ullapool in Wester Ross, Tobermory in Mull, and Lochbay in Skye. The last of these villages never lived up to expectations but the other two were more successful. Ullapool was laid out on a blunt peninsula protruding into Loch Broom. The loch was sheltered with deep water and had attracted earlier ventures. The Forfeited Estates Commissioners had attempted to create a settlement of discharged soldiers and seamen here in the 1760s but it had failed to develop. More successfully, two herring curing centres had been built upon adjacent islands. The Society laid out a spacious grid of streets on a 60ha (150a) site which was never fully built up. There were five main streets, all designed to be parallel, but the main street, which was reserved for warehouses and public buildings, was built following the gentle curve of the shore and is not quite in line with the others. The individual houses were built by their occupiers but the Society financed a warehouse, inn and pier. The three-storey warehouse with an external stone staircase leading to the first floor still stands near the pier, functioning now as a shop and museum. The growth of Ullapool was rapid; by 1794 there were 72 houses and a population of up to 600.

Although more distant from the herring fishing grounds, Tobermory had a fine harbour. Tobermory's layout was controlled to a greater degree by the topography of its site, built in a gentle curve around the bay. The street which ran along the shore had most of the commercial property and a parallel one above was lined by the houses of the ordinary inhabitants. The harbour attracted general trade as well as fishing vessels and by 1793 the settlement had a population of some 300. Lochbay on the west coast of Skye was more remote and lacked good local building stone. Although the Society erected a school, an inn and warehouses the settlers, who numbered around 150 at the maximum, seem to have preferred crofting to fishing and the centre never thrived.

The Society's largest and most successful settlement was Pulteneytown, named after one of its directors, which was grafted on to the existing burgh of Wick. This venture was far more expensive than the Society's earlier efforts. The harbour alone cost £14,000, half of the money coming from the Forfeited Estates Commission. The harbour and the plan of the settlement was designed by Thomas Telford and work began in 1803. Fishermen living in Pulteneytown were forbidden to own land so they were not diverted from full-time fishing into agriculture. By 1819 the population had grown to around 1,200. One of the herring curing yards now houses a local heritage centre with exhibits illustrating the history of the herring fishing industry.

Other fishing villages were set up by private landowners while some grew as a result of the displacement of population from the interior glens with the coming of sheep farming. Plockton in Wester Ross is a good example of a village of crofter-fishermen established by a local landowner. The Earl of Seaforth originally planned the settlement in 1794 but development did not get under way on a large scale until the early years of the nineteenth century. One of the first houses, a traditional Highland cottage with a low thatched roof, small windows and whitewashed rubble walls, still stands in the village.

The coming of the sheep

The clearance of population in the Highlands caused by the 'coming of the sheep' is one of the most potent images in post-Jacobite Highland history. Many aspects of it are still widely misunderstood by the Scots themselves as well as by visitors to the Highlands. First it is important to appreciate that the clearance of population in the Highlands in the later eighteenth century was not undertaken solely to promote commercial sheep farming. Displacement of population often accompanied schemes for farm amalgamation undertaken to improve cattle rearing and mixed farming in the southern and eastern Highlands, as well as in conjunction with the establishment of planned villages.

As we have noted, early experiments with specialist cattle ranching had shown that the Highlands would be far more profitable for landowners under systems of extensive livestock farming. Livestock had a key role in the traditional farming system in the Highlands. With the rise of the droving trade the Highlands were already heavily stocked with cattle but the lack of attention to producing winter fodder ensured that around a fifth of the animals which were wintered perished in most years. The Highlanders also kept large numbers of horses for ploughing and transport. Most tenants had a few sheep as well, which provided milk, wool and mutton. Numbers of sheep were approximately equivalent to those of cattle in most areas. However, when the market demand for sheep rose in the later eighteenth century commercial sheep farming became increasingly attractive.

Nobody ever tried to prove that sheep farming was better in the long term than cattle raising; this was just assumed and the disadvantages were never taken into consideration. Sheep, being more selective grazers than cattle and grazing the pastures all year round, caused the quality of a stretch of pasture to deteriorate if they were kept on it for too long, leading to a long-term impoverishment of the environment. Sheep left only the coarse rough grasses which would have been eaten by cattle. They also encouraged the spread of bracken which was kept in check by the trampling hooves of heavier cattle. However, as so often in human history, long-term environmental effects, if appreciated at all, were ignored in the interests of short-term profits. There was also a widespread but unfounded belief that sheep farming would give rise to a woollen textile industry in the Highlands.

Commercial sheep farming was introduced to the southern Highlands in the 1760s when farmers from the Borders began leasing land in Argyll, Dunbartonshire and Perthshire. They offered higher rents than cattle farmers and introduced the black-faced Linton sheep which could be wintered outdoors, unlike the native Highland breed. Later they brought in the Cheviot which, although less hardy and requiring more winter fodder, produced much more valuable wool. By the end of the eighteenth century sheep farming had spread over much of the Highlands south of the Great Glen. From the 1790s it began to penetrate the far north and west, an area which was only just being opened up by improved communications (Chapter 9).

Some areas, like the peaty wastes of central Lewis or the rocky coast of Morar, were unsuitable for sheep because the terrain was too rugged or lacking in sheltered glens. In most areas, however, sheep were able to pasture on rocky ground which was unsuitable for cattle. The profits from sheep farming were, initially at least, spectacular. A farm which had previously been stocked mainly with cattle could be let at twice the rent if grazed with black-faced sheep and as much as four times with Cheviots.

By 1790 complaints began to be heard of evictions caused by the engrossing of farms to create large sheep walks. As contemporary writers on agriculture like Sir John Sinclair pointed out, it was impossible for the old peasant system of mixed farming and the new one of commercial sheep raising to coexist. The arable land and hay meadows of the small tenants were needed as winter feeding grounds for the large flocks of sheep while the cattle's summer shieling areas were also encroached upon by the wide-ranging animals. Sheep farming needed to be done on a large scale to be viable; it required a flock of at least 600 sheep to keep a shepherd in full-time employment. There was no chance for small farmers to build up a flock over a period of years because landowners rented out their lands in large blocks at initially high rents. Where small-scale sheep farming was tried, as on the Morar estate, it was unsuccessful.

Sheep farmers sometimes moved initially to the heads of the glens taking over mainly the existing shieling grounds and displacing relatively few people. On the Lochiel estate the process began with the establishment of sheep farms in remote Glen Pean and Glendessary. After a few years new sheep farms were created further down the main valley along the sides of Loch Arkaig, and small tenants were increasingly displaced to new settlements on mossland and stony raised beaches at Corpach, Corran, Onich and North Ballachulish. Many of them found work helping to build the Caledonian Canal. In areas like these changes were gradual and there were enough alternative sources of employment to accommodate the displaced tenants. In parts of the Grampians like Strathdon whole touns were deserted and replaced by sheep farms but again the transition was a progressive rather than a sudden one.

The clearance of population from the interior glens to make way for sheep farming produced distinctive landscapes which still dominate large parts of the Highlands. The floors of the larger glens are divided into regular enclosures by neat stone walls with groups of sheep pens at intervals. In upper parts of the glens, or on plateaux like the interior of Caithness, sheep farms stand in the middle of the waste, defined by ring fences. In many cases these sheep farms are close to the ruined townships which they replaced. Higher on the mountainsides and among the side valleys sheepfolds often stand adjacent to clusters of shieling huts and have frequently been constructed from their stones. Today the sheep farms too are sometimes deserted, the shepherds' cottages roofless, the enclosure walls tumbled. The sheep farming boom did not last. By the 1870s refrigeration was allowing the import of mutton and lamb from Australia and New Zealand and sheep prices plummeted. In desperation Highland landowners turned their estates over to deer forest and grouse moor. The shooting lodge replaced the shepherd's cottage and, in the eastern Highlands, hillsides became dotted with lines of grouse butts.

Deserted settlements dating from the late eighteenth and early nineteenth centuries are found throughout the Highlands and have been mentioned in Chapter 1. They were due to estate reorganisation and, in the north and west, were generally the result of the introduction of sheep farming. In most parts of the Highlands you are seldom very far from one of these deserted townships. Often they lie just beyond the modern improved area, yet they have received remarkable little attention from landscape historians. Many of them, together with their shielings, are marked on the most recent Ordnance Survey 1:25,000 maps. Although popular accounts of the Highland clearances are often highly coloured by emphasis on a few unusually brutal evictions, like those on the Sutherland estates in the early nineteenth century, it is impossible to walk through these abandoned townships without a sense of poignancy and regret for the passing of an ancient way of life. In the north-west townships may contain three dozen buildings or more, reflecting the build-up of population in the decades immediately preceding clearance. Most settlements contain a mill; often a horizontal water-mill but sometimes a primitive vertical water-mill like the settlement at Drumgarve in Kintyre (NR 773264) where the mill is combined with the miller's house in a single long range. Corn-drying kilns are another common feature and around the buildings you will see traces of rig cultivation and lazy beds.

The creation of the crofting landscape

During most clearances for sheep farming the aim was not to remove the existing population but merely to relocate it within the estate so that the inhabitants could engage in profitable activities like kelp burning and fishing. This generally involved moving them from the interior glens down to the coast or, on landlocked estates, down to the main valleys. There was no incentive to evict people completely in the north-west Highlands when the kelp industry was booming and elsewhere in the West Highlands fishing and other activities provided some alternative employment. This process created the crofting system.

As defined in various parliamentary statutes, crofts in legal terms are tenanted smallholdings under 20ha (50a) in extent or paying less than £50 rent a year, whose occupants have security of tenure and who are obliged to take on an additional occupation because they cannot make a full living from agriculture. The seven northern and westernmost of the old Highland counties – Shetland, Orkney, Caithness, Sutherland, Ross and Cromarty, Inverness and Argyll – were designated as the 'crofting counties' because of the prevalence of this system. Undoubtedly these are the areas where crofting is still most obvious in the modern landscape, but the nature of crofting and its appearance differs markedly from one part of the Highlands to another. The crofting landscape is most dramatic in the north west, particularly in the Outer Hebrides. There the townships have a very distinctive appearance. With their lotted lands running back from a central road in long narrow strips and a house or cottage placed on each one, generally by the roadside, they give the impression that you are on the fringe of a densely built-up area which never materialises.

The present crofting area is only a shrunken remnant of what was once a more extensive system of small farms which, in other parts of the Highlands, differed only slightly from West Highland crofts. In the Grampians many crofts were carved out from the waste at the uphill margins of settlement in the later eighteenth and early nineteenth centuries. Crofts were also common in some moorland areas among the north-east Lowlands; on the interior plateau of Buchan for instance. They formed part of a graded system of holdings, providing a valuable reservoir of labour for the larger farms. In the Grampians the existence of a range of holding sizes allowed some people to start as crofters and work their way up to the tenancy of a larger farm. In the present century, however, many of these crofts have been amalgamated or added to larger farms. In Easter

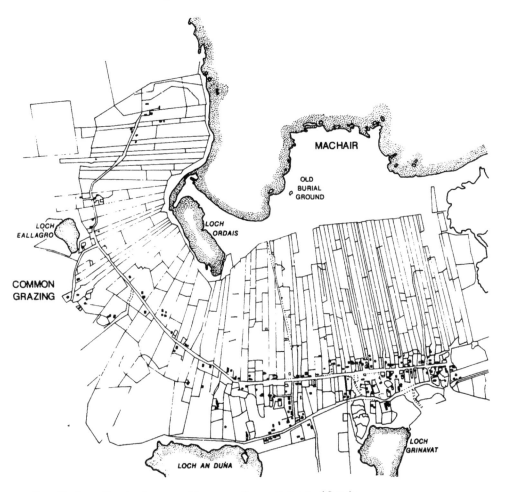

MACHAIR

OLD
BURIAL
GROUND

LOCH
EALLAGRO

LOCH
ORDAIS

COMMON
GRAZING

LOCH
GRINAVAT

LOCH AN DUNA

Map 13 A crofting landscape at Bragar on the west coast of Lewis.

Ross, an area which is transitional between Highland and Lowland, holdings of under 20ha (50a) are still common, even in fertile areas like the
Black Isle. Some crofts were created when existing multiple-tenant farms
were split into separate smallholdings. Others were created on waste land
like the moorland spine of the Black Isle. Around Ferintosh, at the
eastern end of the peninsula, the regular pattern of small rectangular fields
belonging to these intakes is still clearly visible. In the southern and
eastern Highlands crofts were more often laid out individually rather than
in large townships and so form a less dramatic element in the landscape.
Nevertheless, they still form a major part of the settlement pattern in
some areas.

In 1800 the crofting system was just starting to develop in a few areas
but within twenty years it was established all along the west and north

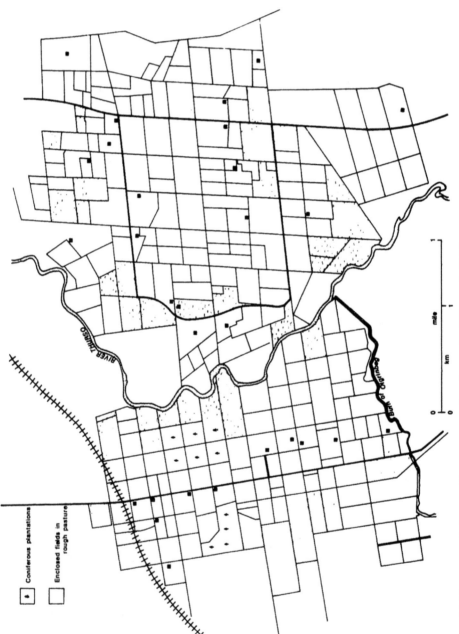

Map 14 The geometric layout of two systems of crofts south of Thurso in Caithness.

coasts and among the islands. The change from the old townships to a crofting system did not necessarily involve much real agricultural improvement. Getting rid of runrig by consolidating each holding into compact blocks was the main benefit. The advantage of laying out crofts, apart from potential increases in efficiency, was that by consolidating smallholdings into single compact blocks the individual tenants' lands were clearly demarcated on the ground. This prevented excessive subletting to cottars and gave landowners greater direct control, allowing them to manipulate rents more easily. The origins of the regularly laid out crofting townships have been sought in some of the early settlements of discharged soldiers and seamen established by the Forfeited Estates Commissioners but it is just as likely that it was the logical outcome of creating clusters of similarly sized smallholdings within a geometrical framework. In some parts of the Outer Hebrides, like the rocky south-east coast of Harris, the terrain was too rugged to allow regular townships to be laid out and irregular scatters of single crofts are more normal. The distribution of large crofting townships even within the 'crofting counties' is restricted. They are especially common in the Outer Hebrides where there may be 20 or even 50 crofts in a single settlement, as well as in Skye and Tiree and along the mainland coast north of Skye. Crofts are common in Shetland but as individual units and not in large regular townships.

In the Outer Hebrides the crofting system was created as an adjunct to the kelp industry, freezing a pattern of peasant smallholdings and preventing any further development. In this area the change often only involved remodelling existing settlements to remove runrig. A comparison of 'before and after' estate surveys shows that the change from the old landscape of clachans and runrig arable land to a crofting township with consolidated holdings simply involved a regularisation of the existing system into a more rigidly geometric pattern. Nevertheless, the tenants were frequently bitterly opposed to such reorganisation even though no displacement was involved. On Lord MacDonald's estates in North Uist and Skye a survey was carried out in 1799 with the intention of converting the existing hamlet clusters and runrig fields to groups of crofts. Due to opposition from the tenants the actual lotting of the crofts was delayed until 1814. In the townships on North Uist which were divided into crofts at this time the layout of the turf dykes from the old runrig system is sometimes visible cutting across the regular croft boundaries. In some cases the location of the township shifted slightly when lotting took place. At Arnol on the west coast of Lewis traces of small, round-cornered houses dating from the later eighteenth century together with their fields and a string of horizontal water-mills can be seen a short distance north of the present regularly planned township.

The attraction of creating crofts in association with kelp was such that in some areas large consolidated farms were subdivided. This was done on the Argyll estates on Mull and Tiree at the end of the eighteenth century. On Tiree five of the Duke of Argyll's farms were occupied by over 1,000 people after they were split into crofts and the island became one of the most overpopulated and congested of the Hebrides as a result.

In areas where people were displaced from the interior glens to make way for sheep they were often settled in completely new townships established along the coast on land which had formerly been uncultivated moorland. In the south-west Highlands single crofts and small farms were normal and townships are rare. On Islay migration to the industrial centres of the south allowed a more gradual process of change which prevented population from building up to crisis level and led to the creation of fewer small crofts. The Campbells of Shawfield, enlightened proprietors, reduced the numbers of holdings slowly and encouraged the development of a range of non-agricultural occupations including fishing, lead mining, distilling and forestry.

An important aspect of the opening up of the Highlands during the later eighteenth century was the construction of improved roads and the provision of better harbours. This focuses attention on the key role of transport and communications in the development of Scotland between 1500 and 1800. Improvements in transport were significant in themselves but also in terms of their impact on agriculture and industry. Different systems of transport have left a fascinating series of traces in the modern Scottish landscape and it is to these that we now turn.

8

Transport and communication

In a country like Scotland, with varied, often rugged topography, and a climate that is frequently harsh, transport can still be difficult even with modern technology. The physical problems of overland travel in the past are obvious for areas like the Highlands, the Borders or Galloway, but it is easy to forget how difficult movement could be through the Lowlands too. In such a recently glaciated country the legacy of the ice sheets was a thick but irregular mantle of boulder clays, sands and gravels. The result was an interrupted drainage pattern with innumerable bogs and small lochs. Many of these have vanished as a result of three centuries of drainage and reclamation.

The strategic significance of particular routes and focal points can be appreciated only if these problems are realised. For instance the crossing of the River Forth at Stirling Bridge was so important in Scottish history because, before the later eighteenth century, the Forth valley above Stirling was an expanse of peat moss which could only be crossed in one or two places, along winding belts of moraine. Internal transport was further hampered by the lack of navigable rivers. The indented coastline, particularly in the West Highlands with its numerous islands and deep sea lochs, meant that movement by sea was often far easier than by land. Inland, lochs like Loch Ness and Loch Lomond acted as miniature seas linking the communities around their shores. The small size of vessels used in coastal trading and fishing meant that almost any creek or open beach could serve as a port. On the debit side, navigation in Scottish coastal waters was frequently hazardous, particularly along rocky coasts like Buchan or where tidal races were strong, as in the Pentland Firth.

The most dramatic phase of the 'transport revolution' lies outside our period; the full development of a network of all-weather roads, the building of many of the canals, the development of large wet dock systems and the coming of the railways all belong to nineteenth-century Scotland. Nevertheless there were important changes in the character of transport in Scotland between 1500 and 1800, particularly during the second half of the eighteenth century. Such developments were themselves agents of landscape change. The ability to transport larger volumes of goods over longer distances at lower costs helped to transform both agriculture and industry, the countryside as well as the town.

Early roads

Scotland has often been portrayed as a country almost without roads before the later eighteenth century, a place where wheeled vehicles were almost unknown. There is an element of truth in this. Because Scotland was a rugged and relatively poor country, packhorse and sled were far more important than cart or wagon. Into the eighteenth century pack-horses were the normal means of transporting even bulky commodities like grain and coal in many areas; this was as much a sensible adaptation to difficult terrain as a sign of backwardness. Carts were in use in many areas before the later eighteenth century but they were often lightweight with solid wheels and rotating axles, appropriately named 'tumblers'. Heavier carts with spoked, iron-rimmed wheels became much more common from the later seventeenth century but tumblers were still common in many rural areas into the mid-eighteenth century.

There is plenty of evidence in early charters that roads for wheeled vehicles, perhaps with some element of deliberate construction, existed in medieval times. The king's highway is often referred to, running between major burghs. Detailed study of the movements of the baggage trains and siege engines used by English armies in Scotland during the Wars of Independence in the late thirteenth and early fourteenth centuries is also instructive. Not only do they indicate the main lines of movement, but calculations of distances covered in specific time periods sometimes indi-cate surprisingly high average speeds. Of course military baggage trains were likely to have had more manpower available for hauling vehicles out of bogs than civilian carriers!

It has been suggested that road conditions in Scotland may have deteriorated after 1400 but the evidence for this is far from clear. In England the state of the roads, particularly in clay areas, does seem to have worsened during the seventeenth century due to the greater wear caused by an increasing volume of traffic. Something similar may have occurred in Scotland during the seventeenth and early eighteenth centuries as there is evidence of increased internal trading and movement of goods, but this has yet to be demonstrated. It may be that more frequent reports

Figure 36 The line of the Roman Dere Street near Jedburgh. The route continued in use through the medieval period and still serves as a farm track.

of the bad quality of the roads at this time merely reflects more abundant documentation.

Although transport conditions in Scotland may not have been as bad as they have sometimes been painted, it is true that during the sixteenth and seventeenth centuries there were, outside the towns, few roads with properly constructed surfaces. Most roads were merely worn by use, broad bands of intertwining trackways which narrowed in at river crossings, on steep slopes, and between obstructions like the policy walls of estates and then spread out once more as each traveller picked his own way. Special efforts were sometimes made to improve specific routes such as the road between Edinburgh and Glasgow or the Causey Mounth, the coast road between Stonehaven and Aberdeen. However, even in the later seventeenth century long stretches of road fit for regular use by substantial numbers of wheeled vehicles were rare. The Earl of Hopetoun had been authorised to improve the road from the mines at Leadhills via Biggar to Leith to facilitate the export of lead ore. The fact that he had to undertake this as a private venture demonstrates that the authorities were powerless to effect any real improvements in road conditions.

The inadequacy of even main roads is indicated by the preparations for James VI's visit to Scotland in 1617. The efforts to improve the road from Berwick to Edinburgh and north to Perth have a panic-stricken air about them. The resources of landowners and tenants along the line of the planned royal progress were carefully inventoried so that they could be mobilised for road mending but the lists of men, horses and equipment were not easily transformed into action on the ground. In 1617 the Scottish Parliament, presided over by King James with his experience of Scottish roads fresh in his memory, passed legislation requiring Justices of the Peace to maintain roads leading to market towns, ports and parish churches. But as the powers of these officials existed on paper rather than in reality nothing was done in practice. In 1624 the main road from Edinburgh southwards to the Tweed over Soutra Hill was described as impassable on horseback or on foot.

In 1669 an act was passed instituting a system of statute labour for road maintenance comparable to the one introduced in England in 1555. Scottish Sheriffs and Justices of the Peace were constituted as local road authorities and were required to meet annually to prepare lists of roads, bridges and ferries needing repair. They were given the power to call out the local population with their horses for up to six days a year in June and July to repair the roads, and to appoint overseers to superintend the work. They were authorised to raise money for road repairs by imposing an assessment on landowners, in proportion to the value of their rented incomes, and by charging tolls. Administration of the system was organised at county level instead of parish by parish as in England and in 1686 the Justices and Sheriffs were joined in the work by the larger landowners in each shire.

How well did this system work? In England, where central authority had considerable control over local affairs, the system worked poorly at best. In Scotland, where government had little power to force local authorities to act, it has been assumed that the system did not work at all. The pace of economic development was increasing and the volume of internal trade, and hence road traffic, was growing. It is possible that this was accompanied by greater efforts at road maintenance which, because they are not well recorded in contemporary sources, have yet to be highlighted. Certainly in the eighteenth century the increasing practice of commuting road service to money payments allowed skilled labour to be hired and this led to some improvement in road conditions.

Something of the character of these early roads can be gained from surviving traces in the landscape although the precise dating of old roads is difficult. The problem is to distinguish between the periods during which a particular route was in use, and the date of the visible features on the ground. Thus the route over Minchmoor, between Innerleithen and Selkirk, is known from documents to have been used from at least the thirteenth century. The visible remains are more likely to date from the latest period at which the road was in regular use, the eighteenth century, than from medieval times. In the more intensively cultivated lowland areas there are few traces of old road networks which are likely to predate the eighteenth century. They have either been incorporated in the modern road system or have been ploughed out.

In hill areas, however, old roads can often be traced for long distances. Traffic tended to follow the ridges rather than the valleys because the former were often better drained and movement along them was easier, avoiding cultivated land and frequent stream crossings. In such terrain old roads often appear as terraces where they cross hillsides, and as deeply cut hollow ways where they descend steep slopes. An old road through the Lammermuirs, between Gifford and Longformacus, runs parallel with the modern road and where it climbs up the steepest section south-east of Gifford (NT 589657-599654) it takes the form of a band of hollow ways up to 140m (450ft) wide with as many as sixteen separate tracks being visible. On more level ground roads sometimes vanish altogether or appear as single hollowed tracks cut through the thin skin of hill peat. These often show up from a distance as a difference in vegetation, the roads being light, grassy bands among the darker heather. Many roads in such areas were for purely local use. You can sometimes see trackways slanting up the hillside from each farm. Many of these were peat roads, down which fuel was brought by sled; if followed uphill they often terminate against an old peat bank.

Other roads carried long-distance traffic. A number of old roads crossed

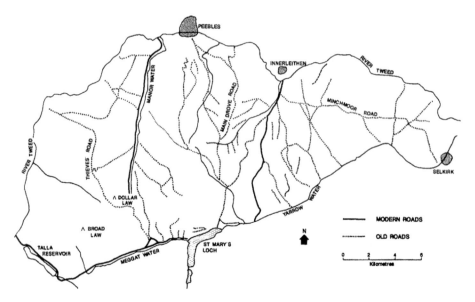

Map 15 Old road networks in the Tweedsmuir Hills.

the Mounth, the line of hills which separates the lowlands of Strathmore and the Angus glens from Deeside, using passes of varying height and difficulty. The Herring Road over the Lammermuirs from East Lothian to the Merse, traces of which can still be seen, got its name because farmers from the Tweed valley used it to bring home packhorse loads of salt fish from Dunbar. A remarkable old routeway is the 'Thieves' Road' through the Tweedsmuir Hills. For many miles it runs at an altitude of over 600m (2,000ft) with feeder roads joining it from each side valley. In places it has clearly been worn by use but sections of it have been improved with careful construction. This is especially evident where the road runs along hillsides, with traces of drainage ditches on the uphill side and revetments downslope, while steep slopes are climbed by carefully graded zig-zags. Such roads were clearly intended for use by vehicles and are likely to date from the eighteenth century but before the establishment of a network of turnpikes opened the valleys up to wheeled transport, when the ridgeway routes fell out of use.

Main roads through the lowlands are harder to follow but sections of the old road from Edinburgh to Berwick have been bypassed by modern traffic and can still be walked or cycled in safety. In the eighteenth century this route was known as the 'Great Post Road' and was the first Scottish road to be turnpiked. For much of its course it is followed by the modern A1 but a section north of Haddington was almost abandoned when the new turnpike was built through the town. It runs from Cantyhall (NT 434752) near Longniddry to Phantassie (NT 510757) north of Haddington. The gently sinuous course of the road contrasts with the right-angled

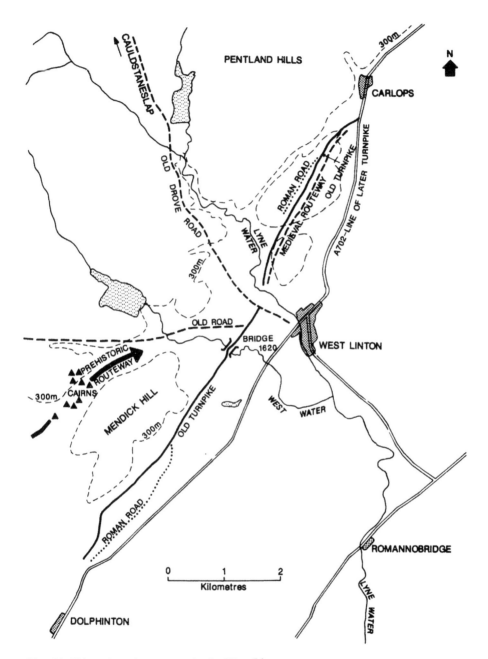

Map 16 Old roads and routeways in the West Linton area.

enclosures on either side of it which were laid out at a later date. From Phantassie eastwards the road vanishes but a curving field boundary probably preserves its original course. Further on, past Beanston Mains (NT 553765), the road continues as a cart track to Pencraig Wood (NT 569765) where a deeply worn hollow way may mark the line of the old road that preceded the turnpike. Further south the line of the Great Post Road can be followed for several kilometres over Coldingham Moor as a minor road heading for the Eye Water near Ayton Castle. Deep hollow ways can be seen cutting the slopes on either side of the stream here. The road then continues its characteristically high-lying route over Lamberton Moor as a farm track.

Drove roads

A special category of road was the drove road. These were used by cattle and other livestock on their long walk from the Highlands and the Southern Uplands to English markets. Droving from destinations as distant as Skye was well established by the late seventeenth century and a network of roads developed by which the herds were moved to the Lowlands and then across the Border. Highland drove roads converged on the main cattle 'trysts' or markets at Crieff and later at Falkirk. Many routes in the Highlands now used only by walkers were once drove roads, like the Lairig Ghru pass through the Cairngorms. Cattle from the West Highlands and Islands made for Doune and then crossed the Forth several miles above Stirling at the Fords of Frew (NS 670960), where a deeply worn hollow way can be seen descending the river bank.

The numbers of livestock involved in the droving trade increased during the eighteenth century and reached a peak in the early nineteenth century before the coming of the railways provided a less arduous means of transporting livestock. Drove roads kept to high ground as far as possible, avoiding cultivated areas where movement of the large herds was difficult. The occurrence of wheel ruts and hollow ways shows that they were often used by other traffic but their most characteristic feature, where they have survived undisturbed, is their great width, to allow for droves which might contain hundreds of cattle. Efforts were often made to fence in such roads to prevent the animals from straying. On open ground drove roads may be defined by old turf dykes as along the Sheriffmuir Road north of Stirling (NS 826016–805969) which was the main route to Falkirk for cattle coming from the north. Through improved ground drove roads often appear as broad tracks around 15m (50ft) wide defined by stone dykes. The main drove road southwards from the cattle trysts at Crieff and Falkirk takes this form in several places. It crossed the Pentland Hills by the Cauldstaneslap pass (NT 118589), leaving remarkably little trace on the open peaty moorland to mark the passage of millions of animals.

Figure 37 The main drove road south to the Border near Carlisle crosses the Liddel Water at Castleton. The broad road is here defined by banks and ditches.

Between Romannobridge and Peebles some stretches are identifiable as a broad 'green road' between parallel enclosure walls. South of Peebles the road climbs Kailzie Hill between two stone dykes 100m (350ft) apart.

The animals covered around 20km (12 miles) a day and were halted for the night at recognised stopping places or 'stances'. A number of these simple change houses were established to provide the drovers with whisky, and many modern Highland hotels originated in this way. Large rectangular enclosures beside drove roads, like those which stand next to the Wheel Causeway in the Cheviots, sometimes indicate the existence of former stances. There is little to see at the sites of most of the great cattle trysts. These fairs were first held at Crieff during the later seventeenth century. Falkirk tryst developed after the Union of 1707 and took over from Crieff around 1770. The tryst was held at three successive sites in the Falkirk area until the later nineteenth century. At a lesser tryst, Hill of Balgair NS (6191), a stretch of level moorland, a series of small enclosures and mounds spread over 1km (0.5 miles) are probably associated with the sale of livestock, though their actual function is not clear.

Early bridges

The principal form of investment in overland communication before the eighteenth century was bridge building. Compared with England bridges were few and far between. One estimate is that in 1630 there were only around 220 sizable bridges in the whole of Scotland, though many small, local ones may not have been recorded. The erratic regimes of Scottish rivers like the Tay, Tweed and Spey, which were liable to sudden spates as a result of heavy rainfall in their upland source areas, worked against bridge construction as even stone bridges could easily be swept away. Following the destruction of the medieval bridge at Roxburgh only a single bridge at Peebles spanned the Tweed above the one at Berwick until the mid-eighteenth century. At Perth a stone bridge built in 1616 was swept away in 1621 and was not replaced until the late 1760s. When bridges fell into disrepair it sometimes took decades to organise the finance to repair them. As a result, ferries remained common on major rivers into the eighteenth century. A series of place names scattered down the Spey valley such as Boat of Garten and Boat of Insh pinpoints the location of old ferries.

Most of the early bridges which have survived or for which records exist spanned major rivers in the immediate vicinity of burghs, and were financed by towns because of the benefits to their trade. Many of them, such as the bridges at Dumfries, Ayr and Stirling were located at the lowest bridging point of a river, close to the head of navigation. Others, like the bridge at Peebles and the lost one at Roxburgh, spanned major rivers at inland burghs.

Early medieval bridges were built of timber but these began to be replaced by stone ones from the fifteenth century. In contrast to the poor state of contemporary roads these bridges are often superbly built and a number of them carried increasing volumes of traffic into recent times. Bridge building was seen as an act of piety and charity while it also had the advantage of being relatively finite in terms of cost compared with building and maintaining a stretch of road. The Bridge of Balgownie near Aberdeen (NJ 940047) is one of the oldest surviving stone bridges, supposedly dating from the early fourteenth century but partly rebuilt in 1597. Such bridges were solidly constructed using squared masonry with many small arches, often semicircular, and thick piers with massive triangular cutwaters which extended upwards into refuges. Their carriageways were fairly narrow, just wide enough for wheeled traffic though often sharply humped. Surviving medieval bridges have generally been repaired on several later occasions and it can be hard to date their earliest phase of construction. An examination of their sites, often in tidal water, gives one considerable respect for the masons who built them. They placed their abutments and piers on solid rock above the surface wherever possible but where piers had to be founded on submerged rocks, as at Ayr and Bridge of Dee, they may have used earth coffer dams to keep the water out while the foundations were being laid.

The six-arched bridge at Dumfries, dating from the fifteenth century, is one of the oldest surviving multiple-arched bridges in Scotland. Originally it had nine arches but three were later removed. It is known as Devorgilla's Bridge, a name it probably inherited from a timber predecessor for it owed its construction not to Lady Devorgilla de Balliol, but to the Douglas family. Although damaged by floods in 1620 the bridge continued to carry all traffic across the Nith in and out of Dumfries until the end of the eighteenth century when a wider replacement was built nearby. Guard Bridge in northern Fife (NO 451188) may date from around the same period, supposedly having been built by a fifteenth-century bishop of St Andrews.

Given that most goods were transported by pack horses rather than wheeled vehicles, one might expect small, simple packhorse bridges to have been widespread in Scotland, as they are in northern England. Surprisingly few have survived, though. One at Coaltown of Balgonie in Fife (NT 307983) may date from the seventeenth century or earlier and was used by packhorses carrying coal from local pits to the coast. Similar narrow bridges with low parapets can be seen in the north east crossing the Isla at Old Keith and at Charleston of Aberlour. Two simple bridges of medieval date can be seen spanning the main water-supply canal at Melrose Abbey. Some stone clapper bridges of indeterminate date with drystone piers spanned by flat slabs occur in parts of the Highlands; there are a number on the old packhorse track round the north coast of Applecross. Some examples are known to have been built as recently as the nineteenth century but their design is so basic that they are likely to have existed in earlier centuries too. One or two comparable bridges occur in Orkney, where the flagstones readily split into suitable slabs. It is possible that other examples have been washed away by floods but the impression is that before the eighteenth century most minor streams were crossed by fords rather than bridges.

Before the Reformation the church was a major source of finance for bridge construction. Examples include the fine sixteenth-century bridge on the outskirts of Jedburgh, provided by the monks of Jedburgh Abbey, and the Abbey Bridge downstream from Haddington which was associated with a nearby nunnery. Aberdeen, Dunkeld and Glasgow all had early bridges provided by their bishops. After the Reformation the initiative for the building and repair of bridges outside the towns passed to lay landowners, either as private individuals or as Commissioners of Supply for their respective shires. Landowners had a vested interest in improving communications but the church often helped them indirectly. Ministers might be prompted to make special collections in their parishes to help finance new bridges which served the common good. During the later seventeenth and early eighteenth centuries a number of simple bridges, mostly single arched, were built, often rather narrow and generally with rough rubble masonry and arches, something which was cheaper than dressed stone. Their purpose was often simply to provide better access to

Figure 38 Now restricted to pedestrians, this modest bridge at Innerleithen was built in 1701 using local funds to improve access to the parish church.

the parish church for local residents. The old bridge over the Gala Water at Stow (1654–5) and one at Innerleithen (1701) are good examples. Diverting the minister's stipend when a parish was vacant was another way of financing bridge construction. Old Manor Bridge near Peebles (NT 231394) was built by these means in 1702.

Bridges in the later eighteenth century

In the eighteenth century, as internal trade and traffic increased, the need for more bridges and better roads became widely appreciated. Despite developments in design and materials, many simple bridges of rubble masonry with semicircular arches continued to be built. County authorities; the Justices of the Peace and Commissioners of Supply, played an increasingly important part in road and bridge construction. This can often be seen from inscriptions on surviving bridges, as at Chartershall near Stirling (NS 792902) where a panel records that the bridge was built by the Justices in 1696 and repaired by them in 1747. Other bridges were financed privately by local people who realised the advantages of better communications. The solid, four-arched bridge which spans the River Forth at Drip, above Stirling, was built in the mid-eighteenth century on the initiative of local farmers, who helped to finance its construction. The peat-covered carselands of the Forth valley had been a major barrier to communications for centuries. The new bridge allowed farmers on the northern side of the carse to bring lime from near Stirling to improve their lands as well as coal for domestic heating. Ramsay of Ochtertyre, a local landowner, recorded in his memoirs that the building of the bridge had allowed local farmers to burn more coal than gentlemen had been able to afford forty years earlier.

From the 1760s the pace of bridge building quickened and many multi-arch ones were built across major rivers, some of the most important being aided by government finance. In a single county, Roxburgh, 24 major bridges were built between 1764 and 1813. Over Scotland as a whole one survey has estimated that an average of between 10 and 15 bridges were being built every year in the later eighteenth century. The new bridge at Perth was one of the earliest of these ventures. The prime mover in the project was the ninth earl of Kinnoul, who owned estates around Perth on both sides of the river and who was well placed in government circles to lobby for finance. Money was raised locally for the project but in the end two-thirds came from the government. The bridge, designed by engineer John Smeaton, was completed in 1770 at a much higher cost than originally estimated. It was a great benefit to the inhabitants of Perth, encouraging local agriculture and industry, but its advantages were reduced by the fact that its construction was not linked to any effort to improve local roads. Such a scheme had been planned but the bridge had used up all the money!

Bridges from this period incorporated a range of new design features. Although many early Scottish bridges had been built with segmental rather than semicircular arches, the design of arches became much flatter, their spans wider and piers slimmer. Dressed stone masonry for the wing walls and spandrels of bridges rather than merely the arch rings became normal and on some bridges the spandrels were pierced with circular holes to reduce the weight of the structure and provide extra outlets for flood water. Smeaton's seven-arch bridge at Coldstream, finished in 1767, shows these features while Thomas Telford's bridge at Tongland, opened in 1808, was the first to incorporate hollow arches and spandrels.

Turnpikes

The later eighteenth century, particularly its last twenty years, saw a revolution in road construction throughout the Lowlands. The idea of turnpike roads had developed in England from the later seventeenth century. They were managed by groups of trustees who raised finance for road improvement, had specific highways upgraded or totally rebuilt by professional surveyors and then charged tolls on traffic to maintain them in good order and, hopefully, to pay a dividend to the subscribers. Tolls were not new in Scotland; for centuries they had been levied on an *ad hoc* basis for maintaining bridges and stretches of road but they had never been applied as part of a properly organised system of road improvement.

By the mid-eighteenth century many counties were using the statute labour system more effectively by having the labour commuted to money payments and using the funds to employ professional road-builders. In Fife, for instance, the system was working so well that the introduction of turnpikes over most of the county was delayed until the 1790s. Nevertheless, the statute labour system was not effective in many areas and turnpikes held considerable promise for improving Scotland's communications. The first turnpikes were authorised in Midlothian in 1713 but nothing effective was done until the 1750s when turnpike trusts were set up to improve the main roads radiating out from Edinburgh. By the end of the eighteenth century over 3,000 miles of turnpikes were in operation in Scotland and a comprehensive network of improved roads ran through most parts of the Lowlands as far north as Aberdeen.

The turnpike trusts, unlike English ones, were established at a county level, the trustees mainly being the larger landowners in the shire. The detailed work of building and maintaining particular roads was delegated to district committees. The trusts borrowed money on the security of the expected income from tolls; most of this came directly from landowners who expected to benefit from the improved roads rather than from investors looking for a profit from their capital. Provision was made to raise additional revenue from an assessment on all landowners within a county. The landowners, in turn, could pass on three-quarters of this sum to their tenants.

Turnpike road construction in the late eighteenth century usually embodied variants of the system used by Thomas Telford and adapted ultimately from the Romans. First a sound bottoming of large stones was laid with smaller stones above and then gravel on top. The disadvantage of this system was its high cost but even more importantly the fact that it was not very durable. The permeable surface layers of gravel and small stones allowed water to seep under the foundations and break them up so that the larger stones tended to rise to the surface of the road and jolt cart and wagon wheels. The solution was developed by John MacAdam, who was appointed a trustee for the Ayrshire turnpikes in 1787. He dispensed with the expensive bottoming of large stones and pounded a layer of angular stones about the size of a hen's egg until they interlocked into an impermeable mass which shed water and resisted erosion. It took time for MacAdam's new system to be generally adopted and many turnpikes which had originally been built using Telford's system had to be resurfaced using MacAdam's methods a decade or two later.

Some turnpikes were simply existing roads upgraded, retaining their original alignments. These often involved steep gradients which had to be eased by later realignment. Most late eighteenth-century turnpikes have been overlain by modern 'A' and 'B' class roads, a tribute to the skill of the early turnpike engineers. Along modern roads the principal legacies of the turnpike era are milestones and tollhouses. The milestones often have a characteristic 'house style' within the areas administered by particular turnpike trusts. Tollhouses were usually single-storey buildings with a bow window in front to enable the tollkeeper to keep an eye on traffic in either direction. Most tollhouses date from the early decades of the nineteenth century. An early tollhouse dating from 1756 can still be seen at Jamestown, between Inverkeithing and North Queensferry (NT 127819). Like milestones, tollhouse design often varies in detail from county to county. As well as occurring along the new roads, often at junctions, they were also built at some bridges like the one at Coldstream.

Because so many turnpikes have been developed into modern roads it is difficult to appreciate their original character. Some abandoned turnpikes exist, however, and make interesting walks. On the eastern side of the Pentlands you can follow a turnpike for over six miles between Carlops and Dolphinton. The road runs parallel to the modern A702 about 1km (0.5 mile) nearer the hills. It follows fairly closely the line of a Roman Road and a set of hollow ways which marked the main route from Edinburgh to Clydesdale before the later eighteenth century. The turnpike crosses the Lyne Water upstream of West Linton, whose inhabitants were annoyed at being bypassed. Further on you can find evidence that the line of the road was not entirely new, for the West Water is crossed by a bridge dated 1620. This stretch of road remained in use until 1830 when it was replaced by a new one, now the A702, which followed an easier line and passed through West Linton.

Military roads in the Highlands

The most famous programme of road construction in eighteenth-century Scotland was the building of a network of military roads, mainly in the Highlands. In 1724, following the Jacobite rebellions of 1715 and 1719, Major-General George Wade was sent to Scotland to report on conditions in the Highlands and to suggest measures for the further pacification of the region. Wade, a regular soldier and not an engineer, made wide-ranging proposals including raising locally recruited independent companies of troops, and the establishment of more government garrisons. However, it is as a road-maker that he is best known. Having strengthened the defences of Fort William and Fort George at opposite ends of the Great Glen he planned a new outpost, Fort Augustus, midway between them at the south end of Loch Ness. It made sense to improve the 96km (60 miles) long road between the three forts. However, Wade's vision was wider than this. The difficulty of moving regular troops through the Highlands with their rugged, and virtually unmapped topography, had long been appreciated. What was needed, Wade believed, was a system of roads to link the main forts with the smaller outposts and to allow ready access from the Lowlands in the event of a further rebellion.

In 1725 Wade started improving the road through the Great Glen. His original road ran well above the eastern shores of Loch Ness where the ground was less steep but it proved to be too exposed and easily blocked by snow. In 1732 a new stretch of road was made close to the lochside and a considerable amount of blasting was required to clear the ground for it. A contemporary writer has left a vivid description of how the miners who carried out the blasting operations had to hang over the cliffs on the ends of ropes in order to bore the holes for the gunpowder. With the three Great Glen forts connected, Wade turned his attention to linking the system to the Lowlands.

Wade's main road through the Highlands, 164km (102 miles) long, connected the strategic centres of Perth and Inverness. It began at Dunkeld, following the Tay and the Garry through the gorge of Killiecrankie, over the bleak pass of Drummochter, and then across rolling moorland to reach the Spey at Ruthven Barracks. Beyond Aviemore the road left Speyside and cut through the Slochd pass to Inverness. To improve access to the road from central Scotland Wade had a branch built northwards from Crieff via Amulree and the Sma' Glen. It crossed the Tay and then the Tummel to reach the main road at Dalnacardoch north of Blair Castle.

Wade's main road linked the eastern end of the Great Glen to the south but there was also a need for a road that turned westwards towards Lochaber. Wade's most famous road, made notorious by the descriptions of faint-hearted eighteenth-century travellers, branched off from the main road in upper Speyside and led to Fort Augustus over the Monadhliath mountains via the Corrieyairack pass, climbing to 775m (2,543ft). It followed an existing drove road westwards from the Spey into the steep armchair-shaped hollow of Corrie Yairack, with crags and broken rocky slopes all round. The road escaped from this dead end by a side valley to the west, climbing by means of eighteen zig-zag traverses at a gradient which, though steep, was just practicable for wheeled vehicles.

In some respects Wade's bold decision to drive a direct road over this high pass was a mistake. The road was blocked by snow for long periods in winter. In the first year of its use eleven soldiers are believed to have died of exposure crossing the pass. In an age before mountain scenery became fashionable the Corrieyairack road had a grim reputation and, significantly, this route is not followed by a modern road, unlike most of Wade's routes. As a result, it is the longest stretch of military road in the Highlands surviving more or less in its original state. The zig-zag traverses, faced with stone retaining walls, are still impressive and although the scenery is bleak rather than spectacular it emphasises how alien and hostile was this country to the Hanoverian soldiers who built the road.

The roads were laid out by army surveyors and built by ordinary soldiers working between April and October. The troops received extra money for their work but, living in tented camps on basic army rations in unfamiliar country whose climate, inhabitants and midges were equally hostile, their job was a hard one. Working parties normally consisted of around 100 men and a couple of officers. Up to 500 soldiers were employed on the roads at any time. The speed at which they worked was impressive. The road from Dunkeld to Inverness was completed in two summers, the Corrieyairack road in a single season. Each soldier was expected to complete a yard and a half of road a day.

The roads were laid straight across country, like Roman ones, where topography permitted and tended to follow high ground as far as possible to make drainage easier. This sometimes led to steep descents to river crossings with gradients of up to 1 in 6. They had a maximum width of 5m (16ft) although where the ground was difficult they were often narrower. The general practice was first to clear the ground of large boulders and dig it out until a solid bottom of rock or gravel was uncovered. The excavated material was piled into banks on either side of the road and large stones were set up at regular intervals to mark the line of the road in snowy conditions. These stones were the ancestors of the modern guide posts which mark Highland roads today. The banks and markers were a characteristic feature of Wade's roads and can still be seen clearly today in some places. A layer of stones was laid over the bed of the road and then gravel was beaten down on top. On sloping ground a drainage channel was generally dug on the uphill side with a stone revetment downhill. Detailed sectioning of parts of Wade's road between Dunkeld and Inverness in advance of the construction of the new A9 trunk road showed that in places the surface of Wade's road lay directly on glacial boulder clay without any additional bottoming or metal. On soft ground the roads were floated on layers of brushwood.

Given that the officers were not skilled engineers, and considering how quickly the roads were built, it is not surprising that standards of construction were sometimes poor. The major problem faced by the builders was not so much the rugged topography but drainage difficulties caused by the high rainfall. At first water was channelled across the roads by open drains and streams were crossed by cobbled fords, but these proved too vulnerable to sudden floods and required annual repairs. Later the practice was to carry small streams under the roads in culverts and to build bridges over the larger ones. The smaller bridges, with their distinctive narrow arches, were sometimes unable to cope with floods and several were washed away, but in fairness to the builders they were not used to such an extreme climate.

Wade did not attempt to span the widest rivers like the Spey at Ruthven and the Tay at Dunkeld but other large streams required bigger bridges, several of which are still in use. The road from Fort George at Inverness to Fort William crossed the River Spean by High Bridge (NN 200820), 85m (280ft) long with three arches. Sadly this structure is badly ruined today. Still complete, with a high single arch, is Whitebridge on the same road south of Foyers (NH 489154). The most imposing and stylish Wade bridge, built of dressed stone rather than the usual rubble masonry, crosses the Tay at Aberfeldy. Ninety metres (300ft) long, with five arches, it is ornamented by four classical-style obelisks, the result of a design by the architect William Adam. More functional but equally effective is the bridge over the Tummel further north on the same road (NN 762592).

By 1736 Wade had overseen the construction of around 400km (250 miles) of new road with 40 major bridges. This was a great achievement, particularly in difficult terrain. The lines chosen by Wade's surveyors were often followed by later road engineers, including Thomas Telford, who sometimes merely upgraded the existing road surfaces and bridges. When Wade left Scotland in 1740 the work of building military roads continued under his successor, Major William Caulfeild, who had been Wade's chief surveyor.

Following the 1745 rebellion another 1,200km (750 miles) of roads were built under Caulfeild's direction with nearly 1,000 bridges. Caulfeild's roads were often better built than Wade's, with more extensive use of cuttings and embankments although steep gradients were still allowed. The post-1745 military roads included some over difficult passes. One ran from Perth to Braemar via the Devil's Elbow and then on by the Lecht

Figure 39 This stone at the Well of Lecht was set up in 1759 to commemorate the completion of the military road from the Dee to the Spey.

pass to the new Fort George, east of Inverness. Another linked Fort
William directly with the south, skirting the bleak wasteland of Rannoch
Moor and climbing the hills to the north by a series of traverses known
as the Devil's Staircase. A third route ran from Dumbarton to Inveraray.
Caulfeild's cra also produced some fine bridges. The one spanning the
Dee at Invercauld (NO 187909) with its six graduated arches is one of the
finest.

The sites of many of the soldiers' camps along the new roads became
inns. Known as 'King's Houses', they were spaced out at intervals of about
16km (10 miles). A number of modern Highland hotels originated as
King's Houses, like the one at Whitebridge near Foyers. Sometimes the
original name has survived, as with the Kingshouse Hotel on the military
road at the head of Glencoe. At Garvamore, on the Corrieyairack road
(NN 528943), there is an original King's House, dating from about 1740.
The inn is a long, unadorned range of two-storey, slate-roofed buildings.
At one end is a stable with a loft above which probably once accommodated soldiers. It continued to function into the nineteenth century as a
stance for drovers and their herds.

In the later eighteenth century the military road network in the Highlands began to fall into disrepair. The mileage of roads which had been
built, often hurriedly and over difficult terrain, needed more maintenance
than the limited manpower or finance that the army could spare. By 1799
under 965km (600 miles) of the network was in some sort of repair. By
this time, however, the civil authorities were beginning to build roads and
bridges in the Highlands and were soon to take over and upgrade the
network of military roads.

Roads and bridges in the Highlands at the end of the eighteenth century

As we saw in Chapter 7, by the later eighteenth century the economy and
society of the Highlands were changing rapidly. The influences behind this
included rapid population growth and the increasing integration of this
once isolated region with the the rest of Britain. Highland landowners
and official bodies like the Commissioners for Annexed Forfeited Estates
and the British Fisheries Society realised the importance of improved
roads in the development of agriculture, fishing and industry in the Highlands. In such an isolated region it was unrealistic to expect that the
statute labour system would work, while the volume of traffic was not yet
sufficient for turnpikes to be a viable proposition. The question was how
to raise finance for road improvement and bridge building. Towards the
end of the eighteenth century a number of schemes were started by local
landowners raising money by public subscription and completed with the
aid of funds provided by the government from the revenues of the estates
of Jacobite families which had been forfeited after the rebellion of 1745

and retained in crown hands. For example in 1779 the shire authorities for Argyll applied to the Commissioners of Forfeited Estates for £600 to complete a bridge over the River Awe and in the following year they received £350 from the same source for another bridge over the River Orchy.

By the end of the eighteenth century the need to stem emigration from the Highlands by providing employment was seen as another reason for improving communications in the Highlands. Thomas Telford, who was already adviser and surveyor to the British Fisheries Society in their projects to build new fishing settlements in the Highlands, was asked to prepare a report on communications in the region. As a result of this two government commissions were formed in 1803, one to oversee the building of the Caledonian Canal (see next section), the other for Highland Roads and Bridges. They were designed to complement each other and Telford acted as engineer to both projects. It was decided to construct new roads on the basis that half the finance would be provided by the government and half by local landowners. The work went ahead rapidly. Groups of landowners would petition for a road in their district and were often able to provide their share of the costs by means of loans. Telford employed different contractors to build the roads using mainly local labour but keeping a watchful eye on the overall design and standards of construction. His carefully constructed roads were a considerable improvement on the earlier military roads and were far better graded. While Wade and Caulfeild had tolerated gradients of up to 1 in 6, Telford's maximum in most circumstances was only 1 in 30.

The greater part of the military road network had been built south of the Great Glen. Although Telford's contractors upgraded and realigned many existing roads in this area their greatest achievement was to build a network of new roads in the more remote north-west Highlands beyond the Great Glen, and also on some of the larger islands such as Skye, Islay and Arran. Between 1803 and 1828 around 1,480km (920 miles) of new roads were laid and over 1,117 bridges built. Southey's pun about Telford being the 'Colossus of Roads' was appropriate! It is a tribute to Telford's engineering skills that most of this mileage is still in use as modern motor roads so that it is difficult to find stretches of his roads in anything like their original condition. Hence it is the bridges which remain as his most tangible monument. Among his most impressive achievements are the bridge over the Tay at Dunkeld completed in 1809. It has seven arches with a tollhouse at one end and another chamber, formerly used as the local prison, at the other! At Craigellachie on the Spey he built the earliest surviving iron bridge in Scotland in 1815. It has a single wide arch with crenellated turrets on the abutments and was high enough to survive the great Spey floods of 1829. The rapid influx of tourists into the more distant parts of the Highlands in the early nineteenth century, using Telford's new network of roads, is an indication of how effectively he opened up this once remote area.

Canals and wagonways

Although Scotland shared in the enthusiasm for canals which swept England during the later eighteenth century, comparatively few were built. The reasons were largely topographical. Scotland was a smaller country than England, deeply indented by the sea and with rugged relief inland which made canal construction difficult. Most major towns and industrial centres were on or close to the coast. While the agriculture of some rural areas such as the Berwickshire Merse would undoubtedly have benefited from access to a canal there was insufficient profit in building canals purely to serve farmers. There was not the scope for laying out an integrated network of canals in the way that was done through the English lowlands. The canals which were built in Scotland in the eighteenth and early nineteenth centuries were mainly short through routes crossing peninsulas or serving as feeders into the main estuaries.

The earliest Scottish canal scheme, an ambitious one for its day, was for a link between the Forth and Clyde estuaries. In the 1760s Glasgow still lacked direct access to the sea for vessels of any size and her merchants had considerable trade with the Baltic and other European countries. Much of this was undertaken through the port of Bo'ness on the Firth of Forth but overland carriage to Glasgow was difficult and expensive. In 1762 Lord Napier undertook a private survey to determine the feasibility of a canal linking the two estuaries. Results were encouraging and the engineer John Smeaton was called in. Starting from near the mouth of the River Carron on the east his projected canal followed the low, marshy valleys of the Bonny Water and the River Kelvin to reach the Clyde at Yoker, downstream of Glasgow. His plan was for a waterway deep enough to take sea-going vessels. Glasgow merchants, fearing that their trade would be hit if the canal bypassed the city in this way, retaliated with a counter-proposal for a smaller barge canal coming right into the city. In the end a compromise was reached in which Smeaton's original plan was adopted with an additional branch from the main canal to the outskirts of Glasgow.

Parliamentary approval for the scheme was given in 1768 and work began immediately. By 1775 the canal had been completed from the Forth to Stockingfield, 3 miles north of Glasgow. The costs of construction had greatly exceeded estimates and work stopped when finance ran out. The last section to the Clyde was expensive, requiring eighteen locks, and was only completed in 1790, twenty-two years after work had begun, with the aid of a large government loan.

The Forth and Clyde canal never succeeded as a ship canal due to changes in patterns of commerce as Glasgow's merchants became heavily involved with transatlantic trade, and as the size of vessels increased. However, as a more conventional canal, serving local needs by transporting grain, coal and other commodities, it was more useful. In the early 1960s it was finally closed to traffic but although sections of it have been filled in, several lengths are still walkable. Particularly interesting is the canal basin at Port Dundas in Glasgow where the branch from the Forth and Clyde canal connected with the Monklands canal. The early nineteenth-century custom house and a series of bonded warehouses which were originally a distillery, grain mills and a sugar refinery have been preserved.

The Monkland Canal was conceived in 1769 as a means of improving transport between Glasgow and the north Lanarkshire coalfields. The price of coal in Glasgow was increased considerably by the high cost of overland carriage and it was hoped that a canal might ease the city's fuel supply problems in the way that the Sankey Navigation had already done for Liverpool. James Watt surveyed the route and provided estimates for a shallow barge canal to the outskirts of Glasgow with a tramway from there into the city centre. Work began the following year but in 1773 construction was halted. As with the Forth and Clyde Canal, expenditure had greatly exceeded original estimates and the subscribed capital for the company had been exhausted. Economic conditions were unfavourable for the raising of new finance for several years and it was not until 1781 that the company was reconstituted and work continued. The revised plan for a link-up with the Forth and Clyde canal involved an expensive set of locks at Blackhill, where there was a rise of 29m (96ft). The full canal was not opened until 1792. Although only 20km (12 miles) long, and despite its early financial problems, the Monkland canal was the most successful and profitable Scottish canal. Even so, it was built in advance of real need. Glasgow's demand for fuel did not increase as quickly as expected and it was only from the 1820s, when a series of branches were built from the canal to nearby ironworks, that its full potential was realised. The canal was finally closed in the 1950s and large sections of it were filled in. Today its line into Glasgow is followed by a totally different transport system, a motorway.

The last canal in west-central Scotland that was planned in the late eighteenth century ran from Glasgow to Paisley and Johnstone. It was first proposed in the early 1790s when the Earl of Eglinton was planning a large harbour at Ardrossan on the Firth of Clyde coast. At this time the Clyde had not been fully deepened to Glasgow and it was thought that a canal from Glasgow, passing through the major textile centre of Paisley, and following the valley between Lochwinnoch and Kilbirnie, would allow Ardrossan to develop as Glasgow's major outport on the Atlantic, a second Liverpool. The act approving the canal was not passed until 1805, by which time inflation caused by the Napoleonic Wars was running at a high level. Funds ran out when only a few miles of the canal had been constructed from Glasgow to Johnstone. All efforts to obtain finance from the government to finish the scheme failed. The canal proved useful for bringing cotton to Paisley's textile mills and for a time a successful passenger service operated on it but virtually all of it was filled in during the later nineteenth century.

The Highlands, with their rugged topography, might seem an unlikely place for canal building but two major links planned at the end of the eighteenth century are still in use: the Crinan and Caledonian Canals. The Crinan Canal was designed to improve communications between the Clyde and the Minch for fishing vessels and coasters by cutting out the long and dangerous passage around the Mull of Kintyre. A survey of various short cuts across the narrow Kintyre peninsula was made by James Watt in 1771 but nothing further was done until 1792 when John Rennie made a further survey and opted for a route between Crinan and Ardrishaig.

Work began in 1794 but the link was not completed until 1809. Looking at a small-scale map it might seem that the canal would have been an easy undertaking. In fact it proved more difficult to construct than had been anticipated. As the canal was designed to accommodate sea-going vessels a minimum depth of 3.6m (12ft) was planned. Because of the shallowness of the sea lochs at either end of the isthmus the canal had to be prolonged for 3 kilometres in each direction to reach deeper water. The central section of the canal rose to 19m (63ft), and had to be cut through very resistant rock in order to avoid a deep, unstable bog. Even after it had been opened the canal suffered from construction problems; shoddily built locks collapsed and one entire section of canal was washed away in a flood. Costs greatly exceeded original estimates, much of the extra finance being provided by the government. The Crinan Canal is still open today although it is used largely by pleasure boats. The towpath provides an attractive and interesting walk of 14.5km between the two small basins at either end.

The idea of a canal down the Great Glen between Inverness and Fort William had been mooted early in the eighteenth century and more serious surveys were undertaken in the 1770s and 1780s. Much of the Great Glen was occupied by a series of deep lochs – Loch Ness, Loch Lochy and Loch Oich – so that only relatively short sections of canal would be required to link them. The advantages of such a link were that fishing vessels and coasters could make an easier passage from the North Sea to the Minch, avoiding the often perilous voyage around the north of Scotland through the Pentland Firth. The canal would also provide a good deal of temporary employment and, when finished, might encourage the development of local industries. A more pressing consideration, in the middle of the Napoleonic Wars, was its possible strategic advantages in allowing the quick passage of warships between the east and west coasts of Scotland.

Thomas Telford was appointed as engineer and work began in 1804. Telford designed a canal 6m (20ft) deep with locks large enough to take a 32-gun frigate, the largest locks which had yet been built on a canal. The depth was later reduced to 3.6m (12ft) due to technical difficulties. Despite this reduction the canal could still accommodate vessels twice the size of those using the Crinan Canal. The scale of the enterprise was immense compared to most previous British canal projects. A number of locks were needed, most impressive being the flight of eight at Banavie known as 'Neptune's Staircase'. An aqueduct had to be built to carry the canal over the River Loy and elsewhere earthworks on a massive scale were needed. Rising costs of labour and materials during wartime added to the usual financial difficulties of canal construction and the Caledonian Canal was not completed until 1822. The canal still functions today, but mainly for pleasure craft.

Other canals have left fewer traces in the landscape but their remains can nevertheless be fascinating to search for. An example is the Aberdeenshire canal. It was first planned in 1793; construction began in 1799 and was completed in 1805. It ran from Aberdeen harbour up the valley of the River Don to Inverurie. The canal was built to allow the export of agricultural produce and stone and the import of coal and lime. Although it never made a great profit it was successful in a modest way. It was closed in the 1850s and the greater part of its length has been filled in. There are few traces of it in the vicinity of Aberdeen itself. Part of its course through the city has been reused as a railway line; the railway company had to deepen the canal to provide enough headroom for engines to pass under the original canal bridges and they had problems in smoothing out the gradients at the sites of former locks. A number of canal distance markers have survived: they can be distinguished from roadside ones because they were placed every half mile instead of every mile. Further up the Don valley, through more open country, the line of the canal can be followed in many places as a depression. At Blackburn (NJ 8832153) a former aqueduct has been converted into a road bridge. The last half mile of the canal near Inverurie still has water in it although it has been converted into a lade supplying a paper-mill.

The development of railways lies outside our period but it is worth mentioning that some short wagonways were built in Scotland during the eighteenth century, mostly between collieries and nearby harbours. The earliest was constructed in 1722 from pits at Tranent to the sea at Cockenzie. It had wooden rails and a gauge of 1m (3.3ft). The loaded wagons ran downhill under gravity and the empty ones were hauled back by horses. The line of the wagonway ran just west of the centre of Tranent and can still be followed running northwards down a deep gully known as the Heugh which opens out on to more level ground near the old parish church of Tranent. Other wagonways were built from collieries to the

Clyde in the 1750s and in 1768 one was laid out near Alloa. These lines were all short and were designed solely for moving coal. However, in 1810 the Kilmarnock and Troon Railway was opened, running for nearly 16km (10 miles) and designed to carry passengers as well as coal. This was the first step in the transition from wagonway to true railway and one of its original bridges over the River Irvine can still be seen.

Harbours

In a country where topography was rugged and there were few navigable rivers coastal shipping was of vital importance. In the sixteenth and seventeenth centuries most of the major towns were coastal or, like Perth and Dumfries, on tidal stretches of rivers. The proliferation of small burghs, particularly between the Tay and Forth estuaries, all engaging in trade as well as fishing, created a large number of harbours. In the nineteenth century some of these were developed into major ports with wet dock systems while many others were extended and rebuilt, but Scotland's coastline is still dotted with small simple harbours.

Until the later sixteenth century few burghs had real harbour works. Vessels were berthed in rocky creeks or grounded on sand and mud in shallow estuaries. Beaches might be cleared of rocks and some outcrops levelled or trimmed to facilitate access but otherwise they remained completely natural. Many harbours remained like this throughout our period. Around the Solway Firth, relatively sheltered from severe gales, most small ports had no artificial harbour works at all or only a quayed wharf. On the more exposed North Sea coast artificial protection began to be provided at one or two sites such as Arbroath from the late fourteenth century, but more frequently in the sixteenth century as the volume of trade increased. Even here many small havens and fishing communities continued to use open beaches or unimproved creeks until the nineteenth century.

At Tantallon in East Lothian, immediately below the cliffs on which the formidable medieval castle stands, is a small creek with traces of a landing place which may have served a small fishing community as well as the castle itself. Below the west corner of the castle bailey an area of flat rocks is pitted with depressions which appear to have been post holes supporting a timber landing stage. Beside the post holes a channel in the rocks up to 10m (33ft) wide seems to have been deliberately cleared of boulders to provide an anchorage for small vessels. The date of this landing place is uncertain but it was probably contemporary with the period during which the castle was in use – from the fourteenth to the seventeenth centuries.

A few miles to the east Aberlady Bay illustrates another early type of harbour. Here the Peffer Burn flows into a large bay backed by sand

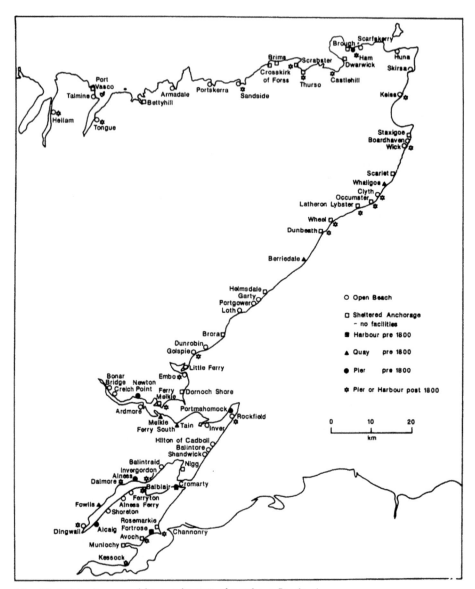

Map 17 Old harbours and havens in part of northern Scotland.

Figure 40 The harbour at Annan, a good example of a quayed river mouth, was an active port in the sixteenth, seventeenth and eighteenth centuries.

dunes and filled with mudflats. Aberlady was the official port for the inland burgh of Haddington and, latterly, a burgh of barony in its own right. Yet there are no indications that there were ever any harbour works here. Vessels were merely beached in the estuary.

It is impossible to establish an exact chronological sequence of harbour development in Scotland as different harbours were developed at different times and in different ways depending on the characteristics of their sites. Some very simple, crudely built harbours continued to be constructed into the nineteenth century, but a general evolution from simple to more sophisticated forms of protection can be traced. Many early harbours were merely quays at tidal river mouths. Major ports like Inverness, Leith and Perth originated in this way. Several of them, including Dumfries and Annan, were originally established to serve early castles around which towns subsequently developed. At Dumfries there are quays close to the town but difficulties of navigation led to the development of quays further downstream at Kingholm and Glencaple in the mid-eighteenth century.

Cramond is a good example of a quayed river mouth which has not been greatly developed. The Romans originally used the mouth of the River Almond and may even have built harbour works but the present quay dates from the eighteenth century when the shallow river mouth was a thriving little port serving a series of water-powered iron forges upstream. The picturesque cottages which line the quay and which have been attractively restored were occupied not by fishermen but by workers in the iron mills. Today the river mouth has silted up and is only occupied by pleasure craft.

On rocky coastlines such as those of Berwickshire, Buchan and Caithness harbours of refuge were built to shelter passing vessels during bad weather. Eyemouth, Fraserburgh and Peterhead originated in this way. On rugged coasts like these the local inhabitants often went to great lengths to create harbours in unlikely locations. One of the most spectacular examples is Whaligoe in Caithness (ND 321402). Here a narrow creek at the base of the cliffs is reached by a flight of 330 steps cut into the cliffs. The steps descend from a fish-curing station on the clifftops with some wider resting places to break the ascent or descent. The harbour dates from the mid-eighteenth century and has a simple quay against which fishing boats were moored. The fishermen's wives carried the fish in creels up the steps to the curing plant. On the Berwickshire coast, Cove harbour (NT 780718) has a similar character on a more developed scale. The village stands on the clifftops and a steep, narrow road winds down the cliff face to the harbour. The last stretch is a tunnel cut through a rocky headland. The harbour works date from as late as the 1830s after two previous attempts to build piers were given up when they were destroyed by the sea.

The construction of breakwaters was a feature of many east-coast burghs in the later sixteenth and seventeenth centuries. Early examples can be seen at St Andrews and Dunbar. Massive and crude in their construction, with outer parapets and inner quays, they were often built across the mouths of rocky bays to create a sheltered tidal harbour, sometimes with a smaller, less massive pier to enclose the bay completely. They sometimes took advantage of existing rocky promontories and occasionally an off-shore reef might have a detached breakwater built on it to shelter a stretch of water inshore, as at Limekilns and Torry in Fife. Sometimes the shore at the head of the bay was left undeveloped but more frequently a quay was built. On a completely open shore protection could be achieved by constructing two piers with curving ends. The first harbour at Newhaven was built in this way.

A more complex harbour was one which incorporated a stilling basin. Here two piers were built with a sloping ramp or stretch of foreshore between them to reduce the energy of waves, giving a calm entrance to the main harbour which was entered at right angles. Keiss, in Caithness (ND 351609), although dating from the early nineteenth century, is a good example but the older harbours at Anstruther and Dunbar have been constructed on the same principle.

Many early harbours were financed by royal burghs but sometimes landowners provided the revenue to develop a new port. Fraserburgh was founded by Sir Alexander Fraser of Philorth in the late sixteenth century. Other fishing and trading harbours were founded by landowners at a later date; Portsoy, established by Sir Patrick Ogilvie of Boyne in 1701, is one. In the later eighteenth century many new harbours were built by landowners who were interested in promoting the fishing industry or creating an export outlet for the produce of their estates. The harbour at Charlestown in Fife was built to allow the export of lime from a nearby battery of limekilns. Macduff, Rosehearty and Portgordon were all founded by major north-east landowners in the late eighteenth century.

Smuggling was an active pursuit on many stretches of Scotland's coasts during the eighteenth century. The Solway was especially notorious because of its easy access to the Isle of Man, which was not fully incorporated into the United Kingdom for customs purposes until 1876. At Balcary Bay, a sheltered anchorage used by smugglers, there are no harbour works but the nucleus of Balcary House is an eighteenth-century building with vaulted cellars that were used for storing contraband by a well-organised company of smugglers. Gunsgreen House, overlooking the Berwickshire port of Eyemouth, has a similar tradition. Berwickshire, with its many remote rocky coves, was a notorious haunt of smugglers. At Redheugh (NT 825695), is a small natural harbour, difficult of access from above, which provided a secluded spot for landing goods. You can still see the iron staples fixed into the rocks where boats were moored. Smuggling ceased in the 1820s with the establishment of a coastguard station on the cliffs above. The ruins of this are still visible as is the coastguards' boathouse beside the shore.

In addition to breakwaters and piers, many habours preserve warehouses and other buildings which are a reminder of their past activities. Quayside granaries, some of which have been converted to modern housing, can be seen at Dunbar and North Berwick. They probably date from the eighteenth century. Some older examples can be seen in Shetland where the Hanseatic trade was important in the fifteenth and sixteenth centuries. Hanseatic merchants came to Shetland for a summer's trading, buying local fish and wool and selling cloth. They rented warehouses or booths from which to operate. At Symbister on the island of Whalsay the Bremen Bod is an early example of one of these. It is a small stone building at the end of a jetty which has now been restored as a visitor centre. It has an outside forestair leading to the first-floor living quarters; the ground floor provided storage space. It may date from the sixteenth century and there are other old storehouses nearby. The Bod of Grimista near Lerwick is another example of uncertain date. Ice houses are also found at many east-coast harbours from the Tay to Sutherland where salmon fishing was important. In 1765 a Perth merchant discovered that salmon packed in ice and transported by fast sailing vessels could be sold fresh in London, and a new industry developed. The ice was collected in shallow ponds during the winter and stored in stone and brick vaulted buildings which were sunk into a hillside or roofed with turf for insulation.

The ice was finely crushed and packed in tightly using a door in the roof. The largest set of ice houses is at Spey Bay where three brick-vaulted ones stand side by side.

In the later seventeenth and early eighteenth centuries Glasgow was the most dynamic of Scotland's larger towns, growing rapidly with the development of transatlantic trade. The only problem was that Glasgow was virtually an inland town with the nearest navigable water for sizeable vessels being 24km (15 miles) downriver. The Clyde near Glasgow Bridge was a mere 0.4m (15in) deep at low water in places and only small boats could berth there. The city's merchants established Port Glasgow as an outport but the settlement was hemmed in by steep slopes, limiting scope for development. The nearby baronial burgh of Greenock had a more open site and was promoted vigorously by its proprietors, but the disadvantage of having to offload all cargo into shallow lighters for the journey upriver to Glasgow still remained.

In 1755 John Smeaton was commissioned to examine the river and see whether any improvement in navigation could be made but nothing was done until 1768 when an engineer called John Golborne was employed. He proposed the construction of a series of jetties to narrow the channel of the Clyde, so that the scouring action of the river would deepen the channel. This simple and comparatively cheap solution worked well and gave a depth of water of between 1.8 and 2.7m (6–9ft) at the Broomilaw quay in Glasgow. In 1773 Golborne got a new contract to try to deepen the lower stretches of the river. At Dumbuck ford where the river had only been knee deep at low water his dredging operations, assisted by tidal scour, created a channel with a minimum depth of 4.2m (14ft). Further improvements were necessary during the nineteenth century to allow the largest sea-going vessels to reach Glasgow and turn it into a major world port but by the end of the eighteenth century the deepening of the Clyde had already transformed Glasgow's position and set it on a course of development that would one day make it the 'second city' of the British Empire.

Scotland's rugged coastline has always presented dangers to shipping so it is not surprising that the provision of navigational aids should have been considered at quite an early date. Scotland's earliest surviving lighthouse is on the Isle of May in the entrance to the Firth of Forth. It was built in 1636, a simple tower on top of which a large coal fire was lit to warn shipping. The beacon consumed some 400 tons of coal a year, using up to 3 tons on long, windy nights. At Southerness at the mouth of the Nith (NX 977542), Dumfries town council financed the building of a beacon tower in 1748 to guide shipping into the estuary. The tower was heightened later in the eighteenth century and again in the nineteenth century when it was converted to a modern lighthouse. Another eighteenth-century

Figure 41 The lighthouse at Southerness, built in 1748 by Dumfries town council to improve access to the port, was one of the first Scottish lighthouses.

lighthouse stands on Little Cumbrae in the Firth of Clyde. The circular tower and keepers' cottages have been restored in modern times.

In 1786 the Northern Lighthouse Trust was set up to establish lighthouses on a more regular basis. Their first four towers were on Eilean Glas in Harris, the Mull of Kintyre, Kinnaird Head in Aberdeenshire and North Ronaldsay in Orkney. The one on Kinnaird Head, still in use, is the most distinctive; it is simply a sixteenth-century tower house which belonged to the Lairds of Philorth with a light-tower built on top. It retains its original machiolated parapet and still looks like a castle despite its whitewashed exterior. On Dennis Head, North Ronaldsay, the circular tower of the old lighthouse still stands intact with the ruins of the lighthouse keepers' cottages beside it. Originally, like other eighteenth-century lighthouses, the tower held a battery of whale-oil lamps each with its own reflector. At a later date it was converted into a daytime marker with a large stone ball on top. It was replaced in the mid-nineteenth century by a more modern lighthouse nearby, the tallest land-based lighthouse in Scotland. Thomas Smith, who designed these first lighthouses for the Northern Lighthouse Trust, took his stepson, Robert Stevenson into partnership. Throughout the nineteenth century and into the twentieth the Stevenson family have designed and built dozens of lighthouses around the coasts of Scotland.

As we have seen, the nature of agriculture in Scotland was transformed by the improvement of existing systems of transport and the introduction of new ones. However, the impact of developments in transport was probably felt most dramatically in industry. As the end of our period witnessed the movement of the Scottish economy into the first phases of the Industrial Revolution it is appropriate to conclude our survey of the changing Scottish landscape between 1500 and 1800 with a review of the contribution of different industries to changes in the countryside.

9

Industry in the landscape

In 1500, 1600, and indeed in 1700, Scotland had a limited range of industries operating on a modest scale and producing only a small effect on the landscape in most areas. Some activities, such as spinning and weaving woollen and linen yarn, required the simplest equipment and were almost ubiquitous at a domestic level. Others, such as grain milling and the fulling of cloth, required more investment in fixed plant but were still widely distributed because of the universal demand for their products, the small scale of their operation, and because the water and sometimes wind power which they used was universally available. Some industries like coal mining, iron smelting and salt making, were concentrated in specific areas because the resources they exploited, or the fuel supply they needed, were more limited in their occurrence. Most manufacturing operated at the scale of the individual household or small workshop. The quality of many home-produced articles, notably linen and woollens, was poor due to the lack of basic skills and lack of demand. In general Scotland exported unprocessed primary products and low-quality manufactures, importing most of the higher-quality products which her wealthier inhabitants required.

Nevertheless, the Scottish economy was far from being purely agricultural. Several industrial products, notably linen, woollens, coal, salt and lead ore, were among her most valuable exports. There were some significant technological advances in the seventeenth century, notably in mining, but it was not until the eighteenth century that the pace of industrial change began to accelerate markedly. Access to England and English colonial markets following the Union of 1707, as well as a growing population and rising standards of living at home, increased the demand for industrial products. There was a substantial growth in the scale of production in many industries, often linked to developments in technology. For example a sixteenth-century bloomery forge might produce a few stones of iron a year, an early eighteenth-century charcoal blast furnace around 700 tons, and by the end of the eighteenth century a fully integrated ironworks might produce 7,000 tons.

The last two decades of the eighteenth century witnessed more change in the nature, scale and location of industries in Scotland than the previous two centuries. There was also the development of a new power source – steam. The first primitive Newcomen steam engine was installed in a Scottish colliery around 1719 but there was only a handful of these machines in Scotland during the first half of the eighteenth century. Although the number of steam engines in Scotland increased greatly in the later eighteenth century and they were applied to an ever-widening range of uses, water was still the principal power source for large-scale industry at the turn of the nineteenth century. By 1800 Scotland was only on the threshold of the Industrial Revolution but already many of its classic features were evident; the increase in the scale of production, the size of the units involved, and the concentration of population in rapidly growing towns.

Inevitably it is the industrial legacy from the later eighteenth century which is most prominent in the Scottish landscape today. Even this is fragmentary as so much has been obliterated by later, larger-scale industrial activity. In addition many important monuments, such as the early textile mills at Catrine and Deanston, have been demolished in recent years. Nevertheless, some early industrial sites like the cotton mill at Spinningdale in Sutherland survive, albeit derelict. Others, like Bonawe furnace, have been carefully restored and are open to the public. Some industries have left more evidence in the landscape than others. The mining of lead and copper was often undertaken in remote upland areas where their remains have been little disturbed. By contrast the early small-scale workings for coal in more densely populated lowland areas have mostly been obliterated by later mining operations. The visible remains of some industries are harder to interpret and date than others especially as documentation before the eighteenth century is often sparse. This is particularly the case with activities like quarrying which were often undertaken intermittently over very long time periods. Partly because of these difficulties the legacy of early industrial activity in Scotland's landscape has been neglected and there is much scope for fieldwork, especially in tracing the history of water power sites. This chapter reviews the impact on the landscape of a number of Scotland's most significant industries from the sixteenth to the end of the eighteenth centuries. Each industry is considered separately but it should be remembered that in their day they were often closely linked.

Coal mining

In Scotland coal occurs among the strata of the carboniferous period in a diagonal belt across the Midland Valley from Ayrshire and north Lanarkshire to the Lothians and Fife. Smaller outcrops around Sanquhar in Nithsdale, Canonbie in Dumfriesshire, Campbeltown in Argyll and Brora in Sutherland have also been worked. Coal was mined from medieval times where it outcropped at the surface, particularly along the coast. The monks of Newbattle Abbey are recorded as among the earliest miners in the twelfth century. Where coal outcropped at the surface it was extracted by simple opencast techniques. Where the seams lay a short distance below ground, bell pits were used. Coal was removed by sinking a shallow shaft from the surface and then excavating the coal for short distances around the base of the shaft, producing a bell-shaped cross-section. When sufficient coal had been removed to make extensive timbering necessary, or when drainage problems developed, the pit was abandoned and another one sunk.

Remains of these early workings are hard to date, for in some areas the use of primitive bell pits continued into the eighteenth century. They sometimes appear today as slight hollows. Examples can be seen in the fields around Ormiston and Tranent in East Lothian. The best example, at Birsley Brae (NT 393729) near Tranent, has been preserved as an historical monument. Where the topography of a coalfield area was varied, extensive underground workings could be opened by cutting horizontal levels known graphically as 'in-gaun e'en' (in-going eyes). These shallow drift workings were sometimes provided with ventilating or winding shafts, but were quickly abandoned whenever drainage difficulties were encountered. In some areas such simple mining technology sufficed well into the nineteenth century for it could be afforded by landowners who did not have a lot of capital. This type of mine was characteristic of outlying coal-producing areas like Canonbie where the coal was worked mainly to provide fuel for local limekilns.

By the early seventeenth century improved mining and drainage technology from England and Flanders was being applied at some collieries, allowing deeper seams to be worked. The most famous example was Sir George Bruce of Carnock's mine at Culross in Fife, which was one of the wonders of its day. Before Bruce took over the colliery in 1575 it had been worked to a shallow depth by Cistercian monks and then abandoned due to drainage difficulties. Traces of Bruce's original shaft at the Castlehill pit can still be seen north of Blairburn at the west end of Culross. The workings were extended further and further under the Firth of Forth. Problems of seepage of water into the workings and especially of ventilation were tackled by sinking the Moat Pit, a shaft from an artificial island situated at the lowest part of the foreshore. At high tide the top of the shaft was surrounded by water, allowing coal to be brought up the shaft and loaded straight on to vessels by means of a pier. Unfortunately a storm in 1625 submerged the island and flooded the pit, so it was abandoned and mining activities were transferred to the east end of Culross. Bruce's artificial island is still visible at low tide as a small mound. The Moat Pit was an advanced idea for its time but other mines along the Fife coast also extended out under the estuary.

In order to work deeper seams it was necessary to install more effective drainage systems. In some coalfields, notably the Lothians, this was done by cutting long drainage levels which emerged at low points on the surface and drained the seams above. One level cut from mines at Duddingston near Edinburgh during the mid-eighteenth century ran for 4.8km (3 miles) to sea level at the Firth of Forth. A number of very long levels were driven in the Fife coalfield where deeply cut valleys or 'dens' emerging at the coast provided suitable outlets. At least twenty-seven major schemes are recorded in this area, mostly dating from the eighteenth century. One of the longest, the Fordel Level (NT 148852), driven around 1750, was 8.7km (5.5 miles) long while the Pitfirrane Level (NT 068857), constructed in 1773, was 6.8km (4.2 miles) in length.

In the Fife coalfield and around Alloa the accent was also upon mechanical aids for drainage. Horse gins, water-wheels and windmills were used. By the end of the sixteenth century elaborate systems of reservoirs, dams and lades had been built in the vicinity of some Fife pits to provide sufficient water for keeping water-wheels pumping continuously. Waterwheels could raise water from a depth of around 30 fathoms and this was adequate for many mines, particularly if water was raised to an underground drainage level rather than all the way to the surface.

Even in the eighteenth century Scottish mines were not as deep as many English ones. As a consequence steam engines were slow to be adopted for mine drainage. Only four Newcomen engines are known to have been in use at Scottish collieries in the 1730s, only six or seven by 1760. The ruins of the engine house of one of these can still be seen near Saltcoats (NS 257414). At Thornton near Markinch (NT 292973) there is a remarkable set of late eighteenth-century colliery buildings, including the engine house, now converted into a farmstead. Old shafts and other colliery workings from before the nineteenth century can still be seen in Fife, the Lothians and other areas but unless detailed plans are available dating them even approximately can be difficult. Old Scottish coal mines used the 'pillar and stall' system of extraction whereby pillars of rock were left at regular intervals to support the roof and the workings took on a honeycomb pattern. This system can sometimes be seen in old mines like ones at Hill of Airth (NS 893876) which were discovered some years ago. Such workings are highly dangerous, and should not be entered! Pillar and stall extraction was replaced during the eighteenth century by the more efficient system of 'longwall' working in which the unwanted rubbish was piled up behind the working face to support the roof.

From the 1760s the whole scale and character of mining was transformed. Steam engines were used much more widely for pumping and for winding coal to the surface. In 1769 there were only 14 or 15 colliery steam engines in Scotland; by the 1790s there were around 70. Underground haulage was improved and surface transport revolutionised by the construction of wagonways, canals and turnpikes. These changes were a response to a rapidly growing home market for coal. Coke-smelting ironworks were using nearly 250,000 tons of coal a year by the end of the eighteenth century while lime burning, distilling, glass and chemical manufacture were also substantial consumers. Demand for coal for domestic use was growing too: the inhabitants of Edinburgh burnt over 200,000 tons of coal a year and those of Glasgow a comparable amount. Coal production increased overall by around four times during the eighteenth century but the output from the Lanarkshire and Ayrshire coalfields grew much faster.

Salt making

Alongside the expansion of coal mining went the growth of the salt industry. Coal and salt production were frequently combined during the seventeenth and eighteenth centuries. In the sixteenth century Scotland had imported much French salt but the dislocation of this trade during the later part of the century stimulated production at home, while exports to Holland and the Baltic also increased. Much of the better quality or 'great' coal mined along the coast was shipped to the burghs or exported; the dross, appropriately known as 'panwood', was used to evaporate sea water in large iron pans to produce sea salt. Although Scottish salt was not as good a preservative as mined rock salt or Biscay sea salt a considerable export trade developed.

Salt making was widespread around the coasts of the Lothians and Fife giving rise to communities whose names often reflected their activities. Bonhardpans, Grangepans and Kennetpans can still be found on the map with some searching but the largest centres were Bo'ness, Kirkcaldy and Prestonpans. Salt was being made at Saltpreston (the old name for Prestonpans) as early as 1189 but it was only with the expansion of coal mining in the late sixteenth and early seventeenth centuries that the industry grew. By the 1570s there were 38 salt pans at Prestonpans and 23 at Kirkcaldy while Sir William Brereton, visiting the area in the 1635, described the salt pans around the Forth as 'innumerable'. The pans were simply huge shallow iron dishes up to 5.4m (18ft) feet long and 3m (10ft) wide but only 2 feet deep. At high tide the seawater was collected into shallow ponds. Natural evaporation in these made the liquid more saline and it was then transferred to the pans by buckets or, at a later date, mechanical pumps.

By the end of the seventeenth century, it has been estimated, the salt pans around the Forth were consuming around 150,000 tons of coal each year. Overseas markets failed in the late seventeenth century and it was once believed that the Scottish salt industry went into a steep decline after the Union of 1707. However, recent research has established that home demand increased to balance the drop in exports. Salt production was sustained, and even expanded, for much of the eighteenth century and most of the surviving remains of saltworks date from this period. For most of the eighteenth century around 90 per cent of Scotland's production came from the Firth of Forth. Dumfries and Galloway produced small quantities from scattered single pans which burnt peat and which were only operated on a part-time basis. From 1793 with the relaxation of duties on the coastal shipment of coal, new saltworks were established north of the Tay.

Scottish salt making declined in the nineteenth century with growing competition from Cheshire rock salt. Although the industry continued in a small way at Prestonpans until 1959 there is little visible evidence of the industry in this area. Salt was a taxable commodity and so had to be carefully stored and supervised. A warehouse near Cockenzie House may originally have been a salt girnel and another example can be seen near Dunbar harbour. At St Monans (NO 534019) you can see the tower of a windmill which was used for pumping seawater up to a battery of nine pans; a trench cut in the rocks of the foreshore brought seawater to the pumps. On Arran a small rubble building with a bowed end (NS 107633) is part of an eighteenth-century saltworks. A similar building with a chimney at one end stands at Ascog on the island of Bute (NS 107633) but seemingly this saltworks was never actually operational. At Fishertown of Usan on the Angus coast (NO 726545) the remains of a saltworks dating from c. 1783 can be seen. The surviving building was later converted into an ice house. Adjacent to it is a channel cut in the rocks with grooves showing where a sluice gate was once fitted. This allowed seawater to be lifted into a shallow rock pool for preliminary evaporation.

Iron smelting

Before the mid-eighteenth century the Scottish iron industry was hampered by a lack of suitable raw materials and fuel. High-grade haematite ores occurred in only a few localities and although the clayband ores of the carboniferous strata were used in the early seventeenth century the richer blackband ironstone seams of the coalfields were not exploited until much later. As the Lowlands had been largely denuded of trees, charcoal for smelting iron ore was in short supply. In the Highlands, however, there was still plenty of timber. Bog ore was smelted there using primitive bloomery forges. Bloomery sites have been found from Kintyre to Sutherland and are probably far more widespread than has been realised. They have yet to be mapped systematically but in areas like the woods on the eastern side of Loch Lomond they are known to be numerous. Their small size and the indeterminate character of their remains makes them difficult to identify. Exacavated examples have consisted simply of small, shallow pits enclosed by stones which were then sealed with clay. In some cases a clay dome may also have been constructed over the top. Small blooms of iron were produced using hand-operated leather bellows. Heaps of slag close by are the most readily identifiable feature of such sites but even these are small and difficult to spot. Bloomery sites are hard to date and may range from the medieval period to the seventeenth century. For areas like Loch Lomondside where bloomery sites are common it is interesting to speculate on how many bloomeries may have been in use at any time and on their cumulative effect on the local woodlands.

The expansion of the charcoal iron industry in Scotland was hampered by a shortage of fuel and an official policy which attempted to protect surviving woodlands. A statute passed in 1609 forbade the setting up of 'yrne mylnes' in the Highlands to prevent the wholesale destruction of timber which it was thought would result from the development of the industry. Nevertheless, in the early seventeenth century, entrepreneurs from the Lowlands began to look to the Highlands as a possible area for establishing larger, charcoal-using blast furnaces. Sir George Hay was one of a group of 'Fife Adventurers' who made an abortive attempt to establish a Lowland colony on the island of Lewis in 1607. The scheme was frustrated by the hostility of the local chiefs but MacKenzie of Kintail appears to have arranged an exchange whereby Hay assigned to him all his rights in Lewis in return for a cash payment and access to the woods around Loch Maree in Wester Ross.

It is tempting to speculate that, on a visit to Lewis, Hay had seen a bloomery site operating beside Loch Maree – possibly the one whose remains can still be seen at Fasagh – and realised the potential of this region for iron smelting. By 1610 a blast furnace, the first in Scotland, was in operation. In a pattern which was to become a model for later industrial developments in the Highlands, skilled workers from north-west England were brought in to operate the plant and English capital may also have been used. Clayband ore from Fife was shipped to Poolewe and haematite from Cumbria was imported. The plant did not merely smelt iron: it seems to have cast guns as well; there are indications that some of the cannon at least were exported to Spain. It is not known how long the plant remained in operation but it appears to have been functioning in 1626. Later iron-making operations are recorded in this area but without any details of which sites were used.

Three sites around Loch Maree have been linked to Hay's operations; one is at Red Smiddy (NG 861798), at the north end of the loch only 1km (0.6 mile) from the sea. Another is at Letterewe (NG 958705) half-way down the eastern side of the loch. The third is Fasagh at the north end of Loch Maree (NH 011654). The sites are only jumbled earthworks today and it is difficult to reconstruct their original layout and function. Recent limited excavations suggest that Fasagh was only a bloomery site, albeit a large one. At Red Smiddy and Letterewe remains of blast furnaces have been uncovered. The one at Red Smiddy, squat and low, lined with imported sandstone, is certainly an early design and may have been Hay's original furnace. On a nearby terrace faint remains of the charcoal and ore sheds were found.

Hay's venture, surprisingly successful in its day, was ahead of its time. It was not until the early eighteenth century, when the Highlands were more settled and demand for iron throughout Britain was growing steadily, that further iron-making ventures were undertaken on any scale. English ironmasters began to take an interest in the Highlands as the charcoal iron industry in many parts of England had reached the limits of its fuel supply.

Some ventures were undoubtedly ill-judged failures. In 1727 the Cumbrian Backbarrow iron company set up an iron furnace at Invergarry in the Great Glen, leasing surrounding woodlands from MacDonnell of Glengarry. The company, though successful on its home territory, had little knowledge of conditions in the Highlands and chose a poor location for its ironworks. Ore had to be shipped to Fort William then transported 32km (20 miles) up the Great Glen by packhorse and boats. Workmen were brought from Lancashire and Yorkshire, and some of the materials for building and equipping the works also came from England. Production ceased in 1736 with only around 2,500 tons of iron having been smelted. The furnace appears to have been in blast only intermittently due to problems of raw material supply, the hostility of the local population, and possibly a period of drought which affected the water supply. The overgrown remains of the works can be seen beside the River Garry (NH 313010).

Three ironworks in the south-west Highlands had varying degrees of success and are interesting to visit. The most remote site is in Glen Kinglass (NN 082371), a valley which opens out into Loch Etive. It is the least well preserved of the three ironworks, largely because erosion by the river has removed the dam, lade, water-wheel pit, and tailrace but the blast furnace, built of granite boulders, still stands 4m (13ft) high. Excavations have shown that the charcoal and ore sheds were turf-walled structures supported on cruck frames. The ironworks was constructed by an Irish iron company in the early 1720s and used imported ore from England, but it remained in production only between 1725 and 1738. At

Furnace on Loch Fyne (NN 027001), a site also known as Goatfield, are the remains of the ironworks erected in 1755 by the Argyll Furnace Co., a partnership between the Duke of Argyll and a Lake District company. Beside the square blast furnace stands the one-storey casting house, and a charcoal shed survives nearby.

Most fascinating of all are the remains of the ironworks at Bonawe (NN 009318) beside Loch Etive. Restored by the Department of the Environment and open to visitors, they give a vivid impression of the nature and scale of what was, in its day, a large industrial undertaking. The ironworks was established in 1753 by a group of Lakeland ironmasters. By this period the charcoal iron industry in the Lake District had almost reached the limits of its local fuel supply. It was actually economic to ship high-grade haematite ore from Cumbria to the West Highlands, smelt it using local charcoal, and then ship the iron back to north-west England. This was cheaper than merely shipping to Cumbria the vast quantities of Highland charcoal that would have been needed for smelting the iron. The works at Bonawe are particularly interesting because so many of the ancillary buildings have survived. As well as the blast furnace itself you can inspect the charcoal and ore sheds, built into the slope like Lake District bank barns so that the unloading of raw materials and their transfer to the furnace could be done separately on different levels. There are also rows of workers' cottages and a mansion, Bonawe House (not open to the public), which was built for the manager of the ironworks. Bonawe was an English industrial complex transplanted into an alien setting. It even had its own church and school. Nevertheless, the enterprise was a successful one and the furnace operated until 1874, its machinery driven entirely by water power.

Output of iron from Bonawe and Furnace seems to have averaged around 700 tons a year in the later eighteenth century. This may not sound impressive compared with later coke-using ironworks like Carron, but the scale of production was far greater than the simple bloomery sites that preceded them. It has sometimes been suggested that these ironworks, few and scattered though they were, were major contributors to the defor- estation of the Highlands. However, detailed study of woodland manage- ment has shown that coppicing rather than clear felling was widely prac- tised, making the woodland a renewable resource. The coppice stools, mainly oak, if protected from grazing animals, would have produced a crop of new poles every 20 years or so. The blast furnace at Bonawe would have needed the charcoal produced from several hundred acres of coppice woodland a year or around 10,000 acres over a 20-year period, assuming this to be the length of coppice rotation which was used.

Surviving contracts show that the Bonawe works obtained charcoal from a wide area of the south-west Highlands from Kintyre in the south to Loch Eil and Ardnamurchan in the north. The furnace's ready access to coastal shipping allowed charcoal to be brought in from a wide area. The very fact that the furnace remained in operation over such a long period indicates that a regular fuel supply was available from woodlands which were managed as a renewable resource. In the glens immediately around the works, to the south of Loch Etive, where the forests were managed directly by the company, the area of woodland actually increased as a result of the demand for charcoal.

Charcoal-burning stances, or pitsteads, can be found in many parts of the West Highlands. Some are located in areas which still retain remnants of woodland. Others occur in locations which are devoid of trees today but must have been wooded in the eighteenth century. Characteristically these sites are circular platforms around 8m in diameter which have been formed by cutting into the hillside and spreading the waste downslope. The downslope edge of the platform is sometimes revetted with boulders, like the spectacular ones at the head of Loch Etive (NM 1044, 1045). Timber was stacked on the platforms in carefully constructed piles, then covered with earth or turf and set alight. The wood burned slowly for up to ten days and the charcoal was then extracted. Good examples can be seen in Glen Nant south of Bonawe but they occur on Mull and many parts of the adjacent mainland which are known to have supplied charcoal to the furnace at Bonawe. Their full distribution has yet to be studied and they may also occur further north in Torridon and around Loch Maree.

A radically new development in the history of Scottish ironmaking was the foundation of the Carron ironworks near Falkirk in 1759. The Carron company was one of many examples of English entrepreneurship married to Scottish business sense which characterise the early phases of the Industrial Revolution in Scotland. It was launched by a partnership of Samuel Garbett, a merchant and manufacturer from Birmingham, Dr John Roebuck, a chemist, and William Cadell, a merchant from Cockenzie. Roebuck and Garbett had already collaborated in establishing a chemical works to make sulphuric acid at Prestonpans and it was here that they met Cadell, who had interests in the iron and timber trades with the Baltic. The site at the mouth of the River Carron was chosen for its proximity to carboniferous ironstone from the Bo'ness area, an ore which had never previously been used for making iron. In addition the site had access to coal and water power, while its central location facilitated the marketing of its products. From the start Carron was conceived as an integrated operation on a scale hitherto rare in Britain. The company handled every part of the production process from mining the coal and iron ore to selling the finished goods. Although making a range of iron goods the plant specialised in the manufacture of guns. After an uncertain start due to difficulties in boring the cannon exactly, the firm enjoyed a period of great prosperity from the start of the American War in 1775.

The partners who set up the Carron Company made one miscalculation.

They had judged the River Carron to be adequate for their water-power requirements but the plant soon outgrew its water supply. Despite building a series of reservoirs, dams and lades the ironworks still did not have enough water for the eighteen water-wheels that drove the machinery by 1784. The development of the improved steam engine by James Watt (who was originally backed by Roebuck) came just in time to solve their problems. By the later eighteenth century the firm employed 1,600 workers and was producing 6,500 tons of iron a year; roughly ten times as much as the charcoal-fired blast furnaces. The sheer scale of the works turned it into a major attraction for visitors while contemporary prints show the extent to which the fires and smoke from the blast furnaces dominated the landscape of this part of the Forth Valley. By the end of the eighteenth century the Carron Ironworks consumed as much coal as the whole of Edinburgh. More than any development in mid-eighteenth-century Scotland Carron heralded the Industrial Revolution. Nothing remains today of the mid-eighteenth-century works; the oldest building is an engineering shop from the early nineteenth century. However, the lade which supplied water to the works can still be seen: 2.5km (1.6 miles) long, it is up to 9m (30ft) wide and downstream from the works it becomes a canal down which the factory's products were sent to the River Carron, which was itself straightened and canalised by the company, and the original port at Carronshore.

The Carron ironworks remained the only one of its kind in Scotland for many years. Only in the 1780s was a new group of plants established including the Clyde Ironworks near Glasgow, the Muirkirk Company in Ayrshire and the Omoa works at Cleland in Lanarkshire. As most of these sites continued to operate into the present century, remains from their early years are scanty and in some cases have been dismantled and removed in recent decades. The Carron company also had a number of subsidiary plants in which iron was forged into a wide range of articles. The remains of the Cramond Ironworks, on the River Almond just beyond the north-western outskirts of Edinburgh, are interesting to explore. The ruined buildings of some of the water-powered forges can still be seen as well as the manager's house; many of the cottages in the village of Cramond, from whose quays iron was imported and iron goods shipped out, were originally occupied by ironworkers.

The mining of non-ferrous metals

Although non-ferrous metals were mined and smelted in Scotland on a small scale in medieval times it was not until the sixteenth century that mining technology developed sufficiently for larger-scale exploitation to be possible. Gold was the metal which stimulated most excitement in the sixteenth century. The Scottish crown was perennially short of bullion and at times during the sixteenth century there was almost a prospecting fever in different parts of the Lowlands. The discovery of gold on Crawford Muir in upper Clydesdale was the most significant development. In the 1540s the Scottish coins known as Bonnet Pieces were made of gold from this area. Because of a lack of native skills in prospecting and mining the Scottish crown engaged various foreign experts including Dutch, German, French, Flemish and English miners to try their luck in the area.

The most famous prospector was an Englishman, Bevis Bulmer, who undertook the development of the gold workings on Crawford Muir during the 1590s. Most of the gold occurred in alluvial deposits rather than veins and Bulmer employed up to 300 men in summer washing the gravels of the streams to extract the particles of gold. One site he worked was at the head of the Longcleuch Burn (NS 912178). The remains of shallow excavations can be seen and the hillside above, Bulmer Moss, still bears the prospector's name. Nearby (NS 907164), more extensive opencast gold workings are visible. Substantial quantities of gold were produced from Crawford Muir: in one year gold valued at £100,000 sterling is said to have been recovered from the area.

Gold was also found elsewhere in the Borders, notably the streams draining to St Mary's Loch. One site was on the Glengaber Burn, a tributary of the Meggat Water. Along the narrow flats beside the stream (NT 214237) can be seen traces of hollows and channels by which water was diverted for washing the alluvium. The workings may date from the sixteenth century for the locality was mentioned in an early account of mining in Scotland. A deserted settlement on nearby Douglas Burn, also noted as a gold-bearing locality, may have been occupied by gold prospectors.

The most important lead-mining area throughout our period was the Leadhills–Wanlockhead district, straddling the watershed between Clydesdale and Nithsdale. The monks of Newbattle Abbey are the first recorded miners in 1239. Lead ore was extracted sporadically in the sixteenth and early seventeenth centuries but larger-scale development at Leadhills came when the lands passed into the hands of the Hope family in 1638. By the mid-seventeenth century the mines employed 50 workers and were producing 300–400 tons of ore a year. The profits from the mines enabled the family to build up estates and influence: they became the Earls of Hopetoun and were able to afford one of Scotland's finest late seventeenth-century country mansions, Hopetoun House near South Queensferry (Chapter 4).

A thriving mining community grew up at Leadhills in a remote upland setting. An extensive area of moorland around the settlement was improved and still bears the marks of former intensive cultivation. Most of the miners had smallholdings and tried to produce oats, potatoes and other basic foodstuffs for themselves. The hillsides around the village are covered with the remains of mining activity: adits, shafts and spoil heaps. The Hopetoun family and the Scotch Mines Company, which leased a large part of the mining field, spent a good deal of money on providing good accommodation and other facilities for the miners at Leadhills. Many of the mine workers came from England and this encouraged the payment of higher wages. The miners' library, founded in 1741 by the poet Allan Ramsay, whose father was a mine manager there, was the earliest circulating library in Scotland. It is now a visitor centre with exhibits relating to the history of lead mining in the area.

North of the village a great gash in the hillside marks the location of the Susanna vein, the most productive lead vein in the area, which in places had a width of nearly 6m (21ft) of solid ore. During the seventeenth century the ore was smelted using charcoal but this was so expensive that most of the ore was exported unprocessed. Around 1690 the use of peat as a fuel was developed and thereafter most of the ore was smelted locally. Due to the hilly topography of the area many of the veins could be reached by horizontal levels or adits driven into the hillsides; numerous examples can still be seen around the village. As the more accessible ore was extracted deeper workings were needed and drainage became a greater problem. The hard rock made cutting drainage levels more difficult and expensive than in coal-mining areas. By the 1760s a main drainage level had been cut from a low point about two miles north of the village and driven back to drain most of the workings. Deeper workings, which eventually extended 150m (500ft) below this level, had to be drained mechanically by water-driven and steam pumps.

The lead mines at Wanlockhead on the other side of the watershed were developed a little later than those at Leadhills. Lead was supposedly first discovered here by a German prospector in the late sixteenth century but serious mining only began in the 1680s. The land belonged to the dukes of Queensberry who worked the mines directly at some periods and leased out the mineral rights at others. Wanlockhead was a smaller community than Leadhills but equally remote. The landscape remains of mining at Wanlockhead are even more fascinating than those at Leadhills. A small mining museum has been created in one of the cottages and a mining trail laid out nearby. Together they illustrate some of the problems of mining in such a remote location, particularly regarding drainage and the provision of power. Although steam engines became increasingly common at Scottish collieries during the eighteenth century the transport of large quantities of coal to such a remote area as this was uneconomic unless at times when the price of lead was very high. Up to a point horse gins could be used for raising water but they were less effective than steam engines. Horses were also used on tramway systems for hauling the ore from the mines to the crushing plants; examples of old tramways can be seen at Wanlockhead.

Figure 42 This water bucket pumping engine at the lead-mining settlement of Wanlockhead, dating from the nineteenth century but using an earlier design, demonstrates the ingenious solutions which were adopted for providing power to remote industrial sites.

Every effort was made to maximise the use of water power. At Wanlockhead the remains of a simple water bucket pumping engine, possibly dating from *c.* 1770, can be seen. The beam of the engine was raised and lowered by the action of water pouring into a bucket that hung from one end of the beam. The weight of the full bucket pulled one end of the beam down and when the bucket reached ground level it emptied automatically causing the beam to rise once more. The bucket was filled from a wooden flume connecting with a cistern on the hillside. Water for the cistern was collected by drainage channels which contoured the hillside and trapped runoff. As long as water was available this was a simple yet effective system of draining a mine. The ore was raised by means of a horse gin whose circular walkway is still visible next to the beam engine. Towards the end of the eighteenth century high prices for lead combined with the development of more efficient steam engines which burned less coal encouraged the use of steam power at Wanlockhead. Coal had to be brought by pack horse from Sanquhar, 10 miles away. In the valley of Whyte's Cleuch, near the village, a row of massive stone blocks can be seen. These formed the base for the cylinder of a steam engine built by William Symington in 1790.

The Leadhills–Wanlockhead area was the only one in which lead mining was continuous during the seventeenth and eighteenth centuries. Another district where lead mining was carried out on a large scale, though more intermittently, was Strontian in north Argyll. The area was first developed by a Lowland entrepreneur, Sir Alexander Murray of Stanhope, a fanatical mineral prospector who had bought the estates of Sunart and Ardnamurchan in 1723 and was keen to develop the mineral wealth that he had discovered on them. In 1724 Murray leased the mining rights to a group of partners which included Sir Archibald Grant of Monymusk who later became a noted agricultural improver and General Wade the commander-in-chief of the army in Scotland. The mine was worked by the ill-fated York Buildings Company for three years with much activity and expense but no profit. The York Buildings Company ran out of money in 1734 and Murray once again managed the working of the mines himself.

The largest mines at Strontian worked a single vein of ore up to 0.75m (2.5ft) thick over a distance of 2km (1.2 miles). Operations were centred around three sites: Middlehope, Whitesmith and, most productive of all, the Bellsgrove mine (NM 8366). Most of the early workings were simply open clefts or stopes which followed the vein down from the surface. The remains of these can still be seen along with spoil heaps, working floors and remains of the buildings used for processing the ore. As the depth of working increased so did the need for improved drainage leading to the driving of a drainage level, the Grand Level, which was begun during the 1730s and was designed to drain all the workings. Around the mines can be seen the dams and lades which provided water and the pits for the water-wheels which drove the crushing machinery. In the 1750s water power was also applied to the task of draining the mines.

Other mines in this area were worked from the 1750s on a small scale, notably one at Corrantee (NM 8066) on a vein which was an extension of the one at Strontian but which outcropped in a different valley. At Liddesdale (NM 779596) a ruined storehouse is the only survivor of an extensive group of buildings related to the nearby mines at Lurga. A contemporary plan indicates that there was a manager's house, warehouses, barns, stables, malt kilns, and workmen's houses. As with the iron smelter at Bonawe, mining settlements in the Highlands at this time had to be self-sufficient communities. Skilled workers from the Lowlands and England expected better facilities and housing standards than the local inhabitants.

Lead mines were also worked on Islay, supposedly from Norse times, but more extensively from the end of the seventeenth century. At Mulreesh (NR 402688) the remains of a stone steam-engine house dating from the eighteenth century can be seen together with mine workers' cottages. An important group of lead mines were opened at Tyndrum between Loch Lomond and Rannoch Moor. Lead was discovered here in 1741 by Sir Robert Clifton, an Englishman who had spent several years prospecting for minerals on the Breadalbane estates. Mining operations began a year or two later. Initially the ore was carried by packhorse to a smelter at the bottom of Glen Falloch, to which coal was brought by boat up Loch

Lomond from the Lowlands. At a later date, when communications had improved, a smelter was established at the mines themselves, which were worked throughout the later eighteenth century.

Small-scale trial workings for a variety of ores including those of iron, lead and copper can be found in many parts of Scotland. Surface traces are often scanty although such sites are often of interest to mineral collectors. Place names containing elements like 'lead' sometimes help to pinpoint the location of old workings. An example is Lead Law in the Pentland Hills south of Edinburgh. Tradition claims that silver was mined here at a locality called the 'Siller Holes' (NT 145533) during Mary Queen of Scots' reign, and traces of lead ore, possibly containing silver, can still be found. A short distance away an intriguing cave in the side of a glacial meltwater channel near Carlops, known as Jenny Barrie's Cove (NT 154533), may also have been a trial for lead.

Quarrying

Quarrying stone for building or for other purposes, such as making millstones, was widespread throughout our period but has been much less thoroughly studied than the extraction of coal or iron. One difficulty is that quarries can be hard to date. Many outcrops were worked intermittently over very long periods. Quarries at Tor Wood near Stirling appear to have been used for building an Iron Age broch, a Roman road and a medieval castle, as well as later structures. The use of another quarry at Airth is recorded over a 500-year period. In the sixteenth century and earlier quarrying was done on a small scale mainly for the construction of castles and ecclesiastical buildings as most houses, even in the towns, were still timber-framed with insubstantial walls and thatched roofs. Because of the difficulty and expense of transporting such a bulky commodity most stone was quarried as close to the building site as possible.

Quarries were often opened for specific building projects, preferably with a downhill run along a prepared road or 'sled gate'. An example is Bourjo quarry (NT 548327) on the north side of the Eildon Hills. It provided stone for the rebuilding of Melrose Abbey during the fifteenth and early sixteenth centuries. Traces of the sled track leading from it can also be seen. This practice was still being followed in the later eighteenth century, special quarries being opened for projects like the cotton mills at New Lanark and harbour schemes like the one at Portpatrick.

Millstone quarries formed a special category. Scotland did not have rocks as suitable as the famous millstone grits of northern England but many outcrops of hard sandstone were used for millstone making. Around thirty millstone quarries are known from Galloway to Shetland but there is still considerable scope for fieldwork in this neglected area. In some cases single millstones were cut from a small outcrop but in other instances a quarry might be used over long periods. This can be seen on the island of Gigha (NR 635473) where hand querns for local use and for trade with more distant areas were produced from early times until the eighteenth century from a quarry near the shore. At some examples, like Craigmaddie Muir in Stirlingshire (NS 578763–581762), millstones can be seen in different states of completion from rings of holes pecked out on a flat surface to the round hollows where millstones have been extracted. Kaim Hill in Ayrshire (NS 220530) was one of the most important sources of millstones in Scotland in the eighteenth century and pieces of shaped stone can still be found among the waste on the sides of the hill.

Certain kinds of stone were transported over greater distances. This was particularly the case with sandstone that could be tooled and dressed to make quoin stones for the corners of buildings and for door and window surrounds. In areas where easily worked stone was rare, like the West Highlands, sandstone might be brought from a considerable distance and its origin from particular quarries is often easy to establish. Quarries in the Jurassic sandstones at Carsaig on the island of Mull supplied dressed stone for castles and ecclesiastical buildings, including the abbey on Iona, from medieval times onwards over an extensive area of the West Highlands. The Triassic sandstones around Loch Aline on the mainland opposite Mull were exploited in a similar manner.

The nature and scale of quarrying altered in the eighteenth century with the rapid growth of stone as the standard walling material for buildings in both town and country and the spread of slate as a roofing material lower down the social scale. New demands for stone also emerged; for instance in the building of stone enclosure walls, the construction of piers and harbours, and the paving of streets. Even with this huge increase in the demand for stone most needs were still met at a purely local level. In the late eighteenth century quarrying was still a widely dispersed industry with quarries in virtually every parish, each one employing only a handful of workers. However, by the end of the century certain kinds of stone, worked in coastal locations for easy shipment, were generating demand widely within Scotland and further afield. In such situations quarrying was carried out on a larger scale and gave rise to specialist communities. The stone involved was principally slate, flagstone and granite.

In the south-west Highlands a band of slate was worked intensively on some of the islands in the Firth of Lorn and on the mainland at Ballachulish. The quarries at Ballachulish were opened as early as 1693. By the end of the eighteenth century some seventy-four families were employed and slate was being exported to England, Ireland and America. The remains of the workings are still impressive. They were normal surface workings cut into the hillside but further south on the islands of Luing and Seil most of the best slate was located close to or below ground level. The results can be seen around Easdale and Ellanbeich. Quarrying here was greatly developed in the first half of the eighteenth century with an export trade to the Clyde and eastern Scotland. By the mid-eighteenth century half a million slates a year were being produced and by 1771 annual output had risen to five million. For most of the eighteenth century slate was only extracted from above low-water mark. Quarrying below sea level with the aid of windmills and later steam pumping engines was largely a nineteenth-century development, as were the rows of quarry workers' houses. The island of Easdale is split into a patchwork of tiny enclosures which were once smallholdings for the quarrymen. The workings below sea level are now flooded, giving the area a curious and distinctive appearance.

In Caithness the horizontally bedded Old Red Sandstone flagstones were easily worked and were especially suitable for use as paving stones. Quarrying on a considerable scale for distant markets began at the end of the eighteenth century. Extensive remains survive of one of the largest complexes of flagstone quarries at Castlehill (ND 195686), including the stump of a windmill used for drainage and a harbour for exporting the stone. Ham Harbour (ND 240737) was also built for the flagstone trade.

More than any other type of stone Scotland is associated with granite, yet it generally occurs in rugged upland areas remote from markets and transport. Large-scale granite quarrying developed in only two areas, Aberdeenshire and Kirkcudbrightshire and in the latter case not until the mid-nineteenth century. In the north east the first proper granite quarries were close to the city of Aberdeen and the smaller burgh of Peterhead which provided convenient harbours for exporting the stone. In 1764 the Aberdeen quarries were all within 2 miles of the town although by the end of the century new ones were being opened further from the harbour on the northern outskirts of the town. The opening of the Aberdeenshire canal in the early nineteenth century allowed more distant inland locations to be worked but the bulk of the industry remained close to the coast.

In the later eighteenth century the Aberdeenshire granite quarries were still small, each employing only a handful of workers and producing only a few hundred tons of stone a year. Machinery was first used to extract the stone in 1795 for the docks at Portsmouth but real progress had to wait until the introduction of steam power in the nineteenth century. Nevertheless, by 1799 the output of the Aberdeenshire granite quarries had reached around 24,000 tons a year. Some of this was used locally but granite was sent to London in increasing quantities from the 1760s and the stone was also in demand for civil engineering projects like piers, breakwaters and lighthouses. Although the massive growth of the industry – which made Rubislaw quarry on the outskirts of Aberdeen the largest man-made hole in the world in its day – lay in the nineteenth century, the basic features of the Aberdeenshire granite industry were already established by 1800.

Lime burning

Limestone was quarried and burnt in increasing quantities from the seventeenth century to provide lime for building construction and particularly for agriculture, which required much larger quantities. The earliest use of lime for improving crop yields by reducing soil acidity is unknown. However, in the early seventeenth century the widespread adoption of liming in the Lothians and other parts of central Scotland produced a mini agricultural revolution. During the eighteenth century two trends are discernible. First, the scale of some limeworks, principally in the central Lowlands, increased substantially. Second, as the demand for lime grew, more careful exploration led to the discovery of beds of limestone in areas outside the Lowlands and the development of lime burning in remote locations, often using peat rather than coal for fuel. These areas included Nithsdale, Lismore in the Firth of Lorn, Durness in Sutherland, and isolated smaller-scale workings in places as far apart as Islay, Skye, Shetland and upper Deeside.

Early lime burning involved primitive clamp kilns in which the limestone and fuel (often peat or wood rather than coal) was covered in horseshoe-shaped mounds of turf or stone which had to be broken open to remove each load of burnt lime. Clamp kilns were around 12m (40ft) long by 5m (17ft) wide and 2.4m (8ft) in height. With careful rebuilding they could be used several times. Their remains resemble prehistoric cairns and long barrows but they have mostly been obliterated by later larger-scale workings. Examples can still be seen at Bents (NT 175535) and Whitfield (NT 172540) south of Edinburgh and at Barjarg in Nithsdale (NX 883902), but unidentified examples are probably more widely scattered adjacent to later limeworks. During the eighteenth century more sophisticated and permanent draw kilns were introduced. These were vertical stone structures, often square in section but sometimes round. Simple draw kilns were often constructed roughly of unmortared stone but larger, more substantial ones were more carefully built, often with a heat-resistant brick lining. Draw kilns were generally built into a slope so that they could be loaded with limestone and fuel at the top while the lime was extracted at the base of the kiln in a continuous process. Simple kilns had a single draw hole at the base but larger ones might have three facing in different directions.

Major limeworks were often sited on the coast with a quarry and one or more batteries of kilns adjoining a pier from which the lime could be shipped and, sometimes, coal brought in. The most impressive example is Charlestown on the south coast of Fife (NT 064835). Lime was produced here in the seventeenth century but in the 1770s the fifth earl of Elgin greatly expanded the scale of operations with a bank of fourteen draw kilns, the largest group in Scotland, and an improved harbour. By 1790

Figure 43 Limekilns near Carlops, south of Edinburgh, in a landscape pitted with old limestone quarries and kilns.

the port was handling some 1,300 cargoes of lime a year in addition to shiploads of coal and building stone. Some 80–90,000 tons of limestone was being quarried each year. This early industrial complex is well preserved. Similar limeworks on a smaller scale can be seen at Boddin on the Angus coast (NO 713533) where a headland of limestone has been almost entirely removed by quarrying and at Skateraw in East Lothian (NT 738754).

Lime was also transported inland by cart to areas which lacked limestone. The kilns at Skateraw supplied large quantities of lime to the Berwickshire Merse. Those around Carlops south of Edinburgh and at Middleton in Midlothian, where the quarry face was half a mile long, provided lime for the upper Tweed valley. In Nithsdale, lower Annandale and around Canonbie limestone was quarried and burnt on a large scale in the later eighteenth century to allow agricultural improvement. At Barjarg (NX 883902) and Closeburn (NX 912915) extensive limeworks were developed in the 1770s and 1780s using coal brought overland from Sanquhar 22km (14 miles) away. Limeworks near Lockerbie in lower Annandale used coal brought by cart from England. At Canonbie thin seams of coal were mined specifically for burning lime. Lime from the works in Nithsdale had a marked effect on improving local agriculture but was also sent overland considerable distances into Galloway.

A number of large limeworks from this period still preserve traces of subsidiary buildings such as stables, gunpowder sheds and workers' houses. In some areas, like parts of the Lothians, where the limestone was thinly bedded and steeply dipping, it was mined rather than quarried. Good examples can be seen at Hillhouse (NT 006752) and Middleton (NT 355575). Such mines slanted steeply downwards, following the dip of the strata and often required adits or mechanical aids for drainage. At Raw Camps near East Calder the base of a windmill which was used for draining a limestone mine can be seen. Stationary winding engines were also fitted on top of some kilns for hauling stone along light wagonways from the quarry face.

On Lismore, an island made entirely of limestone, a number of specialist lime-burning communities developed. One at An Sailean (NN 8431) is especially interesting. Here limestone was quarried from a natural cliff 50m high overlooking a sheltered bay. At the foot of the cliff are two pairs of limekilns. A number of quarrymen's houses, derelict but still quite well preserved, are scattered around the bay. There is also a quay for shipping out the lime with a ruined storehouse on it. A similar community existed at Port Ramsay (8845) further south but here quarrying was combined with fishing and the single row of workers' cottages is still inhabited with the quarry, limekilns and pier adjacent. In other areas lime burning was done on a smaller scale by estates for purely local use. Some good examples can be seen in the Aberdeenshire valleys of Glenbuchat and Strathdon. Single kilns can be found as far north as Shetland and some, like the one at Girlsta (HU 430504), can be quite large. Around the shores of Wigtown Bay in the late seventeenth century seashells were burnt with peat to produce lime and this simple practice was still being undertaken a century later. Remains of the small, simple kilns that were used can be seen in several places today.

Textiles

Before the later eighteenth century the manufacture of woollen and linen cloth was carried out on a domestic scale in almost every community. Wool was available everywhere, so the woollen industry was widely dispersed. The manufacture of linen, using locally grown flax or imports from the Baltic, was more concentrated in a belt running from Renfrewshire to Fife and Angus. As time went on the production of finer-quality linen focused on west-central Scotland while the making of coarse linen, the bulk of the output, was centred in Fife and Tayside.

Few of the processes of textile manufacture had been mechanised before the eighteenth century, save that the fulling of woollen cloth was carried out using water power from medieval times. Fulling involved beating the cloth under water with wooden hammers, using fullers' earth as a kind of soap, to matt the fibres of the cloth together. The process had originally been done by treading the cloth with bare feet, a technique known as 'waulking' or walking the cloth. Scottish fulling mills were referred to as waulkmills as a consequence. The earliest examples recorded in documents date from the fourteenth century and in later times there were at least 300 of them scattered throughout the Lowlands.

The first main process to be mechanised in the manufacture of linen was scutching, the removal of the woody particles from the stems of the flax plants. Improved scutching machinery was developed in 1729 and 'lint mills', as they were called, were soon almost as widespread as waulkmills. There were some 350 of them by 1750. Very few early waulkmills and lint mills survive and most of these have been altered and extended in later times but some, even in their modernised state, provide an impression of the small-scale nature of early textile production. A good example survives at Lintmill of Boyne near Portsoy (NO 608676), dating from the seventeenth century but altered in the eighteenth. Mill of Aden, at Old Deer in Aberdeenshire (NJ 984470) is an early flax mill, dating from 1789.

Another key process in the manufacture of linen was bleaching. Originally this was done simply by washing the cloth in local streams and laying it out on the ground to bleach naturally in the sun. However, in the early eighteenth century lack of care in bleaching was identified as one of the causes of the very low quality of Scottish cloth. The Board of Trustees for Manufactures, keen to encourage improvements in Scotland's premier industry, provided subsidies for laying out proper bleaching greens where the process could be controlled and supervised. In the 1720s a number of large bleachfields were established. Those at Dalquhurn, in the Vale of Leven north of Dumbarton, were among the earliest using the inexhaustible supply of soft water from the outlet of Loch Lomond to wash and rinse the cloth and remove effluent. Perth was another important bleaching centre and as much as 24ha (60a) of ground around the town were covered by cloth at any time.

The number of large bleachfields increased rapidly during the eighteenth century but the introduction of new chemical methods of bleaching gradually shortened the time that the cloth had to spend outside on the grass and eventually eliminated this space-demanding operation altogether. Most of the old bleaching greens have been built over but some have survived in association with planned textile villages, such as Eaglesham in Renfrewshire and Gifford in East Lothian. At Friockheim in Angus a complex of buildings from a bleachworks, dating from the early eighteenth century onwards, has survived fairly intact (NO 595499).

Large-scale mechanisation of cloth production was applied first to spinning the yarn and only later to weaving, as was the case with the cotton industry. Mechanised teazing, carding and spinning of woollen yarn developed in the 1790s. The earliest example of a large integrated woollen spinning factory was Caerlee Mill at Innerleithen (NT 332370) built around 1790 for Alexander Brodie, a blacksmith who had made a fortune in the Shropshire iron industry and established the mill in his home area for philanthropic as much as business reasons. Other early woollen mills can be found in widely scattered locations which often seem remote from later centres of industry. This reflects the widespread distribution of the raw material that they used and their use of water power. Examples include mills at Huntly, Keith, Knockando and Stuartfield in the north east, Bridgend on Islay, Portree on Skye, Kilmahog outside Callender and Aberfeldy in Perthshire. The spinning of flax was mechanised at about the same time as that of wool. The first large flax mill was built at Brigton in Angus in 1778. It has since been demolished but the associated cluster of workers' cottages at Douglastown still survives.

Most of the early factories for spinning linen and woollen yarn were small; some were merely a couple of cottages knocked together and filled with hand-operated looms or stocking frames. A good example of a small stocking-frame workshop survives in the village of Denholm near Hawick. Other purpose-built factories were still small by comparison with the giants of the nineteenth century. Examples include the small carding mill built at Carlops around 1800 by a local weaver turned entrepreneur in asociation with a community of weavers, or the one at Old Bridge of Urr in Galloway. Many of these early factories have since been converted to houses like the Muckle House at Spittalfield, Caputh (NO 108409), a two-storey linen factory dating from 1767. Some older waulkmills were refurbished and converted into new factories: Bar Mill at Mochrum in Galloway was turned into a carding and spinning mill with carding machines on the

Figure 44 A small wool-carding mill at Carlops, later converted to a grain mill and now a private house.

ground floor and spinning jennies above. From the 1790s new, larger mills began to appear. The waulkmill at Cumloden near Minnigaff, dating from around 1800, is a well-preserved example, a three-storey building with machinery in the basement, spinning machines on the first floor and looms above.

The rise of the cotton industry

The cotton industry introduced to Scotland one of the most dramatic elements of the early Industrial Revolution; large water-powered spinning mills with adjacent planned communities. Even the earliest cotton mills were built on a scale greater than anything previously seen in Scotland. The spinning of cotton was mechanised by a series of inventions in the 1760s and 1770s. The first large-scale cotton mill in Scotland was established in Rothesay on the island of Bute in 1779 but nothing of it survives. In the later 1780s a number of new cotton mills were established. Most of them were located on large, fast-flowing rivers, the scale of their water power requirements emphasising the unusual size of these new mills. Catrine and New Lanark were situated on the margins of the Southern Uplands but the remainder were sited on swift-flowing Highland streams where they emerged into the Lowlands. Because they were some distance from existing industrial centres good housing had to be supplied in order to attract and retain a skilled labour force. For this reason most large, isolated early cotton mills were linked with planned communities for accommodating the workers.

A number of new cotton mills were established in 1785 and immediately after by Sir Richard Arkwright or people associated with him. One of them, planned by Arkwright in association with Sir George Dempster of Dunnichen and a group of Perth merchants, was at Stanley on the Tay above Perth. The mills were sited on the neck of a deeply cut meander and water was brought by a lade which tunnelled through an intervening hill. Today you can see three mill blocks built in a U-shape. The earliest, Bell Mill, dates from the foundation of the factory in 1785 and is the finest surviving early cotton mill in Scotland. It is characteristically narrow with timber floors and little headroom, built of brick above first-floor level. The village stands on level ground above the mill with terraced houses of stone and brick dating mainly from the early nineteenth century. The community had its own church, school and shops. At Spinningdale in Sutherland David Dale and George Dempster, who had established the mill at Stanley, set up a cotton mill between 1792 and 1794. It is unlikely that a mill would have flourished for long in such an isolated location but the building was gutted by fire in 1806. The ruins, with their fine architectural details, can still be seen (NH 675894).

Another early mill at Deanston on the River Teith was established in

Figure 45 Workers' housing and mill, New Lanark, emphasising the scale of the new special-ised factory communities which began to be established in the Scottish countryside at the end of the eighteenth century.

1785 by John Buchanan, originally Arkwright's manager in Scotland, and his brother Archibald who had once worked as an apprentice for Ark-wright. Sadly the original mill at Deanston was demolished in 1947 but a later mill from *c.* 1826 still stands, as do the terraces of workers' houses. Deanston Mill originally relied for labour on the nearby burgh of Doune but the village adjoining the mill had been started by 1811. The dam and lade for the water-wheels are still visible. A further large cotton mill was established at Catrine in Ayrshire by David Dale, of New Lanark fame, and Sir Claud Alexander of Ballochmyle in 1787. Unfortunately the mills, which were the finest examples of their kind in Scotland, have been demolished but, as at Deanston, the weir, lade and workers' houses remain.

The most famous of Scotland's early textile communities, New Lanark, was also founded in 1785 and the community remains the most impressive surviving monument to the early Industrial Revolution in Scotland. It was established by Sir Richard Arkwright in partnership with David Dale, a Glasgow entrepreneur. The mills' location in the narrow, wooded gorge of the River Clyde, utilising its waterfalls, is a classic water-power site. Despite its distance from Glasgow and other large towns a community of around 2,000 had developed here by the end of the eighteenth century. In 1798 Robert Owen, famous for his attempts to humanise the often grim and harsh world of the early Industrial Revolution, was appointed

Figure 46 The weaver's cottage, Kilbarchan, near Glasgow; a good example of a once common type of dwelling (National Trust for Scotland).

manager. Over the next twenty years Owen expanded the mills and improved facilities for the workers. Many structures from his day still survive including the New Buildings, a tenement block built in a sober classical style in 1799. There is also the shop (1810) which was the forerunner of the co-operative movement, a nursery (1809) for 300 pauper apprentices who had previously slept beside their machines, and the Institute for the Formation of Character (1816), a kind of education cum social centre for the workers. The houses occupied by Dale and Owen can also be seen. The mills did not close until 1968 and although the settlement was in a semi-derelict state at that time it has been carefully restored in recent years and is flourishing once more.

The weaving side of textile processes, for linen and woollens as well as cotton, remained unmechanised throughout the eighteenth century. Many of the cottages in early industrial communities, as well as more generally throughout the countryside and in the towns, housed handloom weavers. An early example, dating from 1723, can be seen in the Renfrewshire village of Kilbarchan. Owned by the National Trust for Scotland and open to the public, it is cruck framed and originally had a roof of turf. It is built into a slope with the loomshop below and the family's accommodation above, entered from street level at the upper end. Elsewhere weavers' cottages from the later eighteenth century are often single storeyed. They may have a double window on one side of the entrance to show on which side of the building the loomshop was placed. Good examples can be seen at Dairsie in Fife, Jericho in Angus and Craigie in Perthshire.

Conclusion

In this book we have traced elements of continuity and change in Scotland's landscape from late-medieval rural settlements and field systems to the highly regimented patterns of enclosures created by the improvers, from primitive bloomery forges to sophisticated industrial complexes like the Carron Ironworks and the mills of New Lanark. It has not been possible to cover every aspect of social and economic change that impinged on the Scottish landscape during this period within the compass of a single volume. Many interesting topics have only been touched on or have had to be omitted entirely but we hope that this survey will encourage readers to follow them up elsewhere. To facilitate this we have produced some suggestions for further reading. This list is only an introductory guide; residents and visitors to Scotland alike will find much more material of interest in local libraries. From this it is only a short step to looking at old maps and printed sources and from this to becoming involved in hunting through original archive material. No matter how interesting research in libraries and record offices may be there is nothing like the exhilaration of getting out in the open air and studying the landscape itself for traces of the imprint of humanity in times past. The beauty of the Scottish landscape has often been extolled and its most classic landscape features, whether natural or man-made, are familiar the world over from innumerable photographs. However, as this book has shown, much of the story of human influence on this landscape, even in comparatively recent times, is still unclear and has yet to be examined in detail. Whether in your home area or holiday venue we hope that this book will encourage you to look more closely at the countryside around you. You may start to pose questions about how the countryside has developed and then to begin searching for the answers!

A note on further reading

Many articles relating to aspects of the Scottish landscape *c*. 1500–*c*. 1800 are published in the *Proceedings of the Society of Antiquaries of Scotland* (*PSAS*), the *Scottish Geographical Magazine* (*SGM*), the *Scottish Historical Review* (*SHR*) and *Scottish Studies* (*SS*). These and other journals should be available in good reference libraries; only a sample of articles on key topics is mentioned here. The various county volumes of the Royal Commission on Ancient and Historical Monuments for Scotland provide a wealth of information. The older volumes are more limited in their scope but deal well with features like castles and churches while the more recent ones list a much wider range of landscape features. In compiling this bibliography we have tried to recommend mainly books which have been published within the last few years: many are still in print and others should be readily available through your local library.

General historical background

Mitchison, R. *A History of Scotland* (Methuen, London, 1970) is a good one-volume history.

Three volumes in the New History of Scotland series published by Edward Arnold cover the period 1500–1800:
Brown, J. *Court, Kirk and Community: Scotland 1470–1625*. London. 1981.
Lenman, B. *Integration, Enlightenment and Industrialization: Scotland, 1746–1832*. London. 1981.
Mitchison, R. *Lordship to Patronage: Scotland 1625–1745*. London. 1983.
Smout, T. C. *A History of the Scottish People 1560–1830* (Collins, London, 1972) is excellent for general background reading, combining fine scholarship with readability.

For Scottish society see:
Houston, R. A. and Whyte, I. D. (eds) *Scottish Society 1500–1800*. Cambridge University Press. Cambridge. 1989.

Less specific to the period 1500–1800 but still useful are the following:

Turnock, D. *The Historical Geography of Scotland since 1707*. Cambridge University Press. Cambridge. 1982.

Whittington, G. and Whyte, I. D. *An Historical Geography of Scotland*. Academic Press. London. 1983.

Good overall surveys of the evolution of the Scottish landscape are thin on the ground. The best is:

Parry, M. L. and Slater, T. R. (eds) *The Making of the Scottish Countryside*. Croom Helm. London. 1980.

At a regional level the eight volumes of *Exploring Scotland's Heritage* published by HMSO are excellent.

1 Rural settlement before the improvers

Crawford, I. A. Contributions to history of domestic settlement in North Uist. *SS* 9 (1965) 34–63.

Dodgshon, R. A. *Land and Society in Early Scotland*. Oxford University Press. Oxford. 1981.

Fairhurst, H. The deserted settlement at Lix, West Perthshire. *PSAS* 101 (1968–9) 160–99.

Gailey, R. A. The evolution of Highland rural settlement with particular reference to Argyllshire. *SS* 6 (1960) 155–77.

Pollock, D. The Lunan Valley project: medieval rural settlement in Angus. *PSAS* 115 (1985) 357–401.

Smith, J. S. Deserted farms and shealings in the Braemar district of Deeside. *PSAS* 116 (1986) 447–54.

Whyte, I. D. The evolution of rural settlement in Lowland Scotland in medieval and early-modern times: an exploration. *SGM* 97 (1981) 4–15.

2 The pre-improvement landscape: house and home

Dunbar, J. G. Some cruck framed buildings in the Aberfeldy district of Perthshire. *PSAS* 90 (1956–7) 81–92.

Fenton, A. and Walker, B. *The Rural Architecture of Scotland*. John Donald. Edinburgh. 1981.

Stewart, J. H. and Stewart, M.B. A Highland longhouse – Lianach, Balquhidder. Perthshire. *PSAS* 118 (1988) 301–18.

Walker, B. The vernacular buildings of North East Scotland: an exploration. *SGM* 95 (1979) 45–60.

3 The pre-improvement countryside: field and farm

Caird, J. B. The making of the Scottish rural landscape. *Scottish Geographical Magazine* 80 (1964) 72–80.

Dodgson, R. A. *Land and Society in Early Scotland*. Oxford. Oxford University Press. 1981.

Donnachie, I. L. and Stewart, N. K. Scottish windmills – an outline and inventory. *PSAS* 98 (1967) 176–299.

Fenton, A. *Scottish Country Life*. John Donald. Edinburgh. 1976.

Gaffney, V. Summer shielings. *SHR* 38 (1959) 20–35.

Handley, J. E. *Scottish Farming in the Eighteenth Century*. Faber. London. 1953.
Lebon, J. H. G. Old maps and rural change in Ayrshire. *Scottish Geographical Magazine* 68 (1952) 104–9.
MacSween, M. Transhumance in North Skye. *SGM* 75 (1959) 75–88.
MacSween, M. and Gailey, A. Some shielings in North Skye. *SS* 11 (1967) 193–221.
Miller, R. Land use by summer shielings. *SS* 11 (1967) 193–221.
Whyte, I. D. *Agriculture and Society in Seventeenth-century Scotland*. John Donald. Edinburgh. 1979.

4 From castle to mansion

Cruden, S. *The Scottish Castle*. Scottish Academic Press. London. 1981.
Dunbar, J. G. *The Historic Architecture of Scotland*. Batsford. London. 1981.
Lindsay, I. G. and Cosh, M. *Inveraray and the Dukes of Argyll*. Edinburgh University Press. Edinburgh. 1972.
MacGibbon, D. and Ross, T. *The Castellated and Domestic Architecture of Scotland*. 5 vols. Edinburgh. 1887–92.
Tabraham, C. J. The Scottish medieval towerhouse as lordly residence in the light of recent excavation. *PSAS* 118 (1988) 267–76.
Tranter, N. *The Fortified House in Scotland*. 5 vols. Oliver and Boyd. Edinburgh. 1962–70.

5 The church in the landscape

Cruden, S. *Scottish Abbeys*. HMSO. Edinburgh. 1960.
Di Folco, J. Graveyard monuments in eastern, northern and central Fife. *PSAS* 102 (1969–70) 205–36.
Dunbar, J. G. *The Historic Architecture of Scotland*. Batsford. London. 1981.
Fawcett, R. *Scottish Medieval Churches*. John Donald. Edinburgh. 1985.
Graham, A. Graveyard monuments in East Lothian. *PSAS* 94 (1960–1) 211–21.
MacGibbon, D. and Ross, T. *The Ecclesiastical Architecture of Scotland*. 3 vols. Edinburgh. 1887–92.

6 The landscape of improvement: the Lowlands

Adams, I. H. *Directory of Former Scottish Commonties*. Scottish Record Society. Edinburgh. 1971.
Dodgshon, R. A. The removal of runrig in Roxburghshire and Berwickshire. 1680–1766. *SS* 16 (1972) 121–37.
Handley, J. E. The Agricultural Revolution in Scotland. Burns. Glasgow. 1963.
Lockhart, D. G. Scottish village plans: a preliminary analysis. *SGM* 96 (1980) 158–65.
Naismith, R. J. *Buildings of the Scottish Countryside*. Gollancz. London. 1985.
Walker, B. Glamis: the 'great rebuilding' on a Scottish estate. *SGM* 101 (1985) 139–49.

7 The landscape of improvement: the Highlands

Hunter, J. *The Making of the Crofting Community*. John Donald. Edinburgh. 1976.

Lindsay, J. M. The commercial use of Highland woodland 1750–1870. *SGM* 92 (1976) 30–40.

Lindsay, J. M. Some aspects of timber supply in the Highlands 1700–1850. *SS* 19 (1975) 39–53.

Richards, E. *The History of the Highland Clearances*. Vol. 1. Croom Helm. London. 1982.

Smith, A. *Jacobite Estates of the 'Forty-five'*. John Donald. Edinburgh. 1982.

Turnock, D. *Patterns of Highland Development*. Macmillan. London. 1970.

Turnock, D. Glenlivet: two centuries of rural planning in the Grampian uplands. *SGM* 95 (1979) 165–80.

8 Transport and communication

Curtis, G. R. Roads and bridges in the Scottish Highlands: the route between Dunkeld and Inverness 1725–1925. *PSAS* 110 (1978–80) 475–96.

Fenton, A. and Stell, G. (eds) *Loads and Roads in Scotland and Beyond*. John Donald. Edinburgh. 1984.

Graham, A. More old roads in the Lammermuirs. *PSAS* 53 (1959–60) 217–35.

Graham, A. Archaeology on a Great Post Road. *PSAS* 96 (1962–3) 318–47.

Graham, A. Archaeological notes on some harbours in Eastern Scotland. *PSAS* 101 (1968–9) 200–85.

Graham, A. Old harbours and landing places on the east coast of Scotland. *PSAS* 108 (1976–7) 332–65.

Graham, A. and Gordon, J. Old harbours in northern and western Scotland. *PSAS* 117 (1987) 265–352.

Haldane, A. R. B. *The Drove Roads of Scotland*. Edinburgh University Press. Edinburgh. 1952.

Haldane, A. R. B. *New Ways Through the Glens*. David & Charles. New'on Abbot. 1982.

Lindsay, J. *The Canals of Scotland*. David & Charles. Newton Abbot. 1968.

Taylor, W. *The Military Roads in Scotland*. David & Charles. Newton Abbot. 1976.

The volumes by J. R. Hume listed below contain much information on features such as canals, wagonways, and bridges.

9 Industry in the landscape

Aitken, W. G. Excavation of bloomeries in Rannoch and Perthshire. *PSAS* 102 (1969–70) 188–204.

Donnachie, I. *The Industrial Archaeology of Galloway*. David & Charles. Newton Abbot. 1971.

Duckham, B. F. *History of the Scottish Coal Industry*. David and Charles. Newton Abbot. 1970.

Hume, J. R. *The Industrial Archaeology of Scotland I. The Lowlands and Borders*. Batsford. London. 1976.

Hume, J. R. *The Industrial Archaeology of Scotland II. The Highlands and Islands*. Batsford. London. 1977.

Lewis, J. H. The charcoal fired blast furnaces of Scotland: a review. *PSAS* 114 (1984) 433–80.

Lindsay, J. M. The iron industry in the Highlands: charcoal blast furnaces. *SHR* 56 (1977) 49–63.

Shaw, J. *Water Power in Scotland*. John Donald. Edinburgh. 1984.
Turner, W. H. K. The location of early spinning mills in the historic linen region of Scotland. *SGM* 98 (1982) 77–86.
Turner, W. H. K. The development of flax spinning mills in Scotland 1787–1840. *SGM* 98 (1982) 4–15.

Index

Ingram Content Group UK Ltd.
Milton Keynes UK
UKHW021102170323
418657UK00017B/140